APPLICATIVE HIGH
ORDER PROGRAMMING

CHAPMAN AND HALL COMPUTING SERIES

Computer Operating Systems
For micros, minis and mainframes
2nd edition
David Barron

Microcomputer Graphics
Michael Batty

The Pick Operating System
Malcolm Bull

Programming in FORTRAN
3rd edition
V. J. Calderbank

Expert Systems
Principles and case studies
2nd edition
Edited by Richard Forsyth

Machine Learing
Principles and techniques
Edited by Richard Forsyth

Export Systems
Knowledge, uncertainty and decision
Ian Graham and Peter Llewelyn Jones

Computer Graphics and Applications
Dennis Harris

Artificial Intelligence and Human Learning
Intelligent computer-aided instruction
Edited by John Self

Artificial Intelligence
Principles and applications
Edited by Masoud Yazdani

APPLICATIVE HIGH ORDER PROGRAMMING

The Standard ML perspective

S. Sokolowski

CHAPMAN & HALL COMPUTING
London · New York · Tokyo · Melbourne · Madras

UK	Chapman and Hall, 2–6 Boundary Row, London SE1 8HN
USA	Van Nostrand Reinhold, 115 5th Avenue, New York NY10003
JAPAN	Chapman and Hall Japan, Thomson Publishing Japan, Hirakawacho Nemoto Building, 7F, 1-7-11 Hirakawa-cho, Chiyoda-ku, Tokyo 102
AUSTRALIA	Chapman and Hall Australia, Thomas Nelson Australia, 102 Dodds Street, South Melbourne, Victoria 3205
INDIA	Chapman and Hall India, R. Seshadri, 32 Second Main Road, CIT East, Madras 600 035

First edition 1991

© 1991 S. Sokolowski

Printed in Great Britain
by Page Bros (Norwich) Ltd
ISBN 0 412 392402   0 442 30838 8 (USA)

British Library Cataloguing in Publication Data

Sokolowski, S.
    Applicative high order programming: the standard ML
    perspective.
    1. Computer systems. Functional programming. Programming
    languages: Standard ML language
    I. Title
    005.133

    ISBN 0-412-39240-2

Library of Congress Cataloging-in-Publication Data

Sokolowski, S. (Stefan)
    Applicative high order programming: the standard ML
    perspective/S. Sokolowski.—1st ed.
        p.   cm.—(Chapman and Hall computing series)
    Includes bibliographical references and index.
    ISBN 0-442-30838-8
    1. ML (Computer program language)   I. Title.   II. Series.
    QA76.73.M6S65   1991
    005.13′3–dc20   90-49712
                                                          CIP

Contents

Introduction

Applicative (functional) programming is a style of programming which emphasises the fact that the most important way to view programs is as *functions* and that the most important operation is the *application* of a function to an *argument*. The main distinguishing features of pure applicative programs are the following:

- Expression evaluation rather than computation on states.

- Absence of changing states. Rather than encode input data into a state of variables, transform this state into another state, and then retrieve the result from a current state, as imperative programs do, an applicative program directly relates result to data.

- Consequently, absence of assignments, of time succession of commands (*first* do this and *then* do that) and of loops. Assignments are, to some extent, replaced by definitions of constants, and loops by recursion.

- Absence of side effects. Anything a programmer wants to happen has to be made an explicit result of expression evaluation.

- High order programming. Applicative programs allow for a much higher degree of mathematisation, therefore treating functions as "first class citizens", passing them as parameters and yielding them as values of other functions, come much more naturally than in imperative programs. The same holds for definitions of new types.

- Interactive programming. A program basically consists of an expression preceded by a number of definitions of the objects appearing in the expression. When running, the system is intended to calculate and display the value of any expression immediately after it has been typed in, or to yield an error message.

- Unfortunately, a decreased time and space efficiency when compared to imperative programs. This is the price to pay for relieving the programmer of concern about implementation details.

High order functions (functionals) are functions that take other functions as arguments and/or yield functions as values. A typical mathematical example is the derivative functional

$$\frac{d}{dx} : (real \to real) \to (real \to real)$$

Given a (differentiable) function $f : real \to real$ this yields another function $\frac{d}{dx} f : real \to real$ which is its derivative. High order functions used in programming increase the expressive power of standard programming constructs (e.g. of primitive recursion) and in many cases relieve the programmer of concern about technical details in his algorithms. By high order programming is meant a style of programming that uses high order functions.

Technically, it is also possible to use functionals in imperative languages. For instance, the official report of Pascal states that functions may be arguments (but not results) of functions and procedures. It is, however, difficult to find an implementation of Pascal that would support that feature. The implementors of Pascal have always felt that functionals are not in the spirit of the basically imperative language, and have had no scruples about cutting them off to simplify their task. I think they have been right. High order programming is indeed not in the spirit of imperative languages.

With the increasing capacities of today's computers that make the inefficiencies of applicative and of high order programming less painful, this style has gradually gained ground, not only in academic research but also in industrial applications as a specification and prototyping tool. On the other hand, the interest in functional programming has created new fields of academic research. Although this research is directly motivated by programs arising when implementing functional languages or designing functional programs, its actual relation to "everyday programming" is often overlooked. The main aim of this book is to bring together theory and practice and to illustrate both the gains and the difficulties that a programmer may face.

The workhorse applicative programming language used throughout the text is the Standard ML developed at Edinburgh University between 1983 and 1985[1]. But the reader should be aware of the difference between applicative programming *language* and applicative progamming *style*. To some extent it is possible to write applicative programs in Pascal and also it is possible to write imperative programs in Standard ML.

This text is by no means either a handbook or a reference manual to the Standard ML programming language. This is also not a beginner's guide. The reader is assumed to have some programming practice and at least a superficial familiarity with λ-calculus and related areas. Some prior experience with functional programming would also be an advantage. It is hoped that this book will draw the reader's attention to possibilities he or she might not have thought of. The following is a selection of the issues discussed here that are, to my mind, too sketchily and superficially covered in advanced textbooks on applicative programming:

---

[1]Commented references to the literature are given in Appendix B.

- While technically adequate, mathematical induction is not always readily applicable to proving properties of functional programs: e.g. when $f(n)$ is defined by recursive call to $f(n \ div \ 2)$ rather than to $f(n - 1)$. However, the principle of induction can be reformulated so that it specifically covers that aim.

- High order functions, or functionals, are the very heart of applicative programming. Sequences are functions, dictionaries are functions, curves are functions etc.; and the possibility of directly manipulating them rather than translating them to lists, hash tables or pixels, is an enormous advantage.

- Polymorphism may be treated as functional dependence on types. In order for this to become apparent, polymorphism should be made explicit; this would correspond to making the functionality of, say, x^2+y^2 apparent by denoting it as $\lambda x.x^2+y^2$. Related notions of deep polymorphism and of dependent types are practical tools rather than the toys of theorists.

- While in high order programming languages, such as Standard ML, functions are "first class citizens", the same is not true of types, nor of structures. This can, however, be remedied.

- In a sense, functors are a generalisation of (explicit) polymorphism. Since technically these two notions are independent, their superposition may bring about strange effects.

The book has evolved from lecture notes written for the students of Universität Passau, Germany, who attended my one-semester course on applicative high order programming in the Autumn and Winter of 1988/1989. A chapter roughly corresponds to a single three-hour lecture and the exercises are the ones the students were to work through during the course. Of course, both have been thoroughly revised and edited since, taking into account the students' reaction.

This work has been supported by a visiting professorship of the University of Passau. In the process of transforming the lecture notes into the book the technical criticism by Dave Berry and Mads Tofte has been very helpful. I also have to express my gratitude to Tony Hoare and to Robin Milner for their encouragement and advice. The index to this book has been set up and the camaera ready copy has been prepared with the assistance of ..Polski T_EX" Ltd.

Part I

Advanced Applicative
Programming

Chapter 1

Applicative vs. imperative programming

1.1 A simple example

Consider the following Pascal function that, given a natural number n, calculates the largest natural k such that

$2^k \mid n$

(read: 2^k *divides* n), i.e. the largest power of 2 by which the given number n is still divisible:

```
function power2(n:integer):integer;
  var k:integer;
begin
  k:=0;
  while 2|n do
  begin
    k:=k+1; n:=n div 2
  end;
  power2:=k
end
```

(actually, the divisibility test . . . | . . . does not belong to the Pascal programming language although it *might*; throughout this lecture we are not going to be very dogmatic about this kind of implementation detail of the existing software). In order to understand this piece of program one has to keep track of the way in which the value of the k variable increases while the value of the n variable decreases; this means being aware of the *temporal* synchronisation of changes to the values of variables. To prove that the above function does what it is supposed to, one basically has to demonstrate that

- the operations performed within the body of the while-loop, while affecting the values of variables k and n, keep the value of the expression

$$n \cdot 2^k$$

  invariant at all times when the control enters the while-statement — this accounts for the *safety* of the command,

- every run through the body of the while-loop irreversibly decreases n — this accounts for its *termination*.

Although this small example may appear too simplistic to sound convincing, the temporal properties of programs are sufficiently difficult to make a nightmare out of the verification of a program's logical structure. On the other hand, mathematics, which is our most powerful tool for dealing with the complications of programming, has no notion of time. The mathematical way of depicting changes in time is to produce an unmoving *trajectory*. In the example of power2 there is, however, no need, either explicitly or implicitly, to refer to the time flow; this function should be easy to define in simpler terms. For instance:

```
fun pow2(n) =
      if 2|n
      then pow2(n div 2)+1
      else 0
```

As a matter of fact, this definition of pow2 may be readily run under Standard ML (but for the divisibility test ...|... that does not belong to Standard ML either).

The Pascal definition of power2 consists of the precise recipe for a computer for the steps it should undertake and for the order of these steps: *first* do this, *then* do that.... On the other hand, the above Standard ML definition only explains *what* function pow2 really is. The former is usually referred to as an *imperative* or *procedural* definition; the latter as an *applicative* or *functional* one. The applicative programming style is arguably more programmer friendly, as it relieves him of concern about what should be happening inside a computer, but for the same reason it is less computer friendly. Consider the following Pascal counterpart of the above applicative Standard ML definition of pow2:

```
function pow2(n:integer):integer;
  var k:integer;
begin
  if 2|n
  then pow2:=pow2(n div 2)+1
  else pow2:=0
end
```

The reader can certainly find good reasons why the computation of `pow2` is more time- and space-consuming, thus less efficient, then the computation of `power2`. There are no reasons why the same is not true of Standard ML.

As demonstrated by this small case study, it is also possible to write applicative programs in such languages as Pascal, although for this kind of language this may amount to a poor programming style. Later, however, we will discuss useful features of applicative languages that may not be reduced to imperative ones. In imperative languages these features either do not appear at all, or appear only in restricted form, with the restrictions based on what is good for a computer rather than what is good for a human programmer.

1.2 The common backbone of high-level imperative languages

If the reader knows one imperative language, he may claim he knows all of them.

At the bottom of any high-level imperative language lies an *algebra* of primitive *types* and *operations*. In Pascal, for instance, the basic types are the following:

```
Boolean
char
integer
real
```

and the operations are more or less the following:

```
true, false : Boolean
not : Boolean → Boolean
and, or : Boolean × Boolean → Boolean


'a',..., 'z' : char
= : char × char → Boolean


0, 1, -1, 2, -2, ... : integer
- : integer → integer
+, -, *, div, mod : integer × integer → integer
=, <>, <, <=, >, >= : integer × integer → Boolean
ord : char → integer
chr : integer → char
```

$\ldots, 3.14, \ldots, -6.02E23, \ldots$: real
- : real $\to$ real
+,-,*,/ : real $\times$ real $\to$ real
=,<>,<,<=,>,>= : real $\times$ real $\to$ Boolean
round, trunc : real $\to$ integer

High-level languages usually provide a means of enlarging a primitive algebra of this kind in order to customise it to the user's needs. In Pascal new types may be formed out of old ones using the mechanisms of *enumeration, restriction, arrays, records, files,* and new operations may be defined as Pascal functions.

The *individual objects* a given language may deal with all belong to *types*. This means our set of objects is the set-theoretic union of types:

$Obj = \bigcup Types$

Any high-level imperative language involves the notion of *typed program variable*:

$Var \overset{\text{def}}{=} \ldots$
$type : Var \to Types$

The variables together with the algebra of operations give rise to the set *Expr* of *expressions*. The function *type* used so far to type program variables may be readily extended to typing any expressions, e.g.

$type[\![\text{chr(3+2)}]\!] = \text{char}$
$type[\![\text{x or y}]\!] = \begin{cases} \text{Boolean} & \text{if } type[\![\text{x}]\!] = type[\![\text{y}]\!] = \text{Boolean} \\ Error & \text{otherwise} \end{cases}$

The notion of *state* of a variables is essential for all high-level imperative languages:

$State \overset{\text{def}}{=}$ the set of all functions s defined over *Var*,
such that $s(x)$ is in $type[\![x]\!]$ for any variable x

This means every state is an assignment of appropriately typed objects to variables. This is an example of a state:

	x			a			
			1	2	3	4	
$s_0 =$ ...	0.57	...	'a'	'z'	'p'	'w'	...

This state is, of course, only then legitimate if

$type[\![\text{x}]\!] = \text{real}$
$type[\![\text{a}]\!] = \text{array[1..4] of char}$

In the presence of a state every expression has a *value*:

$$value : Expr \times State \rightarrow Obj$$

moreover, this value is properly typed, i.e.

$$value[\![e, s]\!] \in type[\![e]\!]$$

for any expression e and any state s. For instance,

$$value \ [\![\texttt{a[round(x)]}]\!] \ , s_0 \ ]\!] = \ \texttt{'a'}$$

The main units of an imperative program are *commands*, i.e. the functions that change states:

$$Command \overset{\text{def}}{=} State \rightarrow State$$

The main *primitive* command is the *assignment* of a value to a variable in a given state:

$$\ldots := \ldots : \ Var \times Expr \times State \rightarrow State$$
$$(x := e)(s) \overset{\text{def}}{=} s[value[\![e, s]\!]/x]$$

(by $f[v/a]$ is denoted the function f updated with the value v for the argument a). For instance:

$$(\texttt{x:=x+1.0})(s_0) \ = $$

...	x	...	a				...
			1	2	3	4	
...	1.57	...	'a'	'z'	'p'	'w'	...

High-level languages usually provide mechanisms to define *procedures*, which may be viewed as customised primitive commands.

In every imperative language there is a number of *control structures*, i.e. operations that form new (composite) commands from simpler ones. The main control structures of Pascal are:

`...;...`	—	composition
`if...then...else...`	—	conditional
`while...do...`	—	while-loop
`repeat...until...`	—	repeat-loop
`for...:=...to...do...`	—	upward iteration
`for...:=...downto...do...`	—	downward iteration

This is, in fact, a complete description of an imperative language. Of course, there are also built-in functions, and input/output operations, and side effects, and declarations (which change the function *type* above), and reactions to errors, etc.; but this is the common backbone that should be mastered independently of the particular language one is using. So, when learning a new language, the greatest effort is confined to finding out the language's concrete syntax for the notions discussed in this section.

The imperative style of processing data into results involves, basically, the following stages:

- the creation of an initial state out of available data (*input* operation)

- the transformation of this state into another state, and that one into yet another, ... etc., until a given condition on states is met (proper *computation*)

- the extraction of results out of the final state (*output* operation)

The user is interested in results rather than in states, yet his programs have to deal with states. On the other hand, applicative programming is about taking shortcuts from data to results without going through a sequence of states.

1.3   The common backbone of applicative languages

If the reader knows one applicative language, he may be even more confident he knows all of them. This section is going to be shorter, since applicative programming languages have a simpler structure than imperative ones.

At the bottom of any applicative language lies again an algebra. For instance this is the collection of basic types of Standard ML: real

unit	— one-element type
bool	— logical values
int	— integers
real	— real numbers
string	— finite sequences of characters

Here are the basic operations of Standard ML:

() : unit   —   the only element of unit

true, false : bool
not : bool → bool
andalso, orelse : bool × bool → bool   —   Standard ML's conjunction and disjunction

(if ... then ... else ...)$_T$:
        bool × T × T → T —   a family of operations implicitly indexed by types; neither the **then** part, nor the **else** part may be omitted

$0, 1, \tilde{~}1, 2, \tilde{~}2, \ldots : \text{int}$ — note that ˜ is used
instead of -

$\tilde{~} : \text{int} \to \text{int}$
$+, -, *, \text{div}, \text{mod} : \text{int} \times \text{int} \to \text{int}$
$=, <>, <, <=, >, >= : \text{int} \times \text{int} \to \text{bool}$

$\ldots, 3.14, \ldots, \tilde{~}6.02\text{E}23, \ldots : \text{real}$ — either the dot or the E
have to be present

$\tilde{~} : \text{real} \to \text{real}$
$+, -, *, / : \text{real} \times \text{real} \to \text{real}$
$=, <>, <, <=, >, >= : \text{real} \times \text{real} \to \text{bool}$
$\text{floor} : \text{real} \to \text{int}$ — Pascal's trunc
$\text{real} : \text{int} \to \text{real}$ — explicit type conversion
function

$\ldots, \text{"seq of chars"}, \ldots : \text{string}$
$\ldots \hat{~} \ldots : \text{string} \times \text{string} \to \text{string}$ — string concatenation
$\text{size} : \text{string} \to \text{nat}$ — length of a given string

Like imperative languages, applicative ones provide a means of extending this primitive algebra. For an applicative language to be useful these extension mechanisms have to be much more complex than those in a corresponding imperative language. The reason for this is that in the absence of changing states, data processing may only yield a single result, and so this result has to be complex enough to contain everything a user may require. For example, in screen editing, the results may be whole screen images, to accomodate which the programmer needs tools to extend the underlying primitive algebra with the type of screen images and with appropriate operations.

The type system of Standard ML is therefore quite complex. We are going to study it later. As to the operations, the main means to add new ones is again function definition. In contrast to the case of imperative languages, function definitions are the *main* structuring concept of Standard ML.

Most applicative languages are implemented *interactively*. A user types in either an expression, or a definition. The system's reaction is either to come up with the value of the expression, or to accept and confirm the definition (unless an error has been detected, in which case an error message is issued). The user may then write another expression or definition.

This is in line with the general philosophy of applicative programming: the expression evaluations rather than the computations on states.

1.4   An example session with Standard ML

This section presents a complete Standard ML code for finding *prime* natural numbers. This is carried out by the function

$$prime : \text{int} \to \text{int}$$

that, given a natural number n, yields the n-th least prime number:

$$prime(0) = 2$$
$$prime(1) = 3$$
$$prime(2) = 5$$
$$prime(3) = 7$$
. . .

A natural number is prime if it is not divisible by any prime number smaller than itself. Thus, given the values $prime(i)$ for all $i < n$, we can define $prime(n)$ as the least natural number k such that: $k \geq prime(n-1)+1$ and k is not divisible by $prime(i)$ for any $i < n$. Hence the following definition of *prime*:

$$prime(n) \stackrel{\text{def}}{=} \text{ if } n = 0 \text{ then } 2$$
$$\text{else } next(n, prime(n-1)+1, 0)$$

where

$$next : \text{int} \times \text{int} \times \text{int} \to \text{int}$$
$$next(n, k, i) \stackrel{\text{def}}{=} \text{ if } n \leq i \text{ then } k$$
$$\text{else if } prime(i) \mid k$$
$$\text{then } next(n, k+1, 0)$$
$$\text{else } next(n, k, i+1)$$

The arguments of the above auxiliary function *next* signify the following:

n — we are currently searching for $prime(n)$
k — a candidate for $prime(n)$, all smaller numbers already checked as non-prime
i — k already checked as not divisible by $prime(0),\ldots,prime(\text{i-1})$

The respective Standard ML code follows the above discussion, only the auxiliary functions have to be defined before the main ones. First let us define the divisibility test … | …:

```
- fun divides(k,n) = (n mod k = 0);
> val divides = fn : (int * int) -> bool
```

(the minus sign - is Standard ML's prompt to the user; Standard ML's response is preceded by the > sign). The system has confirmed our definition; actually, the response denotes that *divides* has been accepted as a function of type (int * int) -> bool (star stands for Cartesian product).

Since the functions *next* and *prime* call each other recursively, they either have to be defined jointly, or one of them has to be made *local* to the other. We do not need the auxiliary function *next* for its own sake, so let us make it invisible from outside:

```
- fun prime(n) =
      let
        fun next(n,k,i) =
              if n<=i then k
              else if divides(prime(i),k)
                   then next(n,k+1,0)
                   else next(n,k,i+1)
      in
        if n=0 then 2
        else next(n,prime(n-1)+1,0)
      end;
> val prime = fn : int -> int
```

Now, we can ask the computer about successive prime numbers:

```
- prime(0);
> 2 : int
- prime(1);
> 3 : int
- prime(2);
> 5 : int
- prime(3);
> 7 : int
- prime(10);
> 31 : int
```

The above definition of the function *prime* is rather inefficient; in fact, we have not taken any great pains over it. Note that while evaluating according to this definition the computer has to find lower prime numbers repeatedly. Inefficiency is not a necessary feature of applicative programming, but, admittedly, the applicative style discourages a programmer from paying too much attention to efficiency.

1.5   Exercises

Appendix A contains detailed solutions to all the exercises. But before looking
there, give the exercises a fair try.

Technically speaking, this chapter has not yet given you enough knowledge
to carry out the following two exercises. You may still try to do so by analogy
with the *prime* example from Section 1.4. If this does not work out, then just
refer to the solutions and make sure that you understand them.

Exercise 1

Design a Standard ML definition of a function that, given a natural number n, yields a natural number derived from n by reversing the order of its
(decimal) digits. For instance,

$$1989 \longmapsto 9891$$
$$1000 \longmapsto 1$$

Exercise 2

Design a Standard ML definition of a function that evaluates logarithms
within a given "vertical" precision; i.e given three real numbers $a > 1$, $b > 0$
and $\varepsilon > 0$, it yields a real number c such that

$$(1.1) \quad | c - log_a b | < \varepsilon$$

Chapter 2

The art of applicative programming

2.1 Hand simulation of applicative programs

As has been stated previously, an applicative program consists in principle of a sequence of definitions followed by an expression that may involve defined objects. Fundamental steps of expression evaluation consist in replacing the *definiendum* (defined quantity) by its *definiens* (right hand side of the definition) and then performing basic simplifications. This results in a new expression which is in turn evaluated in the same way until no further replacements are possible. For instance for the program

```
fun gcd(a:int,b:int) =
   if a=b then a
   else if a<b then gcd(a,b-a)
         else gcd(a-b,b);
gcd(24,40);
```

the evaluation proceeds as follows:

gcd(24,40) =   (replacement of gcd)

$$
= \left(\begin{array}{l} \text{if } 24\text{=}40 \text{ then } 24 \\ \text{else if } 24\text{<}40 \text{ then } \text{gcd}(24,40\text{-}24) \\ \qquad \text{else } \text{gcd}(24\text{-}40,40) \end{array} \right) = \text{(simplification)}
$$

= gcd(24,16) =   (replacement of gcd)

$$
= \left(\begin{array}{l} \text{if } 24\text{=}16 \text{ then } 24 \\ \text{else if } 24\text{<}16 \text{ then } \text{gcd}(24,16\text{-}24) \\ \qquad \text{else } \text{gcd}(24\text{-}16,16) \end{array} \right) = \text{(simplification)}
$$

$= \text{gcd}(8,16) =$ (replacement of gcd)

$$= \left(\begin{array}{l} \text{if 8=16 then 8} \\ \text{else if 8<16 then gcd(8,16-8)} \\ \qquad \text{else gcd(8-16,16)} \end{array} \right) = \text{(simplification)}$$

$= \text{gcd}(8,8) =$ (replacement of gcd)

$$= \left(\begin{array}{l} \text{if 8=8 then 8} \\ \text{else if 8<8 then gcd(8,8-8)} \\ \qquad \text{else gcd(8-8,8)} \end{array} \right) = \text{(simplification)}$$

$= 8$

This evaluation principle does not, however, unambiguously define the process of expression evaluation. It may happen that an expression involves more than one occurrence of a function call that, according to the principle, should be replaced by the *definiens*. For instance,

```
fun silly1(x,y) =
   if x then true
   else y;
fun forall(n,f) =
   if n=0 then true
   else forall(n-1,f) andalso f(n);
fun f(n) = (n<3);
silly1(true,forall(2,f));
```

According to the evaluation principle we may now either start by evaluating forall:

```
silly1(true, forall(2,f)) =

= silly1(true,
         (if 2=0 then true
          else forall(2-1,f)
         ) andalso f(2))
        ) =

= silly1(true, forall(1,f) andalso f(2)) =

= silly1(true,
         (if 1=0 then true
```

```
              else forall(1-1,f)
            ) andalso f(1) andalso f(2)
          ) =
```

```
    = silly1(true, forall(0,f) andalso f(1) andalso f(2)) =
```

```
    = silly1(true,
              (if 0=0 then true
               else forall(0-1,f)
              ) andalso f(0) andalso f(1) andalso f(2)
            ) =
```

```
    = silly1(true, f(1) andalso f(2)) =
```

```
    = true
```

or else we may evaluate silly1 first:

```
    silly1(true,forall(3,f)) =
```

```
    = if true then true
      else forall(3,f) =
```

```
    = true
```

The result is in both cases the same but, as we have seen, the evaluation is much shorter in the latter case.

The evaluation *strategy* that in case of doubt prescribes first replacing arguments, starting from the most deeply nested ones and going from left to right, is called *leftmost-innermost*, or *eager evaluation*, or *call-by-value*. The evaluation strategy that prescribes first replacing function names, starting from the most external ones and going from left to right, is referred to as *leftmost-outermost*, or *lazy evaluation*, or *call-by-name*. It is called *lazy* because of the way the interpreter behaves: it postpones the evaluation of the function's arguments for as long as possible in the "hope" that this evaluation may eventually be avoided altogether. These are not all the evaluation strategies, but certainly the two most important ones.

In our example we first applied eager evaluation, and then lazy evaluation, and in both cases the result was the same. It is important to know whether this was due to a lucky coincidence, or whether the result of applying various strategies is *always* the same.

Let us consider the following example with the function silly1 the same as before, and another function silly2:

```
    fun silly1(x,y) =
```

```
      if x then true
      else y;
   fun silly2(y) =
      if y then true
      else silly2(y);
   silly1(true,silly2(false));
```

The lazy evaluation:

```
   silly1(true,silly2(false)) =

   = if true then true
      else silly2(false) =

   = true
```

The eager evaluation:

```
   silly1(true,silly2(false)) =

   = silly1(true,
         (if false then true
          else silly2(false)
         )) =

   = silly1(true,silly2(false)) =
```

```
   . . .
```

— the evaluation is infinite. Thus it is possible for one strategy to yield a value of an expression, and for another to *diverge* over the same expression[1]. But is it also possible to get two different results when applying two different strategies to the same expression?

All would be rosy in the world of applicative programs if a flat "No" could be given as an answer, because this would relieve a programmer of any concern about *how* his expressions are evaluated. Unfortunately, we have to be a bit more cautious.

It *is* possible to get two different results if small, seemingly innocent, imperative details, such as *assignments*, are "compromised" into a basically applicative program. For instance,

```
   val x = ...Boolean variable initialised to true...;
   fun weird1(y) = ...value stored in x...;
   fun weird2(y) = (x:=false; y);
   weird1(weird2(true));
```

---

[1]The term "infinite loop" should be avoided since in applicative languages there are no loops.

By the eager evaluation the argument `weird2(true)` is evaluated first, yield-ing `true` as a value and changing `x` to `false` as a side effect; then `weird1` returns `false` as a result. By the lazy evaluation `weird1` returns `true` as a result and `weird2(true)` is never evaluated. This may serve as a warning against using assignments in applicative languages, although in some of them they are available, for instance in Standard ML[2].

Another dangerous feature is *exception handling,* i.e. user-defined run time errors together with user-defined reaction to these errors. In Standard ML a programmer may create an error situation by a subexpression `raise` *identifier.* This error situation propagates up to the highest-level expression, unless at some point on its way up it is intercepted by a `handle` *identifier* `=>`... clause. For instance, after the declaration

```
exception funny ;
```

we have

the value of	`raise funny`
is	`Failure: funny`
the value of	`3+raise funny`
is	`Failure: funny`
the value of	`5*(3+raise funny)`
is	`Failure: funny`
the value of	`5*(3+raise funny) handle funny => 7`
is	`7`
the value of	`(5*(3+raise funny) handle funny => 7)+2`
is	`9`
...etc.	

Therefore, if the eager strategy is applied to the program

```
exception funny ;
fun funny1(x) = true ;
funny1(raise funny) handle funny => false ;
```

then the evaluation starts with the argument `raise funny`, which results in the error situation `funny` that propagates to the higher level where it is handled by the `handle funny` clause, and the eventual result is `false`. On the other hand, if the lazy strategy is applied to the same program then the definition of function `funny1` yields `true` without ever looking at the function's argument.

Advocates of applicative programming believe that any features that allow for contradictory results of expression evaluation depending on the evaluation

---

[2]The Standard ML syntax for "variable initialised to e" is: `ref`(e); and for "value stored in x" it is: `!x`

strategy are "impure" and should be prohibited, because the programmer must not be burdened with this kind of computer-oriented thinking. From this point of view, assignments and exception handling are dangerous and should not be used. Even without going as far as this we advise the reader to avoid *excessive* use of these features, and always with the greatest caution, because they *are* dangerous.

2.2   The functional counterpart of a loop

The aim of the preceding section has been to explain what is happening during the evaluation of a functional program rather than to suggest any particular method of setting up such programs. Certainly, hand simulation is not an appropriate method.

The first problem a person with a training in imperative languages is likely to encounter when switching to applicative ones is the absence of loops.

Consider the following simple exercise: design a program that, given a sequence *seq* of real numbers, finds the sum of its n leading elements

$$seq_1 + seq_2 + \ldots + seq_n$$

A typical imperative solution is to introduce two auxiliary variables: an integer counter of indices and a real "result" variable in which partial sums would accumulate:

```
type sequence = array[1..verylargeinteger] of real;

function sum(n:integer; seq:sequence):real;
  var res:real; i:integer;
begin
  res:=0.0; i:=1;
  while i<=n do
  begin
    res:=res+seq[i]; i:=i+1
  end;
  sum:=res
end
```

This kind of a loop may be directly coded into an applicative language. The following theorem shows how to do this in general.

Theorem 1   *The following function:*

```
fun prog(x) =
  let fun loop(y) =
    if b(y) then loop(g(y))
    else y
  in h(loop(f(x)))
  end
```

corresponds to the imperative program

(2.1) $y := f(x)$;
```
      while b(y) do
        y := g(y);
      z := h(y)
```

in the sense that the effect of the program's execution is to establish the equality

$$z = \text{prog}(x)$$

for any input data x for which the imperative program halts.

Proof: First demonstrate that the formula

(2.2) $\text{loop}(f(x)) = \text{loop}(y)$

is an invariant of the **while**-loop in the imperative program (2.1). Indeed, if $b(y)$ holds then by the definition of function loop:

$$\text{loop}(y) = \text{loop}(g(y))$$

hence

$$\text{loop}(f(x)) = \text{loop}(y) \ \& \ b(y) \ \Rightarrow \ \text{loop}(f(x)) = \text{loop}(g(y))$$

which means precisely that (2.2) is an invariant.

On the exit of the **while**-loop (2.2) still holds but the condition $b(y)$ is no longer satisfied; therefore, by the definition of function loop

$$y = \text{loop}(f(x))$$

is satisfied. Hence, after the last assignment in the program (2.1)

$$z = h(\text{loop}(f(x)))$$

holds and thus the required equality is satisfied. $\square$

Theorem 1 provides an inefficient but certain way of transcribing imperative into applicative programs. It may be applied to the program that

calculates the sum of a sequence in the following way[3]. First, we find a correspondence between abstract notions from Theorem 1 and concrete ones from
the imperative program:

x	— input data —	(n,seq)
y	— auxiliary program variable —	(res,i)
z	— output values —	sum
$f((\text{n,seq}))$	— initialisation of program variable —	(0.0,1)
$g((\text{res,i}))$	— body of while-loop —	(res+seq(i),i+1)
$h((\text{res,i}))$	— exit operation —	res

Therefore, after obvious simplifications, the corresponding functional program
is:

```
type sequence = int -> real ;
fun sum(n, seq:sequence) =
  let fun loop(res,i) =
      if i<=n then loop(res+seq(i),i+1)
      else (res,i)
  in let val (res,i) = loop(0.0 ,1)
       in res
       end
  end;
```

Here is another example, a bit more complex because of the nested loops:
design a program to find the sum of the sums of the digits of all natural
numbers from 1 to a given n. This is a Pascal solution:

```
function sumofsumsofdigits(n:integer):integer;
  var s,i,j:integer;
begin
  s:=0;
  for i:=1 to n do
  begin {add to s the sum of digits of i}
    j:=i;
    while j>0 do
    begin
      s := s + j mod 10 ; j := j div 10
    end
  end;
  sumofsumsofdigits:=s
end
```

---

[3]Section 2.3 demonstrates equivalent but much simpler applicative programs that correspond to given ones, obtained without the use of Theorem 1.

In order to apply Theorem 1, first transform the `for` iteration in the above program to its `while` counterpart:

```
function sumofsumsofdigits(n:integer):integer;
  var s,i,j:integer;
begin
  s:=0; i:=1;
  while i<=n do
  begin {add to  s  the sum of digits of  i }
    j:=i;
    while j>0 do
    begin
      s := s + j mod 10 ; j := j div 10
    end;
    i:=i+1
  end;
  sumofsumsofdigits:=s
end
```

Next find the functional counterpart of the internal loop, i.e. of the program

```
j:=i;
while j>0 do
begin
  s := s + j mod 10 ; j := j div 10
end;
i:=i+1
```

Note that variable `j` may be made local to this fragment because it is not used outside it:

```
fun jloop(s,i) =
  let fun loop(s,i,j) =
    if j>0 then loop(s + j mod 10 , i , j div 10)
    else (s,i,j)
  in let val (s,i,j) = loop(s,i,i)
     in (s,i+1)
       end
  end
```

The original Pascal program may now be reduced to the following mixed Pascal–Standard ML program:

```
function sumofsumsofdigits(n:integer):integer;
  var s,i,j:integer;
```

```
begin
  s:=0; i:=1;
  while i<=n do
    (s,i) := jloop(s,i);
  sumofsumsofdigits:=s
end
```

which is by Theorem 1 equivalent to

```
fun sumofsumsofdigits(n) =
  let fun iloop(s,i) =
    if i<=n then iloop(jloop(s,i))
    else (s,i)
  in let val (s,i) = iloop(0,1)
     in s
     end
  end
```

After obvious simplifications the complete Standard ML definition is:

```
fun sumofsumsofdigits(n) =
  let fun iloop(s,i) =
    let fun jloop(s,i) =
      let fun loop(s,i,j) =
        if j>0 then loop(s + j mod 10 , i , j div 10)
        else (s,i,j)
      in let val (s,i,j) = loop(s,i,i)
         in (s,i+1)
         end
      end
    in
      if i<=n then iloop(jloop(s,i))
      else (s,i)
    end
  in let val (s,i) = iloop(0,1)
     in s
     end
  end
```

2.3   How to set up functional programs

While programming in a functional language we can, however, do much better than just give an applicative translation of an imperative program. Such translations are a rather poor style of programming. What we did in Sec. 2.2

was first, to code the problem into Pascal, and second, to code that code into Standard ML. No wonder that double coding could not but yield a long and inefficient program. Actually, the original problems were closer to Standard ML than to Pascal.

For instance, a natural Standard ML definition of the sum of a sequence as discussed in the preceding section is:

```
fun sum(n,seq) =
  if n=0 then 0.0
  else sum(n-1,seq)+seq(n);
```

Likewise, a natural Standard ML definition of the sum of the sums of digits is:

```
fun sumofsumofdigits(n) =
  let fun sumofdigits(i) =
    if i=0 then 0
    else i mod 10 + sumofdigits(i div 10)
  in if n=0 then 0
     else sumofsumofdigits(n-1) + sumofdigits(n)
  end
```

The considerations from the preceding section on how to program loops in the functional style, may hardly be considered a methodology for designing functional programs. In this section we give some hints, but the reader should be aware that there are no recipes for programming, and that it always remains a matter of talent and skill.

Respecting the logical structure of a problem

One of the main advantages of the applicative programming style is the possibility of writing programs that directly correspond to the logical structure of a problem. This has been illustrated above by the example of the sum of the sums of digits. Logically, the sum of the sums of digits is obtainable by adding up the sums of digits — this precisely is performed by the main function; and the auxiliary local function evaluates a single sum of digits.

Reduction to smaller subproblems

The main skill that has to be mastered when setting up truely functional programs is organising recursion. A recursive definition is a reduction of a problem to smaller subproblems of the same kind. Consider the following function that finds the maximum of a sequence $s(1),s(2),\ldots,s(n)$:

```
fun max(s:int->real ,n) =
  if n=1 then s(1)
  else let val m = max(s,n-1)
       in if m>s(n) then m
```

```
            else s(n)
        end
```

This definition reduces the problem of finding the maximum of that sequence
to the problem of finding the maximum of a shorter sequence

$$s(1), s(2), \ldots, s(n-1)$$

One thing a programmer is responsible for when organising recursion,
is to ensure the resulting subproblems are indeed simpler than the original
problem. In our case this can be reduced to the obvious

$$n > 1 \;\Rightarrow\; n-1 < n$$

for any natural n.

But for some problems what is meant by a *smaller* problem may not be
as evident. For instance, the definition

```
fun bizarre(n) =
  if n<=1 then 0
  else if n mod 2 = 0 then bizarre(n div 2)
        else bizarre(n+1)
```

reduces the problem from n to n div 2 or to n+1, depending on the parity
of n. In what sense should n+1 be considered smaller than n? A very similar
definition

```
fun bizarre'(n) =
  if n<1 then 0
  else if n mod 2 = 0 then bizarre'(n div 2)
        else bizarre'(n+1)
```

yields a function that is undefined for all n greater than 0, which means
bizarre' does *not* successfully reduce the problem to smaller subproblems.
Still **bizarre** itself is defined for all natural numbers. In order to prove this,
introduce the following "measure" on natural numbers:

$$meas(n) \overset{\text{def}}{=} 2 \cdot uppow_2(n) - n$$

where $uppow_2(n)$ is the least power of 2 greater or equal to n. For instance:

n	$uppow_2(n)$	$meas(n)$
0	1	2
1	1	1
2	2	2
3	4	5
4	4	4
5	8	11
6	8	10
7	8	9
8	8	8
9	16	23
10	16	22
...	...	...

As we see, and may also prove by induction, $meas(n)$ is greater than $meas(n \text{ div } 2)$ for any positive even n; and $meas(n)$ is greater than $meas(n + 1)$ for any odd n with the exception of 1. This exceptional number 1 accounts for the dramatic difference between bizarre and bizarre'.

By any decomposition of a problem into subproblems, a programmer should be aware of the measure according to which the subproblems are smaller than the original problems. Usually, this measure will be something as obvious as one of the arguments itself, or the difference between two arguments; but for some simple definitions it may turn out so complicated that its very existence may constitute an open problem. The so-called Collatz problem is very similar to our function bizarre: is the function

```
fun Collatz(n) =
  if n<=1 then 0
  else if 2|n then Collatz(n div 2)
        else Collatz(3*n+1)
```

defined for every natural n? So far the question remains unanswered.

Generalising

When designing a recursive definition one very often has to generalise the original problem in order to achieve its good inductive properties. The result of the generalisation is usually an auxiliary function.

Consider the following exercise to find the integer part of the square root of a given natural number n. This may be considered as an instance of a general search problem, since, as may easily be proved, a solution may be found in the interval $(0, n + 1)$. By generalising the problem to the one of finding the solution in any interval (a, b) we get the following binary search method:

```
fun sqroot(n) =
  let fun search(a,b) =
    if a+1=b then a
    else let val c = (a+b) div 2
         in if c*c>n then search(a,c)
            else search(c,b)
         end
  in search(0,n+1)
  end
```

Properties of a final program may critically depend on the way the problem has been generalised. It is something of an art to come up with a good generalisation.

2.4   Exercises

Exercise 3

How will the following program evaluate?

```
fun f(n) =
  if n=0 then 1
  else f(n-1)+g(n-1,n-1)
and g(n,k) =
  if k=0 then 0
  else f(n)+g(n,k-1) ;
f(2) ;
```

Exercise 4

How will the following program evaluate under both the eager and the lazy strategies?

```
exception wrong;
exception right;
fun apply(f,e) = f(e);
fun ident(x) =  x
                    handle wrong =>
                    raise right;
apply(ident,raise wrong);
```

Exercise 5

Write down a recursive definition corresponding to the Pascal loop

$y := f(x)$;
repeat
  $y := g(y)$
until $b(y)$;
$z := h(y)$

so that x is the function's argument and z its value; auxiliary variable y above may appear in the functional version only locally.

Exercise 6

Find a Standard ML counterpart of the following imperative bubble-sort algorithm:

```
for i:=n-1 downto 1 do
  for j:=1 to i do
    if a[j]>a[j+1] then swap(a,j,j+1)
```

Chapter 3

Proving properties of recursive functions

This chapter illustrates one of the virtues of applicative programs: the ease of proving their properties.

3.1 Applicative programs as mathematical objects

Applicative programs are mathematical objects to a much greater extent than imperative ones. The latter may, of course, be given a mathematical meaning (semantics) but this meaning does not adequately reflect the idea of a program, as it appears to a programmer. An imperative command is usually perceived as an active entity that *alters* the world, rather than as a function from states, which are functions, to states. In the world of imperative programs there exists a certain psychological discrepancy between intuition and formal apparatus which may endanger reliability.

Applicative programs are formally and psychologically mathematical objects. When defining the semantics of an applicative language one is often haunted by a sense of the futility of one's efforts because the right hand sides of definitions are likely to look very similar to the left hand sides.

Consider for instance the following toy programming language:

$$
\begin{aligned}
Prog \quad &::= \quad Def\,;\ldots;Def\,;Expr \\
Def \quad &::= \quad \texttt{DEF}\ Funname(\,Variable\,) = Expr \\
Expr \quad &::= \quad Number \\
&\quad\ |\quad Variable \\
&\quad\ |\quad (\,Expr + Expr\,) \\
&\quad\ |\quad (\,Expr - Expr\,) \\
&\quad\ |\quad (\,Expr * Expr\,) \\
&\quad\ |\quad \texttt{IF}\ Expr = Expr\ \texttt{THEN}\ Expr\ \texttt{ELSE}\ Expr \\
&\quad\ |\quad Funname(\,Expr\,)
\end{aligned}
$$

$$\left.\begin{array}{l} Funname \\ Variable \\ Number \end{array}\right\} \quad \text{primitive (recognisable) syntactic domains}$$

The reader will undoubtedly understand the intentions behind this syntax. Let us try to define the semantics that would properly reflect these intentions. For the sake of simplicity, we do not discriminate between partial and total functions, although a proper definition of semantics should do that.

We start with expressions. Since an expression may involve variables, its meaning depends on a state of variables:

$$State = Variable \to Nat$$

and since it may also involve function names, its meaning also depends on an environment assigning functions to function names:

$$Env = Funname \to Nat \to Nat$$

The following function gives the meaning of the expressions:

$$E : Expr \to Env \to State \to Nat$$

$$
\begin{array}{ll}
E[\![num]\!]es & = \;\ldots \text{usual understanding of a number} \ldots \\
E[\![var]\!]es & = \; s(var) \\
E[\![(ex_1+ex_2)]\!]es & = \; E[\![ex_1]\!]es + E[\![ex_2]\!]es \\
E[\![(ex_1-ex_2)]\!]es & = \; E[\![ex_1]\!]es - E[\![ex_2]\!]es \\
E[\![(ex_1*ex_2)]\!]es & = \; E[\![ex_1]\!]es \cdot E[\![ex_2]\!]es \\
E[\![\text{ IF } ex_1=ex_2 \text{ THEN } ex_3 & \\
\qquad\qquad \text{ELSE } ex_4]\!]es & = \; \left\{ \begin{array}{ll} E[\![ex_3]\!]es & \text{if } E[\![ex_1]\!]es = E[\![ex_2]\!]es \\ E[\![ex_4]\!]es & \text{if } E[\![ex_1]\!]es \neq E[\![ex_2]\!]es \end{array} \right. \\
E[\![fn(ex)]\!]es & = \; e(fn)(E[\![ex]\!]es)
\end{array}
$$

Thus the meaning of + is explained by the "true" addition, the meaning of the conditional by the "true" case split, the meaning of the function application by the "true" application, etc.

The meaning of a function definition in our toy language is the defined function. Formally:

$$D_1 : Def \to Env \to Nat \to Nat$$

$$D_1[\![\text{DEF } fn(var) = ex]\!]e = \text{the function } f \text{ defined recursively by}$$
$$f(n) = E[\![ex]\!](e[f/fn])(s_0[n/var])$$

where $f[a/x]$ denotes the function f updated with the value a for argument x; and s_0 is the state that assigns 0 to all variables. The meaning of the recursive definition of fn above has thus been explained by the recursive definition of f at a different level of abstraction.

Function definitions also change environments:

$$D_2 \; : \; Def \to Env \to Env$$

$$D_2[\![\text{DEF } fn(var) = ex]\!]e = e[D_1[\![\text{DEF } fn(var) = ex]\!]/fn]$$

Finally, the semantics of a complete program:

$$P \; : \; Prog \to Nat$$

$$P[\![df_1; \ldots; df_n; ex]\!] = E[\![ex]\!](D_2[\![df_n]\!](D_2[\![df_{n-1}]\!](\ldots(D_2[\![df_1]\!]e_0)\ldots)))s_0$$

where e_0 is the environment that assigns to every function name a completely undefined function from $Nat \to Nat$.

This completes the definition of the semantics of our toy language.

We have not, in fact, said what addition, conditional or recursion are; we have just explained them in terms of meta-addition, and meta-conditional, and meta-recursion. A definition of a programming language is certainly not the place to explain the intricacies of arithmetic, or the general nature of recursion, so knowledge of these concepts has had to be assumed. But then the semantic definition does not solve a problem, but only pushes it a stage further.

Unlike imperative programming, applicative programming deals directly with mathematical objects and for this reason it does not need a semantic description any more than geometry or differential equations. This fact accounts also for the more direct proving of properties.

3.2   Simple proofs by mathematical induction

The main tool for proving facts about recursive functions is *mathematical induction*. In its basic form the rule of induction reads as follows:

(3.1)
$$\frac{P(0) \qquad \forall_{n \in Nat} P(n) \Rightarrow P(n+1)}{\forall_{n \in Nat} P(n)}$$

In this rule, P is a property of natural numbers that *a priori* may be true of some numbers and false of some other numbers. The rule (3.1) states that every property P that holds for 0 and is closed under the successor operation, holds for all natural numbers.

To prove the properties of applicative programs, this rule may be readily used as it stands. This should be contrasted with the case of imperative programs where every single property, such as partial correctness or termination, has to come with a theory of its own, e.g. the theory of invariants for partial correctness, and the theory of loop counters for termination. All these theories are specialised forms of the induction rule.

Below we give example proofs of a property of an applicative program, and of a corresponding property of a corresponding imperative program. The reader is urged to go through the details of these proofs, even though they may not be very interesting, in order to appreciate the problems involved.

Let a function sumprod be defined by the following Standard ML code:

```
fun sumprod(matr,n,k) =
  let fun prod(matr,i,k) =
          if k=0 then 1.0
          else prod(matr,i,k-1)*matr(i,k)
  in if n=0 then 0.0
     else sumprod(matr,n-1,k)+prod(matr,n,k)
  end ;
```

Then the following property of sumprod is true:

Theorem 2 *For any matrix*

$$matr \ : \ \text{int} \times \text{int} \to \text{real}$$

and any natural numbers n and k

$$(3.2) \quad \texttt{sumprod}(matr, n, k) = \sum_{i=1}^{n} \prod_{j=1}^{k} matr(i, j)$$

Proof: Since sumprod is defined using an auxiliary function prod, it is natural to start by establishing some properties of this auxiliary function:

Lemma 1 *For any matr as above and any natural numbers k and i*

$$(3.3) \quad \texttt{prod}(matr, i, k) = \prod_{j=1}^{k} matr(i, j)$$

Proof of the Lemma:

Induction on k, which means $P(k)$ from (3.1) is now:

$$\forall_{i \in Nat} \ \texttt{prod}(matr, i, k) = \prod_{j=1}^{k} matr(i, j)$$

for any natural k.

Base step $k = 0$:

According to the definition of prod:

$$\texttt{prod}(matr, i, 0) = 1.0$$

On the other hand, a product of zero real numbers is the neutral element of multiplication:

$$\prod_{j=1}^{0} matr(i,j) = 1.0$$

Inductive step:
Assume (3.3) satisfied. Then

$$\mathbf{prod}(matr, i, k+1) = \quad \text{(definition of } \mathbf{prod})$$

$$= \mathbf{prod}(matr, i, k) \cdot matr(i, k+1) = \quad \text{(inductive assumption (3.3))}$$

$$= \prod_{j=1}^{k} matr(i,j) \cdot matr(i, k+1) =$$

$$= \prod_{j=1}^{k+1} matr(i,j)$$

and this completes the proof of the Lemma.

Proof of the Theorem:
We use induction on n, which means $P(n)$ from (3.1) is now:

$$\forall_{k \in Nat} \, \mathbf{sumprod}(matr, n, k) = \sum_{i=1}^{n} \prod_{j=1}^{k} matr(i,j)$$

for any natural n.
Base step $n = 0$:
According to the definition of $\mathbf{sumprod}$:

$$\mathbf{sumprod}(matr, 0, k) = 0.0$$

On the other hand

$$\sum_{i=1}^{0} \prod_{j=1}^{k} matr(i,j) = 0.0$$

because the summation is trivial and 0.0 is the neutral element of addition.
Inductive step:
Assume (3.2) satisfied. Then

$$\mathbf{sumprod}(matr, n+1, k) = \quad \text{(definition of } \mathbf{sumprod})$$

$$= \mathbf{sumprod}(matr, n, k) + \mathbf{prod}(matr, n+1, k) =$$

(inductive assumption (3.2) and Lemma)

$$= \sum_{i=1}^{n} \prod_{j=1}^{k} matr(i,j) + \prod_{j=1}^{k} matr(n+1,j) =$$

$$= \sum_{i=1}^{n+1} \prod_{j=1}^{k} matr(i,j)$$

□

Compare the above proof with the following proof of the partial correctness of a corresponding imperative program

```
s:=0.0; i:=1;
while i<=n do
begin
  p:=1.0; j:=1;
  while j<=k do
  begin
    p:=p*matr[i,j]; j:=j+1
  end;
  s:=s+p; i:=i+1
end
```

Theorem 3 *The above imperative program is partially correct wrt predicates*

true

and

$$s = \sum_{i'=1}^{n} \prod_{j'=1}^{k} \texttt{matr}[i',j']$$

Proof: Start with the external loop:

Lemma 2 *Predicate*

$$1 \leq \texttt{i} \leq \texttt{n}+1 \ \& \ s = \sum_{i'=1}^{i-1} \prod_{j'=1}^{k} \texttt{matr}[i',j']$$

is an invariant of the external **while**-*loop.*

We postpone the proof of Lemma 2 until later and show first how it implies the hypothesis of the Theorem.

The initialisation command

```
s:=0.0; i:=1
```

is partially correct wrt predicates

true

and

$$1 \leq i \leq n+1 \ \& \ s = \sum_{i'=1}^{i-1} \prod_{j'=1}^{k} \texttt{matr}[i',j']$$

Indeed, the above postcondition reduces to

$$1 \leq 1 \leq n+1 \ \& \ 0.0 = \sum_{i'=1}^{0} \prod_{j'=1}^{k} \texttt{matr}[i',j']$$

which is implied by the precondition because the summation over an empty interval yields 0.0.

Therefore, the initialisation command establishes the invariant, which by Lemma 2 is still satisfied upon exit from the external loop, in conjunction with the negation of the loop condition; therefore the whole imperative program establishes the satisfaction of

$$1 \leq i \leq n+1 \ \& \ s = \sum_{i'=1}^{i-1} \prod_{j'=1}^{k} \texttt{matr}[i',j'] \ \& \ i > n$$

which reduces to

$$i = n+1 \ \& \ s = \sum_{i'=1}^{n} \prod_{j'=1}^{k} \texttt{matr}[i',j']$$

which implies the required postcondition of the program. Thus the proof of the Theorem is complete modulo a proof of Lemma 2.

Proof of Lemma 2:

We have to demonstrate that the body of the external loop, i.e. the command

```
p:=1.0; j:=1;
while j<=k do
begin
 p:=p*matr[i,j]; j:=j+1
end;
s:=s+p; i:=i+1
```

is partially correct wrt predicates

$$1 \leq i \leq n+1 \ \& \ s = \sum_{i'=1}^{i-1} \prod_{j'=1}^{k} \mathtt{matr}\,[i', j'] \ \& \ i \leq n$$

and

$$1 \leq i \leq n+1 \ \& \ s = \sum_{i'=1}^{i-1} \prod_{j'=1}^{k} \mathtt{matr}\,[i', j']$$

To achieve this we need an invariant for the internal loop:

Lemma 3 *Predicate*

$$1 \leq i \leq n \ \& \ s = \sum_{i'=1}^{i-1} \prod_{j'=1}^{k} \mathtt{matr}\,[i', j'] \ \& $$
$$1 \leq j \leq k+1 \ \& \ p = \prod_{j'=1}^{j-1} \mathtt{matr}\,[i', j']$$

is an invariant of the internal while-loop.

We again postpone the proof of Lemma 3 until later and show first how it implies the hypothesis of Lemma 2.

The initialisation command

```
p:=1.0; j:=1
```

is partially correct wrt precondition

$$1 \leq i \leq n+1 \ \& \ s = \sum_{i'=1}^{i-1} \prod_{j'=1}^{k} \mathtt{matr}\,[i', j'] \ \& \ i \leq n$$

and the invariant

$$1 \leq i \leq n \ \& \ s = \sum_{i'=1}^{i-1} \prod_{j'=1}^{k} \mathtt{matr}\,[i', j'] \ \& $$
$$1 \leq j \leq k+1 \ \& \ p = \prod_{j'=1}^{j-1} \mathtt{matr}\,[i', j']$$

Indeed, the above invariant reduces to

$$1 \leq i \leq n \ \& \ s = \sum_{i'=1}^{i-1} \prod_{j'=1}^{k} \mathtt{matr}\,[i', j'] \ \& $$
$$1 \leq 1 \leq k+1 \ \& \ 1.0 = \prod_{j'=1}^{0} \mathtt{matr}\,[i', j']$$

which is implied by the precondition since the product over an empty interval yields 1.0.

Therefore, the initialisation command establishes the invariant, which by Lemma 3 is still satisfied upon exit from the internal loop, in conjunction with the negation of the loop condition:

$$1 \leq i \leq n \ \& \ s = \sum_{i'=1}^{i-1} \prod_{j'=1}^{k} \mathtt{matr}\,[i', j'] \ \& $$
$$1 \leq j \leq k+1 \ \& \ p = \prod_{j'=1}^{j-1} \mathtt{matr}\,[i', j'] \ \& \ j > k$$

It is easy to prove that the command

```
s:=s+p; i:=i+1
```

is partially correct wrt the above predicate and

$$1 \le i \le n+1 \,\&\, s = \sum_{i'=1}^{i-1} \prod_{j'=1}^{k} \mathtt{matr}[i',j']$$

(the reader is strongly urged to carry out the proof!), thus the proof of Lemma 2 is complete modulo a proof of Lemma 3.

Proof of Lemma 3:

  We have to demonstrate now that the command

```
p:=p*matr[i,j]; j:=j+1
```

is partially correct wrt

$$1 \le i \le n \,\&\, s = \sum_{i'=1}^{i-1} \prod_{j'=1}^{k} \mathtt{matr}[i',j'] \,\&\,$$
$$1 \le j \le k+1 \,\&\, p = \prod_{j'=1}^{j-1} \mathtt{matr}[i',j'] \,\&\, j \le k$$

and

$$1 \le i \le n \,\&\, s = \sum_{i'=1}^{i-1} \prod_{j'=1}^{k} \mathtt{matr}[i',j'] \,\&\,$$
$$1 \le j \le k+1 \,\&\, p = \prod_{j'=1}^{j-1} \mathtt{matr}[i',j']$$

The details of this proof we again leave to the reader and urge that the whole thing is written down. □

  Please, note that Theorem 3 gives less information about the imperative code discussed than Theorem 2 about the corresponding applicative code. Firstly, it deals only with partial correctness. Secondly, even total correctness is a relatively weak property of programs as long as no means are provided to distinguish constants from variables; for instance the following trivial program

```
n:=0; s:=0.0
```

is also totally correct wrt

$$true \qquad \text{and} \qquad s = \sum_{i'=1}^{n} \prod_{j'=1}^{k} \mathtt{matr}[i',j']$$

This and similar problems can, of course, be overcome, but always at the cost of adding complication to the proof.

3.3 More complicated induction

Recursion in a function definition may be more complicated than just going from n to $n+1$ (or from $n-1$ to n). For instance, to prove that

(3.4) $\forall_{n \in Nat} \forall_{r \in Real \setminus \{0\}} \ \mathrm{pow}(r, n) = r^n$

where pow is defined by

```
fun pow(r,n) =
  if n=0 then 1.0
  else if n mod 2 = 0 then pow(r*r,n div 2)
        else r*pow(r*r,n div 2)
```

we need

$$\forall_{r \in Real \setminus \{0\}} \ \mathrm{pow}(r \cdot r, n \ div \ 2) = (r \cdot r)^{n \ div \ 2}$$

as the inductive assumption, since this is what the recursive calls within the body of the definition of pow look like.

Since it is often necessary to reach more deeply than to a predecessor, program proving may be better assisted by the following induction rule instead of (3.1):

(3.5) $$\frac{\forall_{n \in Nat} \ (\forall_{k \in Nat} \ k < n \Rightarrow P(k)) \Rightarrow P(n)}{\forall_{n \in Nat} \ P(n)}$$

This reads: if a property P holds for a natural number n provided it holds for *all* predecessors of n, then it holds for all natural numbers.

We may now prove (3.4) using rule (3.5) in the following way. Assume for some natural n

(3.6) $\forall_{k \in Nat} \ k < n \Rightarrow (\forall_{r \in Real \setminus \{0\}} \ \mathrm{pow}(r, k) = r^k)$

holds. Once we have demonstrated that

(3.7) $\forall_{r \in Real \setminus \{0\}} \ \mathrm{pow}(r, n) = r^n$

the premise of rule (3.5) will have been proved and therefore (3.4) will follow by virtue of the rule. To do this, consider the three cases appearing in the definition of function pow.

CASE $n = 0$:
Let r be an arbitrary real number distinct from zero. By virtue of the definition of pow

$$\mathrm{pow}(r, 0) = 1.0$$

On the other hand

$$r^0 = 1.0$$

hence (3.7) is satisfied.

CASE $n \neq 0$ & $n \bmod 2 = 0$:
Let r_0 be an arbitrary real number. By virtue of the definition of pow

(3.8) $\text{pow}(r_0, n) = \text{pow}(r_0 \cdot r_0, n \ div \ 2)$

Since n is even and positive, $n \ div \ 2 = \frac{n}{2}$ is a natural number properly smaller than n, therefore the inductive assumption (3.6) with $n \ div \ 2$ for k yields

$$\forall_{r \in Real \setminus \{0\}} \ \text{pow}(r, n \ div \ 2) = r^{\frac{n}{2}}$$

which implies

(3.9) $\text{pow}(r_0 \cdot r_0, n \ div \ 2) = (r_0 \cdot r_0)^{\frac{n}{2}} = r_0^n$

Now, putting (3.8) and (3.9) together results in (3.7).

CASE $n \neq 0$ & $n \bmod 2 \neq 0$:
Let r_0 be an arbitrary real number. By virtue of the definition of pow

(3.10) $\text{pow}(r_0, n) = r_0 \cdot \text{pow}(r_0 \cdot r_0, n \ div \ 2)$

Since n is odd, $n \ div \ 2 = \frac{n-1}{2}$ is a natural number properly smaller than n, therefore again $n \ div \ 2$ may be substituted for k in the inductive assumption (3.6) yielding

$$\forall_{r \in Real \setminus \{0\}} \ (r, n \ div \ 2) = r^{\frac{n-1}{2}}$$

which implies

(3.11) $\text{pow}(r_0 \cdot r_0, n \ div \ 2) = (r_0 \cdot r_0)^{\frac{n-1}{2}} = r_0^{n-1}$

Now, putting (3.10) and (3.11) together results in (3.7).
This completes the proof of (3.4).

Although the new induction rule (3.5) may look strange (for instance it appears to have no base case) it is fully equivalent to the standard induction rule (3.1). This is proved formally below:

Theorem 4 *The induction rules (3.1) and (3.5) are equivalent.*

Proof: First prove that (3.5) implies (3.1).

Assume P is a property of natural numbers that satisfies the premises

(3.12) $P(0)$

and

(3.13) $\forall_{n \in Nat} P(n) \Rightarrow P(n+1)$

of (3.1). We have to demonstrate (using (3.5)) that P also satisfies the conclusion

(3.14) $\forall_{n \in Nat} P(n)$

of (3.1). Let n be a natural number such that

(3.15) $\forall_{k \in Nat} k < n \Rightarrow P(k)$

In case $n = 0$, $P(n)$ holds by (3.12); if n is positive then $n-1$ is a natural number properly smaller than n, hence $P(n-1)$ holds by (3.15), and hence $P(n)$ by (3.13). This proves (3.14).

Next prove that also (3.1) implies (3.5).

Assume P is a property of natural numbers that satisfies the premise

(3.16) $\forall_{n \in Nat} (\forall_{k \in Nat} k < n \Rightarrow P(k)) \Rightarrow P(n)$

of (3.5). We have to demonstrate (using (3.1)) that P also satisfies the conclusion

(3.17) $\forall_{n \in Nat} P(n)$

of (3.5).

To do this define an auxiliary property Q of natural numbers:

$$Q(n) \Longleftrightarrow \forall_{k \in Nat} k < n \Rightarrow P(k)$$

It is easy to see that Q satisfies the premises of (3.1). Indeed, on the one hand

$$Q(0) \Longleftrightarrow \forall_{k \in Nat} k < 0 \Rightarrow P(k) \Longleftrightarrow true$$

(vacuously); on the other hand, for any natural n

$$Q(n) \Rightarrow Q(n)$$

and by virtue of (3.16)

$$Q(n) \Rightarrow P(n)$$

hence $Q(n)$ implies

$$Q(n) \& P(n)$$

i.e.

$$(\forall_{k\in Nat}\ k < n \Rightarrow P(k))\&P(n)$$

i.e.

$$\forall_{k\in Nat}\ k < n+1 \Rightarrow P(k)$$

i.e. $Q(n)$ implies $Q(n+1)$.

Thus we have proved that rule (3.1) applied to property Q yields

$$\forall_{n\in Nat}\ Q(n)$$

i.e.

$$\forall_{n\in Nat}\ \forall_{k\in Nat}\ k < n \Rightarrow P(k)$$

which yields (3.17) when instantiated with $n+1$ for n and with n for k. $\square$

3.4 Definitions that do not involve natural numbers

For a legitimate use of induction rules (3.1) and (3.5) it is important that the induction parameter be natural. Therefore, when faced with the task of proving a property of a function that operates over other domains, one has to come up with a natural "measure" of the problem and run induction over that measure.

Consider the following function supposed to find the cubic root of a given real number x within a given real positive accuracy *eps*:

```
fun cubroot(x,eps) =
  let fun f(a,b,x,eps) =
          if b-a<eps then a
          else let val c=(a+b)/2.0
               in if x<c*c*c
                  then f(a,c,x,eps)
                  else f(c,b,x,eps)
               end
      in if x<0.0
         then f(x-1.0 , 0.0 , x , eps)
         else f(0.0 , x+1.0 , x , eps)
      end
```

The above definition is so totally committed to real numbers that there seems to be no place left for induction. But since the definition of the auxiliary f in it is by recursion, it does reduce the problem to smaller subproblems and we may try to work out the measure according to which these subproblems are smaller.

Critical for f seems to be the distance between the two limiting arguments a and b: with every recursive call it is halved, and the result is delivered when this distance becomes smaller than eps; this suggests a consideration of $\frac{b-a}{eps}$, which is the distance expressed in eps-units.

Theorem 5 *Function* cubroot *evaluates the cubic root within a given accuracy, i.e.*

$$\forall_{x,\varepsilon\in Real}\ \varepsilon > 0 \Rightarrow \mathtt{cubroot}(x,\varepsilon) \leq \sqrt[3]{x} < \mathtt{cubroot}(x,\varepsilon) + \varepsilon$$

Proof: The lemma that follows shows that $\mathtt{f}(a,b,x,\varepsilon)$ is the required cubic root of x within accuracy ε provided this cubic root lies in the interval $\langle a,b\rangle$; otherwise the result yielded by f is irrelevant. To prove this, consider the following property $P(n)$ of natural numbers:

$$\forall_{a,b,x,\varepsilon\in Real}\ \ \varepsilon > 0\ \&\ a \leq \sqrt[3]{x} < b\ \&\ \tfrac{b-a}{\varepsilon} < n\ \Rightarrow$$
$$\mathtt{f}(a,b,x,\varepsilon) \leq \sqrt[3]{x} < \mathtt{f}(a,b,x,\varepsilon) + \varepsilon$$

Thus $P(n)$ holds if f does what it is supposed to do provided the "measure" of the problem does not exceed n.

Lemma 4 $\forall_{n\in Nat}\ P(n)$

Proof of the Lemma:
  Let $n \in Nat$, assume

(3.18) $\forall_{k\in Nat}\ k < n \Rightarrow P(k)$

We will try to prove $P(n)$. Let $a,b,x,\varepsilon \in Real$ be such that

(3.19) $\varepsilon > 0$

(3.20) $a \leq \sqrt[3]{x} < b$

(3.21) $\dfrac{b-a}{\varepsilon} < n$

We have to demonstrate that

(3.22) $\mathtt{f}(a,b,x,\varepsilon) \leq \sqrt[3]{x} < \mathtt{f}(a,b,x,\varepsilon) + \varepsilon$

CASE $b - a < \varepsilon$:
Then $b < a + \varepsilon$ which together with (3.20) yields

$$a \leq \sqrt[3]{x} < a + \varepsilon$$

and on the other hand $a = \mathbf{f}(a, b, x, \varepsilon)$ by the definition of $\mathbf{f}$; this proves (3.22).

CASE $b - a \geq \varepsilon$ & $x < c^3$, where $c = \frac{a+b}{2}$:
Then

$$(3.23) \quad \frac{c - a}{\varepsilon} = \frac{\frac{a+b}{2} - a}{\varepsilon} = \frac{b - a}{2 \cdot \varepsilon} = \frac{\frac{b-a}{\varepsilon}}{2} < \frac{n}{2} \leq (n + 1) \ div \ 2$$

The equalities above are obvious, the first inequality follows from (3.21), the second one is a simple property of natural numbers (let the reader prove it!). Since in our case $b - a \geq \varepsilon$, then, by (3.19), $\frac{b-a}{\varepsilon} \geq 1$, which, together with (3.21), yields $n > 1$, i.e. $n \geq 2$; it is another simple property of natural numbers that in this case

$$(n + 1) \ div \ 2 < n$$

(let the reader prove it and make sure that the condition $n \geq 2$ is essential). This inequality, together with the induction assumption (3.18), implies $P((n + 1) \ div \ 2)$; when this is instantiated with a for a, c for b, x for x and ε for ε the result is:

$$\varepsilon > 0 \ \& \ a \leq \sqrt[3]{x} < c \ \& \ \frac{c-a}{\varepsilon} < (n + 1) \ div \ 2 \ \Rightarrow$$
$$\mathbf{f}(a, b, x, \varepsilon) \leq \sqrt[3]{x} < \mathbf{f}(a, b, x, \varepsilon) + \varepsilon$$

The satisfaction of the precedent of this implication is easy to verify: $\varepsilon > 0$ by (3.19); $a \leq \sqrt[3]{x}$ by (3.20); $\sqrt[3]{x} < c$ by the entrance condition to the considered case; $\frac{c-a}{\varepsilon} < (n+1) \ div \ 2$ by (3.23). Therefore the consequent of the implication also holds, and this proves (3.22).

CASE $b - a \geq \varepsilon$ & $x < c^3$, where $c = \frac{a+b}{2}$:
This is analogous and left to the reader.
This concludes the proof of the Lemma.

Proof of the Theorem:
Since by virtue of the Lemma, $P(n)$ holds universally for all natural n, this measure is not important, and the simpler

$$(3.24) \quad \forall_{a,b,x,\varepsilon \in Real} \quad \varepsilon > 0 \ \& \ a \leq \sqrt[3]{x} < b \ \Rightarrow$$
$$\mathbf{f}(a, b, x, \varepsilon) \leq \sqrt[3]{x} < \mathbf{f}(a, b, x, \varepsilon) + \varepsilon$$

is true. We have to ensure the values $x - 1$ and 0 (resp. 0 and $x + 1$) are good lower and upper bounds on $\sqrt[3]{x}$, i.e. to prove

$$x < 0 \Rightarrow x - 1 \leq \sqrt[3]{x} < 0$$

and

$$x \geq 0 \Rightarrow 0 \leq \sqrt[3]{x} < x + 1$$

The above is equivalent to

$$x < 0 \Rightarrow x^3 - 3x^2 + 2x - 1 < 0$$

and

$$x \geq 0 \Rightarrow x^3 + 3x^2 + 2x + 1 \geq 0$$

The latter implication is obvious; to prove the former use, for instance, differential calculus to show that the polynome is an increasing function for all $x < 0$, and that it only reaches -1 for $x = 0$, hence that its value is always negative.

Therefore, in the $x < 0$ case, (3.24) instantiated with $x - 1$ for a and with 0 for b yields

$$\forall_{x,\varepsilon \in Real} \; \varepsilon > 0 \Rightarrow \mathbf{f}(x - 1, 0, x, \varepsilon) \leq \sqrt[3]{x} < \mathbf{f}(x - 1, 0, x, \varepsilon) + \varepsilon$$

which, by the definition of cubroot, proves the hypothesis of the Theorem; analogously in the $x \geq 0$ case. $\square$

3.5   Danger points in induction proofs

This section introduces two pseudotheorems that support false claims with pseudoproofs based on misuses of induction. These are probably the most frequently encountered kinds of error, although in everyday practice the pseudotheorems are usually less blatantly nonsensical, which makes the flaws in reasoning even more dangerous.

Pseudotheorem 1   *Every natural number is smaller than itself, i.e.*

$$\forall_{n \in Nat} \; n < n$$

Pseudoproof: Induction on n using (3.5). Let n be a natural number satisfying

$$(3.25) \quad \forall_{k \in Nat} \; k < n \Rightarrow k < k$$

CASE 2 | n:

In this case $\frac{n}{2}$ is a natural number smaller than n, hence by the inductive assumption (3.25) applied to $\frac{n}{2}$ for k:

$$\frac{n}{2} < \frac{n}{2}$$

and hence

$$n < n$$

CASE $\neg 2 \mid n$:

In this case n is at least 1, hence $n - 1$ is a natural number smaller than n, hence by the inductive assumption (3.25) applied to $n - 1$ for k

$$n - 1 < n - 1$$

and hence

$$n < n$$

Since therefore (3.25) implies $n < n$ in all cases, the rule (3.5) implies

$$\forall_{n \in Nat} \, n < n$$

$\square$

Before reading on, the reader should attempt by himself to find an error in the above pseudotheorem.

The problem rests with 0. 0 is an even number, yet it is not true that $\frac{0}{2} < 0$. Therefore the reasoning in the case of even n-s is not correct.

Since the only error committed in the pseudoproof consisted of overlooking a very special property of 0, namely that $\frac{0}{2} = 0$, the reader may wonder whether the same proof works for larger numbers. Try to use the same method to prove

$$\forall_{n \in Nat} \, n > 0 \Rightarrow n < n$$

and observe where the reasoning breaks down.

This lies in the nature of induction, that the effects of an error concerning a single small number may be carried through the whole sequence of natural numbers. An error may of course also arise higher up, but for some psychological reasons people tend to be more careless about smaller numbers.

Pseudotheorem 2   *No positive real numbers exist, i.e.*

$$\forall_{r \in Real} \, r \leq 0$$

Pseudoproof: Induction on r. Assume r satisfies

(3.26) $\forall_{r' \in Real} \, r' < r \Rightarrow r' \leq 0$

and try to prove $r \leq 0$.

CASE $r \leq 0$:

Then of course $r \leq 0$.

CASE $r > 0$:

Then $0 < \frac{r}{2} < r$ and the inductive assumption (3.26) instantiated with $\frac{r}{2}$ for r' implies

$$\frac{r}{2} \leq 0$$

which means that also $r \leq 0$. $\square$

Of course, the problem rests with using induction on real numbers. Admittedly, there exist domains other than natural numbers, the so-called *well-ordered sets*, where induction is a legitimate proof method. But the set of real numbers is not well-ordered.

We can, however, prove theorems about real numbers by induction if we can find some natural "measure" over real numbers that expresses our problem, as discussed in the previous section.

Pseudotheorem 1 warns against too little caution at the start; Pseudotheorem 2 against using induction in the wrong domains. Most mistakes result from a combination of these two flaws in reasoning. For instance, a critical natural number in our proof may be a guaranteed power of 2, from which we conclude that it may be indefinitely divided by 2, yielding smaller and smaller powers of 2, but then it becomes 1 and further divisions result in non-natural numbers.

3.6   Exercises

Exercise 7

Prove that

$$(3.27) \quad \forall_{n \in Nat} \; \mathtt{f}(n) \leq \sqrt{n} < \mathtt{f}(n) + 1$$

where $\mathtt{f}$ is the function defined by

```
fun f(n) =
  let fun g(n,k,a,b) =
    if a>n then k-1
    else g(n,k+1,a+b,b+2)
  in g(n,0,0,1)
  end
```

Hint: Consider the property

$$P(l) \Longleftrightarrow$$
$$\forall_{n,k,a,b \in Nat}$$
$$n - a < l \;\&\; a = k^2 \;\&\; b = 2 \cdot k + 1 \;\&\; k \geq 0 \;\&\; k \leq \sqrt{n} + 1 \Rightarrow$$
$$g(n,k,a,b) \leq \sqrt{n} < g(n,k,a,b) + 1$$

Exercise 8

By analogy with Exercise 7, define a function f that finds the integer cubic root of a given natural number, using only addition, subtraction and comparison, and prove that

$$\forall_{n \in Nat} \; \mathtt{f}(n) \le \sqrt[3]{n} < \mathtt{f}(n) + 1$$

Exercise 9

Design a Standard ML definition of the function that finds the maximal element of a sequence of real numbers, and prove its correctness.

Exercise 10

Find an error in the proof of the following pseudotheorem:

Pseudotheorem 3 *All people in the world have the same colour of eyes*

Pseudoproof: We will try to prove by induction the satisfaction of the predicate

(3.28) $\quad \forall_{n \in Nat} \; P(n)$

where

$$P(n) \Longleftrightarrow \text{within any group of } n \text{ people}$$
$$\text{everyone has the same colour of eyes}$$

Then the hypothesis will follow from the fact that there are only a finite number of people in the world.

To prove (3.28) assume that for a certain $n \in Nat$:

(3.29) $\quad \forall_{k \in Nat} \; k < n \Rightarrow P(k)$

Now, $P(0)$ and $P(1)$ hold trivially even without the inductive assumption (3.29). To prove $P(n)$ for a larger n, take an arbitrary group of n people and select within this group two distinct (overlapping) subgroups of $n - 1$ people each:

The induction assumption (3.29) instantiated with $n - 1$ for k implies that all people in the first subgroup have the same colour of eyes, and also that all people in the second subgroup have the same colour of eyes; hence all people in the whole group have the same colour of eyes. $\Box$

Chapter 4

High order functions

High order functions, or *functionals*, are functions that treat other functions as data; i.e. take functions as arguments and/or yield functions as results. The aim of this chapter is to illustrate their usefulness; and also, to a lesser extent, to discuss the costs involved.

4.1 The dictionary example

Let us consider the general dictionary problem: design a simple system for accessing a given set of records, each consisting of a unique *key* and of *contents*. *Accessing* should be taken as adjoining, finding, updating and deleting a record given its key.

Before the reader decides on arrays, lists, hash tables, trees or any other standard method of implementing databases, let it be understood that all these methods are implementation variants of the same concept: function from key to contents. Finding a record in the dictionary means applying the function to a given key and the other access operations change the function itself.

Standard ML provides a general mechanism for manipulating functions in a similar way to all other objects; they are thus "first class citizens" of Standard ML. This means, functions may be passed as arguments to higher order functions, or yielded as values by higher order functions.

Therefore, we do not really have to worry about how to implement our dictionary, it is enough to specify the higher order functions that operate on it:

```
- exception SORRY ;
> con SORRY : exn

- val initdict =
    fn(key)=>
      raise SORRY ;
```

```
> val initdict = fn : 'a -> 'b

- fun update(cont,key)(dict) =
    fn(key')=>
      if key'=key then cont
      else dict(key') ;
> val update = fn : ('a * ''b) -> ((''b -> 'a) -> (''b ->
'a))

- fun delete(key)(dict) =
    fn(key')=>
      if key'=key then raise SORRY
      else dict(key') ;
> val delete = fn : ''a -> ((''a -> 'b) -> (''a -> 'b))
```

A number of points in the above Standard ML session need explaining.

Exceptions in Standard ML are user-defined error situations. In our example the declared error SORRY is going to be the dictionary's response to any query concerning a non-existent record. The system's response con SORRY : exn to our exception declaration exception SORRY means that a new constant SORRY in the standard type exn of exceptions has been defined. The initial (empty) dictionary responds SORRY to any query.

The construction

   fn x => e

is Standard ML for "the function that given an x yields e", more commonly denoted by $\lambda x.e$. It is used in situations where a function has to be treated as data. The above definition of the empty dictionary as data:

```
- val initdict =
    fn(key)=>
      raise SORRY ;
```

is equivalent to the following definition:

```
- fun initdict(key) =
    raise SORRY ;
```

of the empty dictionary as function. For Standard ML all functions are data, and the distinction between the two definitions lies only in the readability of the program text for the human programmer.

Function update adjoins a new record to the dictionary, or changes an old one. The above definition of update states that update(key,cont)(dict) differs from dict only by the value it assigns to key, namely cont. Function delete removes a record from the dictionary. Both are high order, since they operate on dictionaries which are functions. Of course, these two definitions can be written without the use of fn:

```
fun update(cont,key)(dict)(key') =
  if key'=key then ...
```

This is how this general dictionary mechanism may be used. Setting up a
small English-German dictionary:

```
- val engdeu1 =
  (update("Ameise","ant")
  (update("Katze","cat")
  (update("Pferd","horse")
  (update("Schwein","pig")
   initdict))));
> val engdeu1 = fn : string -> string
```

Enquiries:

```
- engdeu1 "cat" ;
> "Katze" : string
- engdeu1 "pig" ;
> "Schwein" : string
- engdeu1 "cow" ;
Failure: SORRY
```

Deleting entries:

```
- val engdeu1 =
    delete "pig" engdeu1 ;
> val engdeu1 = fn : string -> string

- engdeu1 "cat" ;
> "Katze" : string
- engdeu1 "pig" ;
Failure: SORRY
- engdeu1 "cow" ;
Failure: SORRY
```

In Standard ML there is no obligation to enclose a function's argument in parentheses; and the operation of function application binds
to the left; thus delete "pig" engdeu1 means the same thing as
(delete("pig"))(engdeu1). Please, note the system's reaction to the
"cow" queries above.

The solution presented to the dictionary problem meets the requirements
given at the beginning of this section: it is simple and enables all typical
dictionary operations to be carried out. Moreover, the system is *very* flexible:
it allows for operations we might not have taken into consideration when

designing the dictionary in the first place. For instance, we might, out of
the blue, want to merge our dictionary with another dictionary set up by
somebody else:

```
- val engdeu2 =
    (update("Buche","beech")
    (update("Fichte","spruce")
      initdict));
> val engdeu2 = fn : string -> string

- val engdeu =
    fn(key)=>
      engdeu1(key)
        handle SORRY =>
      engdeu2(key) ;
> val engdeu = fn : string -> string

- engdeu "cat" ;
> "Katze" : string
- engdeu "spruce" ;
> "Fichte" : string
- engdeu "cow" ;
Failure: SORRY
```

The code used above to define engdeu involves a user-defined reaction to
errors. As long as engdeu1(key) is non-error, the value of engdeu(key) is
equal to it. But whenever the call of engdeu1(key) results in the error message SORRY, the handle clause instructs the system to take engdeu2 as the
resulting value. Of course engdeu2(key) may also result in the error message
which might be taken care of by another handle clause, but in the above
example it is not.

We may also perform a certain operation on *all* records in the dictionary.
The following piece of code adds articles to German words in the dictionary,
using the following rule of thumb: anything that ends with "e" is feminine,
everything else is neuter[1]:

```
- val engdeu =
    let fun last(ls) =
      if tl(ls)=nil then hd(ls)
      else last(tl(ls))
    in fn(key)=>
      if last(explode(engdeu(key)))="e"
      then "die " ^ engdeu(key)
```

---

[1]Note that this is *not* a textbook of German.

```
        else "das " ^ engdeu(key)
    end ;
> val engdeu = fn : string -> string
```

The explode function used in the above definition is Standard ML's way
of spreading a string into a list of strings each consisting of one character:

```
- explode "Katze";
> ["K","a","t","z","e"] : string list
```

The last element of this list is selected using the auxiliary function last
defined locally specially for the purpose. Note that the above val statement
redefines the function engdeu. All the references in the body of the definition
concern the old engdeu; but once the definition is accepted the old engdeu
becomes inaccessible. In Standard ML the definition of the form

val $f =$
   fn x => e

differs from the respective definition of the form

fun $f(x) = e$

only in the way they both treat occurrences of f within e: for the former
these occurrences refer to a previously defined f, while for the latter these
are recursive calls.

This is how the new dictionary works:

```
- engdeu "horse" ;
> "das Pferd" : string
- engdeu "spruce" ;
> "die Fichte" : string
- engdeu "cow" ;
Failure: SORRY
```

Does this functional approach to dictionaries render the classical theory
of databases obsolete? Of course not, because the function implementation
mechanism in applicative languages is too general to handle special applications efficiently. The solution proposed above is time and space inefficient to
the degree that it cannot be considered an option in anything that approaches
real life, still it may be used in creating prototypes of software systems. Some
reasons for this inefficiency are discussed in Sec.4.4.

4.2   The determinant example

Let us now switch to a different area of application: design a program to
calculate the determinant of a given matrix of real numbers.

First, the decision has to be made on the representation of matrices in
Standard ML. There are no arrays in Standard ML, nor in most other applicative languages. Simulating a square matrix by a list of lists is ugly and
likely to result in a clumsy code. Again, a promising candidate is function. A
matrix is a function that produces a real value given a pair of integer indices.

The determinant of a $n \times n$ matrix $matr$ can be found by Laplace's resolution as:

$$det(matr, n) = \sum_{j=1}^{n} (-1)^{i+j} \cdot matr(i,j) \cdot minor(matr, n, i, j)$$

where i is an arbitrary integer such that $1 \leq i \leq n$, and $minor(matr, n, i, j)$
is the determinant of the matrix obtained from $matr$ by deleting its i-th row
and its j-th column. For our program it will do to have i always equal to 1,
the first row of the matrix. The auxiliary functions in the definition of det
below are:

delrowcol	— deletes first row and specified column
minor	— evaluates $minor(matr, n, 1, j)$
altsum	— evaluates alternating sum
	$\sum_{j=k}^{n} (-1)^{1+j} \cdot matr(1, j) \cdot minor(matr, n, 1, j)$

Here is a Standard ML definition of det:

```
- fun det(matr,n) =
    let fun delrowcol(matr,j) =
          fn(k,l)=>
            matr(k+1, (if l<j then l
                       else l+1))
        and minor(matr,n,j) =
          det(delrowcol(matr,j),n-1)
        and altsum(matr,n,k) =
          if k>n then 0.0
          else
            matr(1,k)*minor(matr,n,k)-altsum(matr,n,k+1)
    in if n=1 then matr(1,1)
       else altsum(matr,n,1)
    end ;
> val det = fn :
    (((int * int) -> real) * int) -> real
```

Assume now that we want to know the determinants of the initial square matrices cut out of the following quarterplane:

1.0	2.0	3.0	4.0	5.0	...
0.0	2.0	3.0	4.0	5.0	...
0.0	0.0	3.0	4.0	5.0	...
0.0	0.0	0.0	4.0	5.0	...
0.0	0.0	0.0	0.0	5.0	...
		...			

The quarterplane itself may be defined as follows:

```
- val qp =
    fn(k,l)=>
        if k>l then 0.0
        else real(l) ;
> val qp = fn : (int * int) -> real
```

(note that qp is an infinite matrix). Now:

```
- det(qp,1) ;
> 1.0 : real
- det(qp,2) ;
> 2.0 : real
- det(qp,3) ;
> 6.0 : real
- det(qp,4) ;
> 24.0 : real
- det(qp,5) ;
> 120.0 : real
- det(qp,6) ;
> 720.0 : real
```

— the results are hardly surprising since this is just a very inefficient way of calculating factorials.

The reader is encouraged to write a faster-running definition of the determinant by Gaussian elimination (cf. Exercise 15 after this chapter), and to discuss the question of its efficiency problem in comparison with the classical view of the matrix as a table filled with numbers.

4.3   A simple graphic example

A planar *curve*, or a planar *trajectory* is normally defined as a function from real numbers to points on a plane, i.e. to pairs of real numbers. Such a function may be viewed as giving a position of a drawing pencil in a given time instance. For example:

```
fn(t)=> (t,0)                — horizontal axis
fn(t)=> (t*t*t,0)            — horizontal axis drawn at different
                               "speed"
fn(t)=> (cos(t),sin(t))      — unit circle
```

It is not difficult to design a Standard ML function that draws a discretised picture of a fragment of a curve. We precede this definition with some explanations.

The function drawcurve below creates a string that forms a rough picture of a given curve for its time parameter ranging from 0.0 to 1.0 inclusively (unit interval). Only the parts of the curve that lie within the unit square $(0.0, 1.0) \times (0.0, 1.0)$ appear on the picture, the rest are trimmed off by the auxiliary local function displayscreen (see below). The picture is discretised with the resolution depending on auxiliary local constants xscreenresolution and yscreenresolution. A finite number of points on the curve are depicted at the ends of time intervals of length timegrain. Auxiliary local constant initscreen corresponds to the blank discrete screen. Function plot (cf. update in Sec.4.1) marks a pixel of the screen close to point (x,y) by "*". Auxiliary local function curvetoscreen creates the discrete screen image of a curve. Auxiliary local function displayscreen concatenates all the pixels into one string, inserting some abracadabra to make a box around the screen, and to change lines properly. All this need not concern the reader now[2]. Here follows the definition of the function drawcurve:

```
- fun drawcurve(c) =
    let val xscreenresolution = 47
        and yscreenresolution = 20
        and timegrain = 0.005
        and initscreen =
          fn(hor,ver)=> " "
    in

        let fun plot(x,y)screen =
              fn(hor,ver)=>
                  if hor = floor(x*real(xscreenresolution))
                  andalso
```

---

[2]Some of the technical details in the definition of displayscreen are related to the Edinburgh version 3.3 interpreter I am using and may be irrelevant for other versions. For instance, line changing in displayscreen is achieved by overloading the lines with spaces, rather than by the explicit line change character "\n", because this interpreter insists on making line breaks in long strings every 80-th character anyway.

```
                    ver = floor(y*real(yscreenresolution))
                  then "*"
                  else screen(hor,ver)

          and curvetoscreen(c) =
            let fun cts(c,t) =
                    if t<0.0 then initscreen
                    else plot(c(t))(cts(c,t-timegrain))
            in cts(c,1.0)
            end

          and displayscreen(screen) =
            let fun repeat(n,str) =
                    if n=0 then ""
                    else str^repeat(n-1,str)
                and ds(screen,hor,ver) =
                    if ver<0 then ""
                    else
                      if hor=xscreenresolution
                      then
                        "|" ^
                        repeat(76-xscreenresolution," ") ^
                        " |" ^ ds(screen,0,ver-1)
                      else
                        screen(hor,ver) ^
                        ds(screen,hor+1,ver)
            in "|" ^ repeat(xscreenresolution,"-") ^ "|" ^
               repeat(76-xscreenresolution," ") ^" |" ^
               ds(screen,0,yscreenresolution-1) ^
               repeat(xscreenresolution,"-") ^ "|"
            end

      in
         displayscreen(curvetoscreen(c))
         end
      end ;
> val drawcurve = fn : (real -> (real * real)) -> string
```

We can now draw curves as follows:

```
- val pi = 3.14159 ;
> val pi = 3.14159 : real

- fun circle(r) =
    fn(t)=>
      ( r*cos(2.0*pi*t)+0.5 , r*sin(2.0*pi*t)+0.5 ) ;
> val circle = fn : real -> (real -> (real * real))
```

Parameter r is the *radius* of the circle.

```
- drawcurve(circle(0.5));
>
"|---------------------------------------------|
 |            ********************             |
 |         ****              ****              |
 |        ****                ****             |
 |       ***                    ***            |
 |      **                        **           |
 |     *                            *          |
 |    *                              *         |
 |*                                  *|
 |*                                  *|
 |*                                  *|
 |*                                  *|
 |*                                  *|
 |*                                  *|
 |  *                              *          |
 |   *                            *           |
 |    **                        **            |
 |     ***                    ***             |
 |      ****                ****              |
 |       ****              ****              |
 |          ********************             |
 |---------------------------------------------|" : string
```

```
- drawcurve(circle(0.25));
>
"|----------------------------------------------|
 |                                              |
 |                                              |
 |                                              |
 |                                              |
 |                                              |
 |              **************                  |
 |            ***            ***                |
 |           **                **               |
 |           *                  *               |
 |          *                    *              |
 |          *                    *              |
 |           *                  *               |
 |           **                **               |
 |            ***            ***                |
 |              **************                  |
 |                                              |
 |                                              |
 |                                              |
 |                                              |
 |                                              |
 |----------------------------------------------|" : string
```

```
- fun spiral(r) =
    fn(t)=>
      ( r*t*cos(2.0*pi*t)+0.5 , r*t*sin(2.0*pi*t)+0.5 ) ;
> val spiral = fn : real -> (real -> (real * real))
- drawcurve(spiral(0.5));
>
```
```
"|-----------------------------------------------|
 |                                               |
 |                                               |
 |                                               |
 |                                               |
 |                                               |
 |                                               |
 |                                               |
 |              ************                      |
 |           ***           **                     |
 |           **            ***                    |
 |           **                                   |
 |           *                                  * |
 |           **                               ** |
 |            **                             **   |
 |            **                            **    |
 |             **                          ***    |
 |              *****           ******            |
 |                 ****************                |
 |                                               |
 |                                               |
 |-----------------------------------------------|" : string
```

We can also create more complicated drawings by putting curves together.
The following function *addcurve* "speeds up" a first curve so that it is "ready"
over the time $\langle 0.0, 0.5 \rangle$ which leaves another half of the unit time interval to
a second curve:

```
- fun addcurve(c1,c2) =
    fn(t)=>
      if t<0.5 then c1(2.0*t)
      else c2(2.0*(t-0.5)) ;
> val addcurve = fn :
    ((real -> 'a) * (real -> 'a)) -> (real -> 'a)

- drawcurve(addcurve(circle(0.25),circle(0.5)));
>
"|------------------------------------------------|
 |              ** ** ** *** ** ** **             |
 |          ** *                    *  **         |
 |        **                            **        |
 |      **                                **      |
 |    **                                    **    |
 |   *              **************            *   |
 | *              ***            ***            * |
 |*              **                **            *|
 |*             *                    *           *|
 |*            *                      *          *|
 |*            *                      *          *|
 |*             *                    *           *|
 |*              **                **            *|
 | *              ***            ***            * |
 |   *              **************            *   |
 |    **                                    **    |
 |      **                                **      |
 |        **                            **        |
 |          ** *                    *  **         |
 |              ** ** ** *** ** ** **             |
 |------------------------------------------------|" : string
```

4.4   Complex data as functions

Viewing a dictionary or a matrix as a function, rather than as a static collection of data, may seem surprising since it goes against habit. Not only in computer programs but also in everyday life dictionaries are books of entries arranged according to a specific order; and matrices are collections of numbers from a world that is beyond the programmer's concern. In contrast, a function is something that *acts* rather than being acted upon.

On the other hand, mathematicians customarily dismiss this active aspect of functions, and define functions as sets of pairs. Accordingly, enumerable sequences are defined as functions over natural numbers, and curves are defined as functions (or continuous functions) from real numbers to pairs of real numbers.

A function can be an argument or a result of another function. A school example for this situation is differentiation. Functions that operate on other functions are usually referred to as *high order functions* or *functionals*. In our examples the functions update(key,cont) and delete(key) are for any key and cont high order since they act on dictionaries, which are functions; function det is high order since it takes a matrix, which is a function, as one of its arguments; functions drawcurve and addcurve are high order since they operate on curves, which are functions.

As we have seen, this functional approach to compound data results in very simple and flexible programs. There is however a price tag attached.

One problem in treating functions as first class citizens is that they cannot easily be compared. Consider the following two function definitions:

```
- fun ide1(x) = x+0;
> val ide1 = fn : int -> int
- fun ide2(x) = x-0;
> val ide2 = fn : int -> int
```

Obviously, they both define the same function, namely identity over integers. It is, however, beyond the Standard ML interpreter to know that:

```
- ide1=ide2;
Type clash  in:  (ide1 = ide2)
There is no equality defined on type int -> int
```

This is not a temporary shortcoming likely to be cured in the next versions of the interpreter, this is a major theoretical infeasibility. It is *undecidable* whether two given function definitions define the same function, therefore there is no chance of properly implementing the high order equality test.

There is also an efficiency problem when updating functions, as we needed to do in the dictionary example. Processing a function definition in Standard

ML involves type checking and coding, but the text of the definition is then re-membered practically unaltered. It is impossible for further updates to change anything in such a definition; the system has to keep track of all succeeding updates.

For instance, if we introduce and then immediately delete a dictionary entry:

```
delete("ant")(update("Ameise","ant")initdict)
```

then, by the definition of initdict, the result will be equal to:

```
delete("ant")
  ( update("Ameise","ant")
      (fn(key)=> raise SORRY)
  )
```

which, by the definition of update, is equal to:

```
delete("ant")
  ( fn(key)=> if key="ant"
              then "Ameise"
              else raise SORRY
  )
```

which, by the definition of delete, is equal to:

```
fn(key)=> if key="ant"
          then raise SORRY
          else if key="ant"
                  then "Ameise"
                  else raise SORRY
```

and the dictionary is remembered in more or less this form. For a human programmer it is obvious that the internal **then** case above can never be reached, thus the whole thing is further equal to:

```
fn(key)=> if key="ant"
          then raise SORRY
          else raise SORRY
```

(warning: equivalent to `fn(key)=> raise SORRY` only under the eager eval-uation strategy, because the evaluation of **key** may fail to terminate!) but this conclusion may not be achieved by the computer on its own. Therefore, successive **updates** and **deletes** do *not* undo each other. This causes the dic-tionary to grow with every operation, at the same time making the access time longer.

However, before dismissing the high order approach as too expensive, the reader should realise what is bought for the price. The most efficient programs are the ones written directly in the machine code, but then the programmer's effort grows enormously. When using high order functions, one pays in computer time and space, but saves on the programmer's work. If you are not convinced, write Pascal programs corresponding to the three examples in this chapter and see how much time you have spent, how much paper you have used, and how many features you have left uncovered at the end.

4.5   Exercises

Exercise 11
Design a Standard ML definition of a function that, given a natural number n, yields the sequence consisting of

> the maximal k s.t. $2^k \mid n$,
> the maximal k s.t. $3^k \mid n$,
> the maximal k s.t. $4^k \mid n$,
> ...
> etc.

Exercise 12
Design a Standard ML definition of a function that solves the equation

$$f(x) = 0$$

over a given interval with a given "horizontal" precision; i.e. a higher order function *solve* that takes as arguments two real numbers a and b such that $a < b$, a continuous function $f : \texttt{real} \rightarrow \texttt{real}$ such that $f(a)$ and $f(b)$ have different signs, and an $\varepsilon > 0$; and yields a real number x_0 that falls within the ε-distance from a zero of f:

$$\exists_x \, f(x) = 0 \; \& \; \mid x - x_0 \mid < \varepsilon$$

Exercise 13
Write a definition of a Standard ML function that sorts a sequence of reals.

Exercise 14
Design a Standard ML definition of a function that given a natural number n yields the sequence of all primes between 2 and n inclusively using Eratosthenes' sieve algorithm.

Exercise 15
Design a Standard ML definition of matrix diagonalisation by Gaussian elimination.

Chapter 5

Data types

In old programming languages, such as Fortran or PL/I types were secondary features of objects, related to their implementation properties. Declaring an object to be an integer meant chosing a "short" representation of the object in the computer's memory (say 16 bits) and fixed point computer arithmetic. Declaring it real meant chosing a "long" representation with floating point arithmetic. The user was welcome to use type declarations for different purposes from those suggested by the name of a type, as long as implementation properties attached to a given type in a given language satisfied his needs; for instance to store 16 different truth values in one integer variable.

Over time people came to realise the theoretical importance of structuring objects in types. Although the mathematics, as commonly taught, is based on a completely untyped "anarchic" set theory, one feels the urge to introduce a type system *a posteriori*. We would, for instance, intuitively protest if told that 100 Deutsch Marks plus 100 Polish złotys make 200; or if a real number were applied to an argument as if it were a function.

Far from being an implementation issue, the type systems form the backbone of modern programming languages. They are crucial for the proper understanding of underlying concepts by man, rather than by computer, the latter being quite happy with the untyped anarchic strings of bits.

Recall that the primitive types of Standard ML are

unit	— one-element type
bool	— logical values
int	— integers
real	— real numbers
string	— finite sequences of characters

In this chapter we show how to structure them into more complicated types.

5.1 Simple type constructors

In Standard ML there are two simple type constructors:

> ...*... — Cartesian product
> ...->... — function space

These may be arbitrarily nested to produce more complex expressions denoting types, e.g.

```
int * (real->real)
(int*real->string) * int * real -> string
```

By Standard ML convention, * binds more strongly than ->, and -> associates to the right; thus for instance

```
int * real -> string * int -> string
```

means

```
(int * real) -> ((string * int) -> string)
```

To produce a value in a Cartesian product one may use the pair construction

```
(... , ...)
```

To decompose such a value back into its components one may use the same construction on the left hand side of the definition. For instance, the projection functions may be defined as follows:

```
- fun fst(x,y) = x ;
> val fst = fn : ('a * 'b) -> 'a
- fun snd(x,y) = y ;
> val snd = fn : ('a * 'b) -> 'b
- let val ab = (5.0,false)
  in (fst(ab)+1.0 , not(snd(ab)))
  end ;
> (6.0,true) : real * bool
```

To produce a value in a function space $A->B$ one uses the functional notation

> fn x => e

where e is an expression that has a value in B for every x in A. The only decomposition operation for functions is the application to an argument.

5.2 Disjoint union

Another important Standard ML type constructor is *set union*, which, however, comes in a slightly modified version of *disjoint* union or *strong* union.
The reason for this is Standard ML's commitment to strong typing: every
value has a unique type[1]. With the usual set-theoretic union this unique typing would be impossible; for instance, here are some possible types for the
number 0:

```
int
int ∪ real
int ∪ string->bool
...
```

Disjoint union may be thought of as differing from classical union by tags
that bear the additional information on the source of a given element:

$$A \mid B \overset{\text{def}}{=} A \times \{(A, B, l)\} \cup B \times \{(A, B, r)\}$$

(*l* for *left* and *r* for *right*). For instance if $A = \{1, 2\}$ and $B = \{3, 4\}$ then

$$A \cup B = \{1, 2, 3, 4\}$$

while

$$A \mid B = \{(1, (A, B, l)), (2, (A, B, l)), (3, (A, B, r)), (4, (A, B, r))\}$$

In this way, in contrast to the classical case, a set A is not equal to the $A|A$;
and 0 belongs only to int while $(0, (\text{int}, \text{int}, l))$ and $(0, (\text{int}, \text{int}, r))$ are two
distinct elements of int | int.

Unlike Cartesian product and function space, disjoint union may not be
used in Standard ML type expressions right away. Its use is restricted to
definitions of new *data types*. The following definition makes a new type $type_0$
equal to the disjoint union of types $type_1$ and $type_2$:

```
datatype type₀  =  fun₁ of type₁
                |  fun₂ of type₂ ;
```

This defines $type_0$ together with conversion functions fun_1 and fun_2 from the
component types to $type_0$: they ornament their argument with all the appropriate tags.

The **datatype** construction may serve to replace the enumeration types
of Pascal; for instance, the week may be defined in Standard ML as

---

[1]As long as polymorphism, which we discuss in Chapter 6, is not taken into account.

```
datatype week = monday of unit
              | tuesday of unit
              | wednesday of unit
              | thursday of unit
              | friday of unit
              | saturday of unit
              | sunday of unit ;
```

and single days of the week are then monday(), tuesday() etc.; recall that
() is the only element of type unit. In the datatype definition the reference
to unit may be skipped in which case the () argument of the conversion
functions also has to be skipped; the conversion functions turn then into
constants:

```
datatype week =  monday | tuesday | wednesday
               | thursday | friday | saturday | sunday ;
```

5.3   Recursive type definitions

More importantly, however, the datatype construction comes together with
the recursion on types and in many respects replaces the use of pointers. For
instance, the natural way of defining binary trees over real numbers in Pascal
is this:

```
. . . . .
type node = record
                val : real ;
                left,right : ^node
              end ;
       tree = ^node ;
. . . . .
function mktree(r:real; t1,t2:tree):tree ;
   var auxtree:tree ;
begin
   new(auxtree);
   auxtree^.val := r ;
   auxtree^.left := t1 ; auxtree^.right:= t2 ;
   mktree := auxtree
end
. . . . .
```

The definition of type node above is recursive, since its right hand side refers
to node. In Pascal such type recursion must be guarded by a pointer.

In Standard ML the same effect may be achieved by the recursive
datatype definition:

```
- datatype tree = empty
               | mktree of real*tree*tree ;
> datatype tree = empty | mktree of real * tree * tree
  con mktree = fn : (real * tree * tree) -> tree
  con empty = empty : tree
```

This definition states that a tree is either trivial, or it is a Cartesian triple consisting of a real value and two subtrees, and the conversion function from such Cartesian triples to trees is called `mktree`. The constant `empty` and the conversion function `mktree` are our only means of constructing trees:

```
- mktree(5.0,mktree(1.0,empty,empty),empty) ;
> mktree (5.0,mktree (1.0,empty,empty),empty) : tree
```

No functions to decompose elements of a newly defined data type are provided, but the constructors may be used on the left hand sides of definitions, which makes the function definitions look very much like case analysis. This is, for instance, the function that sums up all real numbers sitting in the leaves of a tree:

```
- fun sum(empty) = 0.0
     | sum(mktree(r,t1,t2)) = r + sum(t1) + sum(t2) ;
> val sum = fn : tree -> real
- sum(mktree(5.0,mktree(1.0,empty,empty),empty)) ;
> 6.0 : real
```

The capability of defining types by recursion is a very powerful tool. It alone suffices to define non-trivial entities from scratch. For instance, this is a definition of natural numbers that uses type `unit`, disjoint union and type recursion:

```
- datatype nat = zero
               | succ of nat ;
> datatype nat = zero | succ of nat
  con succ = fn : nat -> nat
  con zero = zero
```

Functions operating on this type must be defined by cases:

```
- fun plus(zero,n) = n
     | plus(succ(k),n) = succ(plus(k,n)) ;
> val plus = fn : (nat * nat) -> nat
- plus(succ(succ(succ(zero))),succ(succ(zero)))
                (* this means 3+2 *) ;
> succ(succ(succ(succ(succ(zero))))) : nat
```

It is often necessary to define several data types by mutual recursion; a
typical example are multiple trees, i.e. trees with arbitrarily (but finitely)
many sons to each node. Assume the values in the nodes are real numbers,
then such a tree is a pair of a real number and a forest, where a forest is
either empty or a pair of one tree and a forest:

```
- datatype multree = mkmult of real*forest
        and forest = empty | mkfor of multree*forest ;
> datatype forest = empty | mkfor of multree * forest
  datatype multree = mkmult of real * forest
  con mkfor = fn : (multree * forest) -> forest
  con empty = empty : forest
  con mkmult = fn : (real * forest) -> multree
- mkmult(3.14,mkfor(mkmult(~1.0,empty),empty));
> mkmult (3.14,mkfor (mkmult (~1.0,empty),empty)) :
multree
```

5.4   Example: describing semantics in Standard ML

The datatype construct is especially useful for investigating relations between
syntax and semantics. Consider for instance the following simple language of
arithmetic expressions:

$Oper$ ::= + | *

Dig ::= 0 | 1 | 2 | 3 | 4 | 5 | 6 | 7 | 8 | 9

$Numb$ ::= Dig | Dig $Numb$

$Expr$ ::= $Numb$ | ($Oper$, $Expr$, $Expr$)

This grammar readily translates to Standard ML:

```
datatype oper = plusoper
              | timesoper
        and dig = zerodig
              | onedig
              | twodig
              | threedig
              | fourdig
              | fivedig
              | sixdig
```

```
            | sevendig
            | eightdig
            | ninedig
    and numb = primnumb of  dig
             | compnumb of  dig * numb
    and expr = primexpr of  numb
             | compexpr of  oper * expr * expr ;
```

Assume now the semantics of the language is defined as follows:

$$O : Oper \rightarrow (Int \times Int \rightarrow Int)$$

$$O[\![+]\!] = \ldots \text{addition} \ldots$$
$$O[\![*]\!] = \ldots \text{multiplication} \ldots$$

$$D : Dig \rightarrow Int$$

$$D[\![0]\!] = 0$$
$$D[\![1]\!] = 1$$
$$D[\![2]\!] = 2$$
$$D[\![3]\!] = 3$$
$$D[\![4]\!] = 4$$
$$D[\![5]\!] = 5$$
$$D[\![6]\!] = 6$$
$$D[\![7]\!] = 7$$
$$D[\![8]\!] = 8$$
$$D[\![9]\!] = 9$$

$$N : Numb \rightarrow Int$$

$$N[\![n]\!] = N'(0)[\![n]\!] \quad \text{where}$$
$$N' : Int \rightarrow Numb \rightarrow Int$$
$$N'(k)[\![d]\!] = k \cdot 10 + D[\![d]\!]$$
$$N'(k)[\![dn]\!] = N'(k \cdot 10 + D[\![d]\!])[\![n]\!]$$

$$E : Expr \rightarrow Int$$

$$E[\![n]\!] = N[\![n]\!]$$
$$E[\![(op, ex_1, ex_2)]\!] = O[\![op]\!](E[\![ex_1]\!], E[\![ex_2]\!])$$

This also translates readily to Standard ML:

```
fun oo(plusoper) = (fn(n,k:int)=>n+k)
  | oo(timesoper) = (fn(n,k:int)=>n*k)
and dd(zerodig) = 0
  | dd(onedig) = 1
  | dd(twodig) = 2
  | dd(threedig) = 3
  | dd(fourdig) = 4
  | dd(fivedig) = 5
  | dd(sixdig) = 6
  | dd(sevendig) = 7
  | dd(eightdig) = 8
  | dd(ninedig) = 9
and nn(n) =
  let fun nn'(k)(primnumb(d)) = k*10+dd(d)
        | nn'(k)(compnumb(d,n)) = nn'(k*10+dd(d))(n)
  in nn'(0)(n)
  end
and ee(primexpr(n)) = nn(n)
  | ee(compexpr(ope,ex1,ex2)) = oo(ope)(ee(ex1),ee(ex2)) ;
```

In fact, the above semantic definition in Standard ML constitutes an interpreter of the language of arithmetic expressions, ready for use. What we still lack is a parser that would turn an input string into an element of the above defined type expr.

To make the programming experiment complete, a recursive descent LL(1) parser for the above language is defined below. The following four functions correspond to the four nonterminals of our grammar. Each function parse$N$ takes as its argument a list of characters, i.e. of one-character strings. If an initial segment of this list may be parsed to N, then the result is the Cartesian pair consisting of a data structure (parse tree) and the end segment of the list (unused characters); if it may not be parsed to N, then an exception is raised. These exceptions are more complex than the ones discussed so far, in so far as they are of type (string)list rather than of type *unit*, because they pass the offending unparsable part of input list so that it can be printed out to make an error message more helpful. The exceptions are sometimes handled, when a calling function thinks it may try a different approach. The new Standard ML constructions used below that have not appeared so far, are the following:

- (string)list — type of lists of strings. Lists of any items are available in Standard ML and [] denotes the empty list, :: (not used below) is the *cons* operator, hd and tl are the *head* and *tail* selectors; when applied to the empty list hd raises exception Hd and tl raises exception Tl.

- **case** ... **of** ... => ... | ... | ... => ... — case expression.
  This should be self-explanatory; the underlined space _ that takes place
  of the last option in the **case**-expression means "if none of the above".
  raise *exc*(it val) — exception with a value. A corresponding **handle**
  clause may make use of the value *val.*

Here follows the parser:

```
exception NON_OPERATOR of (string)list ;
fun parseoper(chlist) =
  case hd(chlist) of
    "+" => (plusoper,tl(chlist))
  | "*" => (timesoper,tl(chlist))
  | _   => raise NON_OPERATOR(chlist) ;

exception NON_DIGIT of (string)list ;
fun parsedig(chlist) =
  case hd(chlist) of
    "0" => (zerodig,tl(chlist))
  | "1" => (onedig,tl(chlist))
  | "2" => (twodig,tl(chlist))
  | "3" => (threedig,tl(chlist))
  | "4" => (fourdig,tl(chlist))
  | "5" => (fivedig,tl(chlist))
  | "6" => (sixdig,tl(chlist))
  | "7" => (sevendig,tl(chlist))
  | "8" => (eightdig,tl(chlist))
  | "9" => (ninedig,tl(chlist))
  | _   => raise NON_DIGIT(chlist) ;

fun parsenumb(chlist) =
  let val (d,chlist') = parsedig(chlist)
  in (let val (n,chlist'') = parsenumb(chlist')
      in (compnumb(d,n),chlist'')
      end) handle NON_DIGIT(_) => (primnumb(d),chlist')
                | Hd => (primnumb(d),chlist')
  end ;
```

The **handle** clause above is activated when the parameterised expression that
precedes it raises an exception. If this exception is

```
NON_DIGIT(chlist0)
```

for some `chlist0:(string)list` then the resulting number is considered
as consisting of a single digit d. The same happens when the exception raised

is Hd, meaning that the remaining input is empty. Function **parsenumb** may only fail when the input does not begin with a digit.

```
exception NON_RIGHT_PAR of (string)list
      and NON_COMMA of (string)list
      and NON_DIGIT_NOR_LEFT_PAR of (string)list ;
fun parseexpr(chlist) =
  if hd(chlist) = "("
  then
    let val (ope,chlist') = parseoper(tl(chlist))
    in if hd(chlist') = ","
       then
         let val (ex1,chlist'') = parseexpr(tl(chlist'))
         in if hd(chlist'') = ","
            then let val (ex2,chlist''') =
                              parseexpr(tl(chlist''))
                 in
                   if hd(chlist''') = ")"
                   then
                     (compexpr(ope,ex1,ex2),tl(chlist'''))
                   else
                     raise NON_RIGHT_PAR(chlist''')
                 end
            else raise NON_COMMA(chlist'')
         end
       else raise NON_COMMA(chlist')
    end
  else (let val (n,chlist') = parsenumb(chlist)
        in (primexpr(n),chlist')
        end) handle NON_DIGIT(_) =>
          raise NON_DIGIT_NOR_LEFT_PAR(chlist) ;
```

Now the parser together with the previously defined semantic functions may be used to set up a simple interpreter of the defined language. Here follows its definition and some examples of its use. The main part of the definition is devoted to exception handling. The auxiliary function **write** is called for its side effect, i.e. displaying a string, rather than for its value which is always 0. Function **explode** turns a string into the list of its one-character substrings and function **implode** does the opposite.

```
- exception EXPR_FOLLOWED_BY_RUBBISH of (string)list ;
> con EXPR_FOLLOWED_BY_RUBBISH = fn : (string)list -> exn
- fun interpreter(str) =
    let fun write(s) =
```

```
              let val x = output(std_out,s)
              in 0
              end
           in
             (let val (ex,chlist) = parseexpr(explode(str))
              in if chlist = [] then ee(ex)
                 else raise EXPR_FOLLOWED_BY_RUBBISH(chlist)
              end
             ) handle Hd =>
                         write("Expression ended prematurely     ")
                     | NON_RIGHT_PAR(s) =>
                         write("Expected right par in: " ^
                                 implode(s) ^ "      ")
                     | NON_OPERATOR(s) =>
                         write("Expected cross or star in: " ^
                                 implode(s) ^ "      ")
                     | NON_COMMA(s) =>
                         write("Expected comma in: " ^
                                 implode(s) ^ "      ")
                     | EXPR_FOLLOWED_BY_RUBBISH(s) =>
                         write("Expression followed by rubbish: " ^
                                 implode(s) ^ "      ")
                     | NON_DIGIT(s) =>
                         write("Expected digit in: " ^
                                 implode(s) ^ "      ")
                     | NON_DIGIT_NOR_LEFT_PAR(s) =>
                         write("Expected digit or left par in: " ^
                                 implode(s) ^ "      ")
           end ;
 > val interpreter = fn : string -> int
 - interpreter "2567" ;
 > 2567 : int
 - interpreter "(*,20,(+,5,3))" ;   (* i.e.  20*(5+3) *)
 > 160 : int
 - interpreter "(*,20,(+,5,3)" ;
 Expression ended prematurely     > 0 : int
 - interpreter "(*,20,(+,5,3)]" ;
 Expected right par in: ]      > 0 : int
 - interpreter "(*,20,(-,5,3))" ;
 Expected cross or star in: -,5,3))     > 0 : int
 - interpreter "(*;20,(+,5,3))" ;
 Expected comma in: ;20,(+,5,3))      > 0 : int
 - interpreter "(*,20,(+,5,3))that's all" ;
```

```
Expression followed by rubbish: that's all      > 0 : int
- interpreter "abcd" ;
Expected digit or left par in: abcd       > 0 : int
```

The aim of this section has been to demonstrate the usefulness of `datatype` definitions in constructing interpreters. The general means of doing this may be summarised as follows:

- set down a grammar for your language

- transcribe it into a sequence of `datatype` definitions

- set down a denotational definition of semantics

- transcribe it into a program operating on defined `datatypes`

- program a parser for the language

5.5 Exercises

Exercise 16

Design a Standard ML definition of the function that sorts a list of reals by: (1) reading all the elements of the list into a binary, initially empty, tree of reals so as to make an ordered tree; and (2) traversing the tree in the *inorder* fashion to make a sorted list.

Exercise 17

Design a Standard ML data type to store a family tree. The tree should satisfy the following conditions:

- Every family member is characterised by his name, year of birth, year of death (set to 0 when still alive)

- There is no upper limit on the number of sons of one family member

- There is a direct access from any family member to his eldest son, and to his next younger brother

Write a Standard ML function that calculates the average length of life in the family, not taking into account the family members that are still alive.

Exercise 18

Design a definition of the function that determines whether two given binary trees of reals are isomorphic; i.e. whether one can be obtained from the other by exchanging the left and right branches in arbitrarily selected nodes.

Part II

Polymorphism and Modularisation

Chapter 6

Polymorphism

6.1   Analogies from imperative languages

Recall the Pascal program for binary trees over real numbers:

```
.....
type elem = real ;
     node = record
                 val : elem ;
                 left,right : ^node
            end ;
     tree = ^node ;
.....
function mktree(el:elem; t1,t2:tree):tree ;
  var auxtree:tree ;
begin
  new(auxtree);
  auxtree^.val := el ;
  auxtree^.left := t1 ; auxtree^.right:= t2 ;
  mktree := auxtree
end
.....
```

The only reference in this program to the fact that the trees are supposed to consist of real numbers is its first line

```
type elem = real ;
```

Had we replaced this line by, say,

```
type elem = integer ;
```

or by any other definition of type elem, the rest of the program would still operate properly on trees over the new type. Yet, this change would require

recompiling, and if we need in our program *both* trees of reals and trees of
integers, we would have to write the corresponding code twice, keeping type
and function identifiers distinct:

```
. . . . .
type elem1 = real ;
     elem2 = integer ;
     node1 = ... ;
     node2 = ... ;
function mktree1 ... ;
function mktree2 ... ;
. . . . .
```

To write the same piece of code twice is a waste of resources and is gen-
erally considered poor programming style. The reluctance to do just that
contributed in the early days of computing to the development of the concept
of *subprogram*, or *subroutine*, or *procedure*.

In Pascal there is no way of parameterising a piece of code with a type, but
the idea is not unknown in imperative languages. The best known example
is that of ADA, where one can define a *generic type* or a *generic function*
so that it becomes a type, or a function respectively, when instantiated with
a type for its *generic parameter*. In our example it would mean defining a
generic type `tree` with a generic function `mktree`, both dependent on `elem`,
and then instantiating `elem` to `real` or to `int`.

6.2 Polymorphism in Standard ML

In Standard ML the dependence of types and objects on types is known as
polymorphism and it constitutes one of the main concepts of the language.
Its practical realisation in the old ML has opened a field for theoretical research which, although far from complete, has contributed to a better understanding of many issues concerning the type systems of modern programming
languages.

The Standard ML definition of the polymorphic type of trees is the following:

```
- datatype ('a)tree = empty
                    | mktree of 'a*('a)tree*('a)tree ;
> datatype 'a tree = empty | mktree of 'a * ('a tree) *
('a tree)
  con mktree = fn : ('a * ('a tree) * ('a tree)) -> ('a
tree)
  con empty = empty : 'a tree
```

Syntactically it differs from the *monomorphic*, i.e. non-polymorphic, type of trees over real numbers in that all the occurrences of type `real` are replaced by the type variable `'a`. By the Standard ML convention, identifiers preceded by the prime are type variables and may be instantiated with type expressions. Monomorphic types are those denoted by type expressions without type variables.

Here are some example instantiations of (`'a`)`tree`:

```
(real)tree        —  trees over reals
((int)tree)tree   —  trees over trees of ints
                     whole trees of ints stand in nodes
(('a)tree)tree    —  polymorphic trees over trees
                     still open for further type instantiation
```

The two constructors, `empty` and `mktree`, are now polymorphic, which means they may be used with any instances of type (`'a`)`tree`. For example:

```
- mktree(5,empty,mktree(7,empty,empty)) ;
> mktree (5,empty,mktree (7,empty,empty)) : int tree
```

— both occurrences of `mktree` and all three occurrences of `empty` above concern (`int`)`tree`;

```
- mktree(mktree(1.0,empty,empty),empty,empty) ;
> mktree (mktree (1.0,empty,empty),empty,empty) : (real
tree) tree
```

— the internal calls of `mktree` and of `empty` construct a (`real`)`tree` which is then made a node of a higher order tree, thus the external occurrences of `mktree` and of `empty` concern ((`real`)`tree`)`tree`;

```
- mktree(1,mktree(1.0,empty,empty),empty) ;
Type clash  in:  (mktree (1,(mktree (%,%,%)),empty))
Looking  for a:  int
I have found a:  real
```

— the internal call of `mktree` produces a (`real`)`tree`, and the external `mktree` attempts to put together this (`real`)`tree` and the `int` value 1; this is impossible and hence the error complaint.

Another example of a polymorphic type and polymorphic objects is the predefined polymorphic type of *lists* which could have been defined as follows:

```
datatype ('a)list = nil
                  | :: of 'a*('a)list ;
```

The Standard ML operator `::` that *conses* an element to a list is infixed, i.e. one should write

```
elem :: list
```

rather than ::(elem,list). There also exists a special shorthand notation
for lists:

$$[a_1, a_2, \ldots, a_n] \quad \text{is equivalent to} \quad a_1::a_2::\ldots::a_n::\text{nil}$$

(in particular, [] is equivalent to nil). In Standard ML there are two predefined polymorphic functions operating on lists, the *head* function and the *tail*
function, which could have been defined as follows:

```
exception Hd
        and Tl ;

fun hd([]) = raise Hd
  | hd(el::lis) = el ;

fun tl([]) = raise Tl
  | tl(el::lis) = lis ;
```

A Standard ML polymorphic type may of course depend on more than
one type parameter. For instance, the type of trees with the values in leaves
belonging to a type possibly different from the type of the values in internal
nodes, may be defined as follows:

```
- datatype ('a,'b)tree2 =
      leaf of 'b
    | node of 'a*('a,'b)tree2*('a,'b)tree2 ;
> datatype ('a,'b) tree2 = leaf of 'b | node of 'a * (('a,
  'b) tree2) * (('a,'b) tree2)
  con node = fn : ('a * (('a,'b) tree2) * (('a,'b) tree2))
-> (('a,'b) tree2)
  con leaf : 'a -> ('b,'a) tree2
- node(false,node(true,leaf(6),leaf(~7)),leaf(15)) ;
> node (false,node (true,leaf 6,leaf ~7),leaf 15) : (bool,
int) tree2
```

The examples given so far may contribute to a false impression that Standard ML polymorphism is somehow related to the datatype construct. Polymorphism and datatype are, however, orthogonal concepts. Admittedly, in
many applications they go together, but we may also define polymorphic objects that have nothing to do with datatype. For instance, one may define
the general notion of function application:

```
- fun apply(f,x) = f(x) ;
> val apply = fn : (('a -> 'b) * 'a) -> 'b
```

which may then be used with concrete functions of various types:

```
- apply((fn(n)=>n+1),2);
> 3 : int
- apply(sin,3.14);
> 0.0015926529164866828 : real
```

Or one may define the general recursor:

```
- fun recur(f)(x) = f(recur(f))(x) ;
> val recur = fn : (('a -> 'b) -> ('a -> 'b)) -> ('a ->
'b)
- fun gcd'(f)(n,k:int) =
      if n=k then n
      else if n<k then f(n,k-n)
            else f(n-k,k) ;
> val gcd' = fn : ((int * int) -> int) -> ((int * int) ->
int)
- val gcd = recur(gcd') ;
> val gcd = fn : (int * int) -> int
- gcd(12,16);
> 4 : int
- gcd(240,375);
> 15 : int
```

6.3 Two views on the nature of polymorphism

Consider again the apply function from the preceding section and try to establish its type. When apply is written to Standard ML's interpreter then the interpreter answers with what it considers the function's *most general* type:

```
- apply ;
> fn : (('a -> 'b) * 'a) -> 'b
```

But a programmer may suggest other types, and as long as they are *compatible* with the most general one, they are accepted by the interpreter:

```
- apply : ('a->'b) * 'a -> 'b ;
> fn : (('a -> 'b) * 'a) -> 'b
- apply : ('a->bool) * 'a -> bool ;
> fn : (('a -> bool) * 'a) -> bool
- apply : (int->bool) * int -> bool ;
```

```
> fn : ((int -> bool) * int) -> bool
- apply : (('a)list->('b)list) * ('a)list -> ('b)list ;
> fn : ((('a list) -> ('b list)) * ('a list)) -> ('b list)
```

If our suggestion happens not to be a specialised form of the most general type then the type checker will try to work out a compromise:

```
- apply : ('a->'b) * 'b -> 'a ;
> fn : (('a -> 'a) * 'a) -> 'a
```

It will only report an error when such a compromise is impossible:

```
- apply : (bool->int) * int -> bool ;
Type clash  in:  apply : ((((%->%)*int)->bool)
Looking  for a:  int
I have found a:  bool
```

It looks as if a polymorphic object could be typed to many different types at the same time. So, what should actually be meant by *the* type of apply? There are two different ways of answering this question: either we accept that one object may have an infinite number of distinct types; or that one expression may denote an infinite number of distinct objects.

One-object-many-types view

We may take the position that a Standard ML expression denotes a single object, and every type expression denotes a single type. There exists a preorder[1] $\sqsubseteq$ on type expressions, $T_1 \sqsubseteq T_2$ reads: type T_1 is more general than type T_2, or: type T_2 is further instantiated than T_1. Formally: if T_1 and T_2 are Standard ML type expressions then $T_1 \sqsubseteq T_2$ is true if and only if there exists an instantiation of type expressions for type variables (i.e. primed variables) that turns T_1 into T_2. For instance,

```
'a ⊑ 'b ⊑
   ⊑ 'a->'b ⊑
   ⊑ int->'b ⊑
   ⊑ int->(bool->'b) ⊑
   ⊑ int->(bool->(real->'b)) ⊑ ...
```

Monomorphic types, i.e. the ones that have no type variables, are evidently the maximal elements of $\sqsubseteq$. Now, each object of a given type is of all less general types as well; i.e.

if $ex : T_1$ and $T_1 \sqsubseteq T_2$ then $ex : T_2$

---

[1]*Preorder* is any reflexive and transitive relation; almost a partial order, but the weak asymmetry is not required.

Moreover, for every object ex there exists the unique most general type
(up to the renaming of type variables), i.e. the minimal element wrt $\sqsubseteq$ in
$\{T \mid ex : T\}$. "To be of type" now means something different from "to belong"; for instance, although the function

```
apply : (int->bool) * int -> bool
```

has a monomorphic type, this does not imply that `apply` is a monomorphic
function. Also the $\sqsubseteq$ preorder is not the set inclusion, e.g.

```
('a)list ⊑ (int)list
```

does not imply that every list is a list of integers; nor is it the reversed set
inclusion, e.g.

```
int->int ⊒ 'a->'b
```

does not imply that integer functions may be applied to elements of an arbitrary type `'a`, which is true of functions from `'a->'b`. The relation $\sqsubseteq$ is
very syntactic in nature and relates *type expressions* rather than types they
denote; in fact, it is difficult to say which *sets* are denoted by polymorphic
type expressions.

One-object-one-type view

We may also take the opposite position that every object, monomorphic
or not, has a unique type; and that "to be of type" is synonymous with "to
belong". Types are therefore sets and the type system of Standard ML is a
family of mutually disjoint sets with operations (type constructors) over this
family. But then we have to accept that the meaning of an expression may
depend on its context; e.g. the `apply`-s in

```
apply((fn(n)=>n+1),2)   and in
apply(sin,3.14)
```

are different functions. By this approach, a polymorphic object is a function
that, given a tuple of types, yields an object; for instance the polymorphic
function

```
recur : (('a -> 'b) -> ('a -> 'b)) -> ('a -> 'b)
```

given the (implicit) pair (int*int,int) yields the monomorphic functional

```
recur : ((int*int -> int) -> (int*int -> int)) ->
              (int*int -> int)
```

which may be later applied to the function

```
gcd' : ((int*int) -> int) -> ((int*int) -> int)
```

as has been done in the end of Sec.6.2; and the result of this application is

```
gcd = recur(gcd') : int*int -> int
```

A polymorphic type is a collection of polymorphic objects; for instance the polymorphic type (`'a,'b)tree2` consists of polymorphic trees, each such tree being a function that, given a pair (`t1,t2`) of types, yields a monomorphic tree in (`t1,t2)tree2`. In Standard ML the type dependence of objects is *implicit*, so whether `recur` denotes a polymorphic function, or one of its monomorphic instances, depends on the context of its use.

The former view is better suited to the needs of a Standard ML implementor because he may not like the idea of the same expression denoting an infinite number of different objects depending on context. The latter view results in a more intuitive understanding of types as sets, of "being of type" as belonging, and of polymorphism as functional dependence on types. It may, however, be proved that both approaches are equivalent.

Since implementations are for the moment not our concern, for the remainder of this chapter we accept the latter viewpoint. So, now that polymorphism is a functional dependence on types, we had better be careful to clarify *what kind* of dependence and on *what* types.

6.4   Implicit polymorphism

It would be annoying always to have to write the necessary type information explicitly; for instance, to have to write

```
fun apply(₍'a,'b₎)(f:'a->'b , x:'a) = f(x) ;
```

instead of

```
fun apply(f,x) = f(x) ;
```

so as not to forget that `apply` depends in the first order on a pair of types. In some theoretical considerations in this chapter we will do so, but remember that explicit type dependences, such as in `apply`₍'a,'b₎, do not belong to Standard ML, and that variable typing suggestions, such as in (`f:'a->'b,x:'a`), are optional. The Standard ML type checker is always able to infer the type of expression on its own[2]. We say that Standard ML polymorphism is *implicit*.

Not surprisingly, the convenience of implicit typing comes at a price. Certain possibilities have been ruled out from Standard ML and certain ambiguities have been solved by what may seem an arbitrary decree. Below in this chapter we discuss what this price amounts to.

Consider the following piece of Standard ML code:

---

[2]One exception is discussed in the next section.

```
- fun id(x) = x ;
> val id = fn : 'a -> 'a
- id(id)(5) ;
```

If we take it that both the occurrences of `id` in the latter expression denote the same function, then the expression is ill-typed: for any type `'a` the function

$$id_{'a} : 'a \text{->} 'a$$

may only take an object of type `'a` as an argument, so $id_{'a}$ as its own argument will not do. On the other hand, if we take it that two occurrences of the same identifier in the same expression *may* have different types, then the whole expression may be typed as follows:

$$id_{int\text{->}int}(id_{int})(5)$$

In fact, the Standard ML type checker chooses this second option, and the answer is

```
> 5 : int
```

We may wonder whether

```
- (fn(f)=>f(f))(id)(5) ;
```

is equivalent to the above. The rule of β-reduction[3] applied to this expression would yield

```
id(id)(5)
```

which makes the properly typed case we have already considered. The Standard ML type checker does *not*, however, use the β-reduction in this context and tries first to complete the typing, which turns out not to be feasible for `(fn(f)=>f(f))`:

```
Type clash  in:  (f f)
Looking  for a:  'a
I have found a:  'a -> 'b
```

Let us compare this behaviour with that of Standard ML's **let** expressions for which there also exists a sort of β-reduction rule:

$$\begin{pmatrix} \text{let val } x = e_1 \\ \text{in } e \\ \text{end} \end{pmatrix} = e[e_1/x]$$

This time, the Standard ML interpreter applies this β-reduction prior to any typing:

---

[3]The evaluation rule of λ-calculus that states that

$$(fn(x)\text{=>}e)(e_1) = e[e_1/x]$$

i.e. expression e with e_1 substituted for all free occurrences of variable x and with all bound variables renamed so as to avoid clashes.

```
- (let val f = id
    in f(f)
    end)(5) ;
> 5 : int
```

At first glance this difference between the `let` expression and the corresponding `fn` expression applied to an argument may look like an arbitrary choice, but there is in fact a fundamental difference between

$$(\text{fn}(x)\text{=>}e)\,(e_1) \quad \text{and} \quad \left(\begin{array}{l} \text{let val } x \text{ = } e_1 \\ \text{in } e \\ \text{end} \end{array}\right)$$

In the former, the first part $(\text{fn}(x)\text{=>}e)$ is an expression on its own, therefore it may be processed independently of its argument e_1, giving rise to typing problems; hence the requirement that its type be found before any evaluation is attempted. The latter is harmless, because

$$\left(\begin{array}{l} \text{let val } x \text{ = } \ldots \\ \text{in } e \\ \text{end} \end{array}\right)$$

does not mean anything without an argument e_1 for the dots.

In Standard ML every object is assumed polymorphic until some restriction on its polymorphism can be found. For instance, a programmer's suggestion, or a monomorphic context, may restrict or eliminate polymorphism. E.g. the type of `(fn(x)=>x)` alone is `'a->'a`; the type of `(fn(x:('a)list)=>x)` is `('a)list->('a)list`, which is less general; the type of `(fn(x)=>x+0)` is `int->int`, which is monomorphic. This means, a programmer cannot explicitly require that an object be polymorphic; on the other hand, he can require that an object be *not* polymorphic.

Another facet of the implicitness of Standard ML's polymorphism is the way polymorphic types are denoted. Polymorphism in type expressions is recognised by the presence of type variables. This resembles the now largely obsolete notation for functions, by which $\cos \pi + \sin \pi$ is a number, while $\cos x + \sin x$ is a function, because it contains variable x. This notation is only convenient for functions of one argument, becomes ambiguous for functions of more arguments, and turns helpless for functionals. If a function is to be treated as a "first class citizen", the expression that denotes it should not involve any free variables; hence Standard ML's notation: `fn(x)=> cos(x)+sin(x)`. But the situation is different at the level of types. Standard ML's polymorphic types are *not* "first class" types.

6.5   Polymorphism vs. overloading

Consider the following type dependent function:

$$\texttt{add'}_a = \begin{cases} \texttt{fn(x:real,y:real)=> x+y} & \text{if } \texttt{'a} = \texttt{real} \\ \texttt{fn(n:int,k:int)=> n+k} & \text{if } \texttt{'a} = \texttt{int} \\ \texttt{fn(p:bool,q:bool)=> p orelse q} & \text{if } \texttt{'a} = \texttt{bool} \\ \texttt{fn(x:'a,y:'a)=> x} & \text{otherwise} \end{cases}$$

A type dependent object that has to be defined anew for each type parameter, as is the case with add$'_a$, is usually referred to as *overloaded*. Examples of Standard ML overloaded objects are arithmetic operations +, ˜ and *. The programmer, however, has no means of defining his own overloaded objects; therefore add$'_a$ may not be defined in Standard ML. There are simply no predicates on types available, in particular, no way of testing whether 'a = real.

In some other programming languages it is, however, possible to define overloaded functions as long as they differ in type. For instance, in ADA a programmer may define the type of rational numbers, and three different operations all denoted by /:

$$\begin{aligned} &\dots / \dots : Int \times Int \to Int & &\text{— integer division} \\ &\dots / \dots : Int \times Int \to Rat & &\text{— constructing a fraction} \\ &\dots / \dots : Rat \times Rat \to Rat & &\text{— rational division} \end{aligned}$$

The meaning of the command

$$x := ex_1 / ex_2$$

depends on types of x, ex_1 and ex_2. But even if we know that the variable x is rational, the command

$$x := (4/3)/(2/1)$$

is still ambiguous. One may either think of the nested /-s as integer divisions and of the external one as a fraction, in which case the value assigned to x is $\frac{1}{2}$; or one may view the nested /-s as fractions and the external one as a rational division, in which case the value assigned to x is $\frac{4}{6}$.

There are two ways of avoiding such ambiguities: either to require explicit type instantiation of operators in expressions, in which case they would no longer be overloaded; or to completely outlaw the programmer's definitions of overloaded objects and to check carefully predefined overloaded objects for nonambiguity. The latter solution has been accepted in Standard ML. Since, however, there exist in Standard ML predefined overloaded operations, the programmer has to "unload" them when using them in his own definitions, either by a non-ambiguous context or by a typing suggestion. For instance,

```
- fun plus(x,y) = x+y ;
```

is illegal:

```
Type checking error in: (syntactic context unknown)
Unresolvable overloaded identifier:  +
Definition cannot be found for the type:  ('a * 'a) -> 'a
```

but it becomes correct with the following small change:

```
- fun plus(x,y) = x+y+0 ;
> val plus = fn : (int * int) -> int
```

Since the integer 0 resolves the ambiguity. It also becomes correct with the typing suggestion:

```
- fun plus(x,y:real) = x+y ;
> val plus = fn : (real * real) -> real
```

The Standard ML polymorphism is not *any* dependence on types, it is rather a *smooth*, or a *uniform* dependence on types. A resulting type must not depend on any special properties of a parameter type. This kind of type dependence is called *parametric*, or *true*, polymorphism, as opposed to *overloading* or *ad hoc* polymorphism.

One should realise that notwithstanding this prejudiced terminology, the ban on user defined overloading is no blessing, but rather a heavy price to pay for implicit typing. It is not easy to tell the parametric polymorphism from the *ad hoc* polymorphism independently of language. This is as though we allowed "uniformly defined" functions, such as

$$f(x) \stackrel{\text{def}}{=} x^2$$

but disallowed "*ad hoc*" functions, such as

$$f(x) \stackrel{\text{def}}{=} \begin{cases} x^2 & \text{if } x \geq 0 \\ 0 & \text{if } x < 0 \end{cases}$$

From the mathematical point of view our add$'_a$ is as good a function on types as any other. But we have to part with this mathematical viewpoint and bow to the necessities of the language.

6.6   Equality on polymorphic types

There is in Standard ML a special overloaded Boolean function ...=... defined on all primitive types and carried over to the types defined using the type constructors * and datatype. This means that equality is defined on $A*B$ provided it is defined both on A and on B, e.g.

```
    - (true,0) = ((1=1),floor(0.5)) ;
    > true : bool
```

— since there is equality on `bool` and on `int`, it carries over to `bool*int`. Equality is also defined on a `datatype` provided it is defined on all its components, e.g.

```
    - datatype multree = mkmultree of real*(multree)list ;
    > datatype multree = mkmultree of real * (multree list)
      con mkmultree = fn : (real * (multree list)) -> multree
    - mkmultree(17.2,[mkmultree(~5.0,[])]) =
        mkmultree(17.2,[]) ;
    > false : bool
```

— since there is equality on `real`, it carries over to `multree`. As has already been stated, equality is not defined on function types:

```
    - fun id(x:int) = x ;
    > val id = fn : int -> int
    - id = id ;
    Type clash  in: (id = id)
    There is no equality defined on type int -> int
```

The function space constructor `->` is the only obstacle to defining equality on *any* type in Standard ML.

But since this exceptional constructor does exist in Standard ML, some caution is necessary when using equality in definitions of polymorphic objects. For instance, the function `update` defined by

```
    fun update(cont,key)dict =
      fn(key')=>
        if key'=key then cont
        else dict(key') ;
```

is not of the polymorphic type

```
    'a*'b -> ('b->'a) -> ('b->'a)
```

because then `update` could be instantiated with, say, `int->int` for `'b` which would lead to applying an equality test on `int->int`. The Standard ML type checker assigns `update` the type

```
    'a*''b -> (''b->'a) -> (''b->'a)
```

An identifier preceded by two primes denotes a different kind of polymorphism, namely the one in which the type variable ranges only over types that admit equality.

A typing suggestion to instantiate `update` with a type that does not admit equality for variable `''b` that requires equality, is rejected by the type checker:

```
- update : real * (int->int) -> ((int->int)->int) ->
           ((int->int)->int) ;
Type clash  in:  update : ((real*(%->%))->((%->%)->(%->
%)))
There is no equality defined on type int -> int
```

If there is no actual equality involved, the type checker will however disregard our typing suggestion that the polymorphism for a function parameter be restricted to the types that admit equality:

```
- fun id(x:''a) = x ;
> val id = fn : 'a -> 'a
```

This is in line with the general principle that Standard ML's typing is implicit and the type checker's responsibility. The programmer has only a limited control over types.

6.7   Shallow polymorphism

Section 6.3 ends with the statement that a polymorphic object is a function from types to objects. This leads to the question, whether a polymorphic object may also be instantiated by a polymorphic type. For instance, list is a polymorphic type that yields type (T)list for any monomorphic type T, thus such types as real or (int)list may be used as type parameters. But is it also possible to instantiate list with list itself?

Standard ML's answer is a flat "no". Type parameters in polymorphic objects may range only over monomorphic types. In order to better understand why, and also to be able to discuss other possibilities, we will have to introduce an auxiliary notation which makes all the type dependences explicit. However, do not forget that no such notation is accepted by Standard ML.

Let *Mono* be the collection of all monomorphic Standard ML types, i.e. the least collection of types that contains unit, bool, int, real and string closed under *, -> and datatype. Thus also monomorphic recursive types, such as (int)list or (bool,int)tree2 belong to *Mono*. Let us denote the polymorphic function that given a monomorphic type α yields the identity function on α by

(6.1) $\mathtt{fn}(\alpha : Mono)\mathtt{=>}\ (\mathtt{fn}(x : \alpha)\mathtt{=>}\ x)$

(Standard ML's way of expressing the same thing is fn(x)=>x). The same notation may be used to make all type dependences explicit in the expressions that denote objects.

Now, for any fixed $\alpha \in Mono$, the type of $\mathtt{fn}(x:\alpha)\mathtt{=>}x$ is $\alpha \to \alpha$; therefore the type of (6.1) is the set of all functions that, given a type $\alpha \in Mono$, yield a value in $\alpha \to \alpha$. This set will be denoted by

$$\prod_{\alpha \in Mono} (\alpha \to \alpha)$$

(in Standard ML: `'a->'a`). In general, $\prod_{a \in A} B_a$ is an accepted notation for the *generalised Cartesian product* of a family $\{B_a \mid a \in A\}$ of sets; this product consists of functions f that assign to any $a \in A$ an element from B_a. In studies in type theory, $\prod$ is sometimes called the *type quantifier*.

Another example of a polymorphic type in this notation is

$$\prod_{\alpha \in Mono} \prod_{\beta \in Mono} (\alpha, \beta)\mathtt{tree2}$$

where `tree2` is as defined in Sec.6.2. The constructors of this type are

```
leaf =
  fn(α : Mono)=>(fn(β : Mono)=>leaf_{α,β})
```
$: \prod_{\alpha \in Mono} \prod_{\beta \in Mono} (\beta \to (\alpha, \beta)\mathtt{tree2})$

and

```
node =
  fn(α : Mono)=>(fn(β : Mono)=>node_{α,β})
```
$: \prod_{\alpha \in Mono} \prod_{\beta \in Mono} (\alpha \times (\alpha, \beta)\mathtt{tree2} \times (\alpha, \beta)\mathtt{tree2} \to (\alpha, \beta)\mathtt{tree2})$

All polymorphic types in Standard ML are of the form

$$\prod_{\alpha_1 \in Mono} \cdots \prod_{\alpha_n \in Mono} typ_{\alpha_1,\dots,\alpha_n}$$

where the type $typ_{\alpha_1,\dots,\alpha_n}$ is monomorphic, i.e. it does not involve any further occurrences of $\prod$. Since all the type quantifiers in Standard ML types are grouped together in front of type expressions, one may skip them, as is done in Standard ML (in fact, in Standard ML one *must* skip them), without introducing any ambiguity. A polymorphic object, such as those available in Standard ML, whose type does not involve nested occurrences of $\prod$, is called *shallowly* polymorphic.

Let us now consider the following object, whose type does involve a nested $\prod$:

$$\Phi = \mathtt{fn}(f : \prod_{\alpha \in Mono} (\alpha \to \mathtt{bool}))\mathtt{=>}f_{\mathtt{int}}$$

Function Φ takes a polymorphic function f and instantiates it with the type `int` for α. The type of Φ is

$$(\prod_{\alpha \in Mono} (\alpha \to \mathtt{bool})) \to (\mathtt{int} \to \mathtt{bool})$$

An object, such as Φ, whose type involves nested type quantifiers, is referred to as *deeply* polymorphic.

Please, note that functions such as Φ cannot be defined at all without explicit type instantiations; therefore a programming language with implicit typing may not contain deep polymorphism. The creators of Standard ML have decided for implicitness and against depth.

6.8   Two "universes" in Standard ML

We have several times emphasised that functions in Standard ML are "first class citizens"; i.e. they have types, they may be passed as arguments to other functions, and they may be yielded as results of other functions. In this respect functions do not differ from simple values such as single numbers. Standard ML *types*, though, are not "first class citizens" in the same sense. They are not typed themselves, and they may be arguments or results of functions only in a restricted way, via polymorphism. The Standard ML world is two-fold: it consists of a universe of types and of a universe of objects (values). The laws governing these two universes are different.

The universe of types may be defined in the following way. First define type expressions by

$$
\begin{array}{lll}
TypeExpr & ::= & \texttt{unit} \mid \texttt{bool} \mid \texttt{int} \mid \\
& & \texttt{real} \mid \texttt{string} & \text{— type constants} \\
& \mid & TypVar & \text{— type variable} \\
& \mid & TypExpr * TypeExpr & \text{— Cartesian prod.} \\
& \mid & TypExpr \texttt{->} TypeExpr & \text{— function space} \\
& \mid & TypExpr \mid TypeExpr & \text{— disjoint union} \\
& \mid & \texttt{rectype } TypVar = TypExpr & \text{— recursive type}
\end{array}
$$

This is not quite in line with the actual syntax of Standard ML, because both disjoint union and recursive type are in Standard ML expressed using **datatype**. For theoretical considerations, however, it is better to separate the two different concepts. Anyway, any Standard ML monomorphic type may be expressed by the above syntax, and any type expressible by the above syntax belongs to Standard ML. For instance, the Standard ML type defined by

```
datatype realtree = empty
                  | mktree of real * realtree * realtree ;
```

may be expressed as

```
rectype 'realtree = unit | real * 'realtree * 'realtree ;
```

(note that the type bound by **rectype** has to be a type variable). The translation also works out the other way; for instance, the Standard ML counterpart of the type expression

```
int | rectype 'aux = 'aux
```

is[4]:

```
local
   datatype aux = f0 of aux
in
   datatype T = f1 of int
              | f2 of aux
end ;
```

(the example is silly, because (`rectype 'aux = 'aux`) is the empty type, but the translation may be performed anyway).

Once we have the definition of type expressions, the monomorphic Standard ML types are the ones denoted by expressions with no free type variables, and the polymorphic types are the ones denoted by

$$(6.2) \quad \prod_{\alpha_1 \in Mono} \prod_{\alpha_2 \in Mono} \cdots \prod_{\alpha_n \in Mono} typ_{\alpha_1, \alpha_2, \ldots, \alpha_n}$$

where $typ_{\alpha_1, \alpha_2, \ldots, \alpha_n}$ is an arbitrary type expression with no free type variables other than $\alpha_1, \alpha_2, \ldots, \alpha_n$. Note that by this definition[5] monomorphic types are a special case of polymorphic ones.

To every polymorphic type there corresponds a function that, given a tuple of monomorphic types, yields a monomorphic type. The function corresponding to (6.2) is

$$\begin{aligned}
&\texttt{fn}(\alpha_1 : Mono) \texttt{=>} \\
&\quad (\texttt{fn}(\alpha_2 : Mono) \texttt{=>} \cdots \\
&\quad\quad (\texttt{fn}(\alpha_n : Mono) \texttt{=>} \\
&\quad\quad\quad typ_{\alpha_1, \alpha_2, \ldots, \alpha_n} \\
&\quad) \ldots)
\end{aligned}$$

(obviously, this function cannot be defined in Standard ML). The other way the statement is not true: although every such function gives rise to a generalised Cartesian product of types, this product may be not expressible as a type expression with type quantifiers.

Via the above described correspondence, polymorphic types may be viewed as functions in the universe of types. In this framework it makes sense to ask whether the Standard ML universe of types allows for high order functions, as does the universe of objects; or whether the functions in the universe of types are "first class citizens" of that universe.

---

[4]The Standard ML construct `local...in...end` makes a definition invisible from outside; it is used here to hide the definition of type **aux**.

[5]This definition is a bit informal because we do not explain the notion of a type *denoted* by a given type expression.

Standard ML's answer to both these questions is "no". High order functions on types, i.e. functions that take functions on types as arguments and/or
yield functions on types as results, would correspond to a deep polymorphism
which is unavailable in Standard ML.

6.9   Unifying the two universes: dependent types

We have already said that deep polymorphism is not compatible with implicit
typing, and is, as such, excluded from Standard ML. In this section we discuss
another useful concept not present in Standard ML.

Let us consider possible functional dependences between the two universes
described in the preceding section. An object-dependent object is just an ordi-
nary function; a type-dependent object or type is referred to as polymorphic;
there remains the possibility of an object-dependent type.

Probably the best known example of an object-dependent type is the type
of matrices. Suppose we want to define them as n^2-tuples of real numbers:

$$
\begin{aligned}
Mat(1) \;&=\; \texttt{real} \\
Mat(2) \;&=\; \texttt{real} \times \texttt{real} \times \texttt{real} \times \texttt{real} \\
&\cdots \\
Mat(n) \;&=\; \underbrace{\texttt{real} \times \ldots \times \texttt{real}}_{n^2}
\end{aligned}
$$

$\cdots$

To describe the concept of matrix as such, rather than matrix of a given size,
one has first to define the type-valued function Cartesian power:

```
fun Cartpow =
  fn(n : Nat)=>
    fn(α : Mono)=>
      if n = 0 then unit
      else α × Cartpow(n − 1)(α);
```

The "type" of *Cartpow* is

$$Cartpow : Nat \rightarrow Mono \rightarrow Mono$$

Now, $Mat(n)$ is the type obtained by applying the following function *Mat* to
the argument n:

```
val Mat =
  fn(n : Nat)=> Cartpow(n ∗ n)(real)
```

and the "type" of this function is

$$Mat : Nat \rightarrow Mono$$

The above defined *Cartpow* and *Mat* are the so-called *dependent types*; this term may be considered as short for *object-dependent types*.

Let $\{det(n) \mid n \in Nat\}$ be the family of functions such that for any natural n

$$det(n) : Mat(n) \to \texttt{real}$$

be the function that, given a matrix of size n, yields its determinant. All these functions are instances of the following:

```
val det =
    fn(n : Nat)=> det(n)
```

Its "type" is

$$det : \prod_{n \in Nat} (Mat(n) \to \texttt{real})$$

The "type" of *det* is closely related to the dependent type

```
fn(n : Nat)=> (Mat(n) → real)
```

Apart from implicit typing there is yet another feature of Standard ML that does not allow the use of this kind of function: static type checking. Before any evaluation of a Standard ML expression may start, the type checker has to establish the type of the expression. In the presence of dependent types this is not, however, feasible. Consider, for instance, the expression

$$(6.3) \quad det(f(0))(m_1, m_2, m_3, m_4)$$

where $f : Nat \to Nat$ is a predefined function and m_1, m_2, m_3 and m_4 are given real numbers. Expression (6.3) is type correct if, and only if, $f(0) = 2$, since no function $det(n)$ with $n \neq 2$ may be applied to a 2×2 matrix. This means that in order to establish the type correctness of (6.3) one has to *evaluate* $f(0)$. Thus the operation of the type checker would have to interleave with the operation of the evaluator rather than precede it.

6.10 Exercises

Exercise 19

Design functions

```
f : (string)list * (string)list -> bool  and
g : (real)list * (real)list -> bool
```

that lexicographically compare two lists of strings, respectively of reals. Make them both special instances of a general polymorphic lexicographic order.

Exercise 20

Design a function

```
f : ((int)list)tree -> (int)tree
```

that simplifies a tree by replacing a list of integers in every node by the sum of these integers. Design another function

```
g : (int)tree -> ((int)list)tree
```

that replaces a natural number in each node of a tree by the list of its digits. Since both definitions involve tree traversal, design a general polymorphic function

```
maptree : ('a->'b) -> (('a)tree -> ('b)tree)
```

and use it to define f and g.

Exercise 21

A binary tree may be viewed as indexed at every node by elements of bool, with true meaning "go left" and false meaning "go right". Thus any path from a root to a node corresponds to a list of logical values. By analogy, lists of integers correspond to paths from root to nodes in a tree that has a countable number of sons to each node.

Generalise this to lists over arbitrary type 'a. Design a tree in which any node has a son for every element of 'a. Use this tree to solve the dictionary problem where keys are of type ('a)list; this means defining a function find that finds in such a tree a *contents*, given its *key*; and the function insert that updates a dictionary with a new contents for a given key.

Chapter 7

Recursors for data types

The most important constructor of types (cf. Chapter 5) is no doubt the function space constructor ->. To support this claim the current chapter demonstrates how other data types may be embedded in function spaces, in other words: how numbers, lists, trees etc. may be viewed as polymorphic functionals. This representation is not merely of theoretical interest — but also it provides powerful tools for constructing functional programs.

7.1 Natural numbers as function iterators

Consider the following polymorphic high order function:

```
fun iter n f a =
  if n=0 then a
  else f(iter (n-1) f a)
```

Its type is

```
iter : int -> ((’a->’a)->’a->’a)
```

and it assigns to any natural number (its value is undefined for negative integers) an "iterator" of functions:

$$(7.1) \quad \text{iter } n \; f = \underbrace{f \circ \ldots \circ f}_{n}$$

The functional `iter` is rather special in that it allows many functions over natural numbers to be defined without the explicit use of recursion. For instance, the natural power of a real number may be defined as iterated multiplication in the following way:

```
fun power(r,k) =
  let fun mul(r1:real)(r2:real) = r1*r2
  in iter k (mul r) 1.0
  end
```

Indeed, according to (7.1) and to the above definition of power:

$$\begin{aligned}
\text{power}(r,k) &= \underbrace{((\text{mul } r) \circ \ldots \circ (\text{mul } r))}_{k} \; 1.0 \;= \\
&= \underbrace{\text{mul } r \; (\ldots (\text{mul } r \; 1.0) \ldots)}_{k} \;= \\
&= \underbrace{r * \ldots * r *}_{k} 1.0 \;= \\
&= r^k
\end{aligned}$$

Here follow a couple of other examples of the use of iter in defining functions on natural numbers without an explicit recursion:

- *Multiple conjunction* is the function

  ```
  mconj : (int-bool)*int -> bool
  ```

  such that

  $$\text{mconj}(f,n) = f(1) \text{ andalso} \ldots \text{andalso } f(n)$$

  Using iter it may be defined as follows:

  ```
  fun mconj(f,n) =
    let val (b,i) =
      iter n (fn(b,i)=>(b andalso f(i),i+1)) (true,1)
    in b
    end
  ```

- *Factorial* may be defined as follows:

  ```
  fun fact(n) =
    let val (f,i) =
          iter n (fn(f,i)=>(f*i,i+1)) (1,1)
    in f
    end
  ```

- *Bubble-sort* over a sequence of reals:

  ```
  fun bubblesort(a,n) =
    let fun bubble(a:int->real,i) =
          let val (a,j) =
                iter (n-1)
                    (fn(a,j)=>
                        if a(j-1)>a(j)
  ```

```
                         then (swap(a,j-1,j),j+1)
                         else (a,j+1)
                    )
                    (a,2)
            in a
            end
      in let val (a,i) =
            iter (n-1) (fn(a,i)=>(bubble(a,i),i-1)) (a,n)
          in a
          end
      end
```

You should ensure that you understand the above examples.

Since the recursion in the definition of iter is quite simple, its power must derive rather from its high order. This order may be made very high indeed, because iter has a polymorphic type and its type parameter 'a may be instantiated by a function space.

Using iter in a functional program is similar to using for-iteration in an imperative program. Unlike while-loops, the for-command may be used only when the desired number of repetitions of a certain action is known in advance. The functional counterpart of a loop

$$state := state_0 \; ;$$
$$\text{for } i := 1 \text{ to } n \text{ do}$$
$$state := f(state, i)$$

is

$$\text{iter } n \; (\text{fn}(state, i) => (f(state, i), i + 1)) \; (state_0, 1)$$

A more sophisticated way of expressing the same thing is to state that iter has the expressive power of *high order primitive recursion*, or that it is a *primitive recursor* for natural numbers. Informally, a function is primitive recursive if it can be defined either non-recursively, or with just a restricted use of recursion that corresponds to the following pattern:

$$(7.2) \; \text{fun } f(n, x) =$$
$$\quad \text{if } n = 0 \text{ then } g(x)$$
$$\quad \text{else } h(f(n - 1, x), n - 1, x)$$

where g and h are known beforehand to be primitive recursive. Primitive recursive functions are of special interest to computer scientists.

That with `iter` at hand one may non-recursively define any function defin-able as in (7.2), is shown by consideration of the following function definition:

(7.3) `fun` $f'(n,x)$ =
      `let fun` $f_1(y,n)$ = $(h(y,n,x),n+1)$
      `in let val` (y_0,n_0) = `iter` n f_1 $(g(x),0)$
         `in` y_0
         `end`
      `end`

Theorem 6 (7.2) and (7.3) define the same function, i.e.

$$f'(n,x) = f(n,x)$$

for any natural n and for any x.

Proof: By virtue of (7.3) this follows from the following equality:

$$\text{iter } n \ f_1 \ (g(x),0) = (f(n,x),n)$$

which may be easily proved by induction on n using the definitions of `iter` and of f. □

The polymorphic functional `iter` may be said to extract the very "essence" of natural numbers. Natural numbers are answers to the ques-tion "How many times?". Incidentally, `iter`(1) means "once", `iter`(2) means "twice", and so on; while the argument f of `iter`(n) is the action that has to be repeated the given number of times.

Questions about the essence of objects are too philosophical to be math-ematically tractable, but we may at least demonstrate that `iter` is a homo-morphic embedding, which means that it maps different natural numbers to different polymorphic functions, and it preserves typical operations on natural numbers. To do this, define the corresponding operations

      `zero` : A
      `succ` : $A \to A$
      `add`, `mul` : $A \to A \to A$

where A = (`'a->'a`)`->'a->'a`, by

(7.4) `fun zero f a = a ;`

(7.5) `fun succ ff f a = f(ff f a) ;`

(7.6) `fun add ff1 ff2 = ff1 succ ff2 ;`

(7.7) `fun mul ff1 ff2 = ff1 (add ff2) zero ;`

The following intuitions lie behind these definitions:

- **zero** is the "0 times"-iterator; this means that, given a function **f**, it does not apply it at all;

- **succ**, given an iterator **ff**, yields another iterator **succ ff** that maps its argument **f** as required by **ff** and then applies **f** once again;

- **add ff1 ff2** is the iterator obtained from **ff2** by repeating **ff1** times the operation **succ**; note the high order of the functionals involved: **ff1** is used to iterate an operation that processes iterators;

- **mul ff1 ff2** is the iterator obtained from the iterator **zero** by repeating **ff1** times the addition of **ff2**.

Theorem 7 *For any natural n, n_1 and n_2:*

(7.8) if $n_1 \neq n_2$ then $\mathtt{iter}(n_1) \neq \mathtt{iter}(n_2)$

(7.9) $\mathtt{iter}(0) = \mathtt{zero}$

(7.10) $\mathtt{iter}(1 + n) = \mathtt{succ}(\mathtt{iter}(n))$

(7.11) $\mathtt{iter}(n_1 + n_2) = \mathtt{add}(\mathtt{iter}\ n_1)(\mathtt{iter}\ n_2)$

(7.12) $\mathtt{iter}(n_1 * n_2) = \mathtt{mul}(\mathtt{iter}\ n_1)(\mathtt{iter}\ n_2)$

Proof: To prove (7.8) assume that

(7.13) $\mathtt{iter}(n_1) = \mathtt{iter}(n_2)$

for some natural n_1 and n_2. The type of both $\mathtt{iter}(n_1)$ and $\mathtt{iter}(n_2)$ is

    ('a->'a) -> ('a->'a)

After instantiating int for the type variable 'a in that type, both functions become of the type

    $\mathtt{iter}(n_1), \mathtt{iter}(n_2) : (\mathtt{int}\texttt{->}\mathtt{int}) \rightarrow (\mathtt{int}\texttt{->}\mathtt{int})$

and the equality (7.13) comes down to

    $\mathtt{iter}(n_1)\ f\ n = \mathtt{iter}(n_2)\ f\ n$

for any function $f : \mathtt{int} \rightarrow \mathtt{int}$ and for any integer n. For instance,

    $\mathtt{iter}(n_1)\ (\mathtt{fn}(k)\texttt{=>}1 + k)\ 0 \;=\; \mathtt{iter}(n_2)\ (\mathtt{fn}(k)\texttt{=>}1 + k)\ 0$

i.e.

$$\underbrace{1 + \ldots + 1}_{n_1} + 0 \;=\; \underbrace{1 + \ldots + 1}_{n_2} + 0$$

which implies $n_1 = n_2$.

The proof of (7.9) follows directly from the definitions of iter and of zero; analogously, the proof of (7.10) follows directly from the definitions of iter and of succ.

(7.11) may be demonstrated as follows:

$$\begin{aligned}
\texttt{iter}(n_1 + n_2) \; &= \\
&= \texttt{iter}(\underbrace{1 + \ldots + 1}_{n_1} + n_2) \; = \\
&= \underbrace{\texttt{succ}(\ldots \texttt{succ}(}_{n_1} \texttt{iter}(n_2))\ldots) \; = \\
&= \texttt{iter}(n_1) \; \texttt{succ} \; (\texttt{iter} \; n_2) \; = \\
&= \texttt{add} \; (\texttt{iter} \; n_1) \; (\texttt{iter} \; n_2)
\end{aligned}$$

(7.12) is proved alike.

□

7.2 Lists and trees as iterators

Now consider the high order function

```
itlist : ('a)list -> (('a*'b->'b)->'b->'b)
```

defined by

```
fun itlist [] f b = b
  | itlist (a::lis) f b =
        f (a , itlist lis f b)
```

This function is defined by analogy to iter from Sec.7.1 and also assigns iterators to lists, only now the iterated function f has two arguments of possibly distinct types:

$$\texttt{itlist} \; [a_1, a_2, \ldots, a_n] \; f \; b \; = \; f(a_1, f(a_2, \ldots f(a_n, b)\ldots))$$

The function itlist has many properties analogous to those of iter. It is a primitive recursor for lists, i.e. it can be used to define, with no explicit use of recursion, the functions definable by the following pattern:

```
(7.14) fun f([],x) = g(x)
         | f(a::lis,x) = h(f(lis,x),a,lis,x)
```

where the functions g and h are known beforehand to be primitive recursive (the proof is analogous to that for iter). It is a homomorphical embedding of ('a)list with the operations [] and :: into ('a*'b->'b)->'b->'b with the corresponding operations

```
fun nl f b = b ;
fun cons a lis f b = f(a,lis f b) ;
```

Practically all functions over lists used in everyday programming are list primitive recursive and as such may be defined by itlist. Here are some examples:

• The *length* of a list may be defined by:

```
fun len lis = itlist lis (fn(a,n)=>1+n) 0
```

• The *concatenation* of two lists may be defined by:

```
(7.15) fun concat(lis1,lis2) =
         itlist lis1 (fn(a,lis')=>a::lis') lis2
```

• *Mapping* a function along a list, usually defined by

```
fun map f [] = []
  | map f (a::lis) =
      f(a)::(map f lis)
```

may be defined by:

```
(7.16)  fun map f lis =
          itlist lis (fn(a,lis')=>f(a)::lis') []
```

In Sec.6.2 the type of polymorphic trees with possibly different types of entries in leaves and in internal nodes were defined by:

```
(7.17) datatype ('a,'b)tree2 =
         leaf of 'b
       | node of 'a * ('a,'b)tree2 * ('a,'b)tree2
```

These trees may also be viewed as function iterators, namely via the polymorphic high order function

```
ittree2 : ('a,'b)tree2 -> ((b'->'c)->('a*'c*'c->'c)->'c)
```

defined as follows:

```
fun ittree2(leaf(b)) f g = f b
  | ittree2(node(a,t1,t2)) f g =
      g(a,ittree2 t1 f g,ittree2 t2 f g)
```

For instance, the function that, given a (real,int)tree2, yields the product of the real numbers that stand in its internal nodes and the sum of the integers that stand in its leaves, may be defined as follows:

```
fun prodsum t =
  ittree2 t
    (fn(n:int)=> (1.0,n))
    (fn(r:real,(prod1,sum1),(prod2,sum2))=>
                        (r*prod1*prod2,sum1+sum2))
```

The function ittree2 has the properties analogous to those of iter for
natural numbers and of itlist for lists. It is a primitive recursor for trees,
with the following definition of the tree primitive recursion:

(7.18) fun f(leaf(b),x) = g(b,x)
         | f(node(a,t1,t2),x) = h(f(t1,x),f(t2,x),a,t1,t2,x)

where g and h are tree primitive recursive. The function ittree2 is a homomorphical embedding of trees into the respective function space. Practically,
all functions on this kind of trees may be defined via ittree2 with no explicit
use of recursion.

7.3   Recursors for other types

General recursion is expensive, and in its full generality hardly ever used.
Since programmers mainly need primitive recursion, it would make sense in
terms of efficiency specially to optimise implementations of primitive recursors
for the available data types, such as iter for natural numbers, itlist for
lists, or ittree2 for trees. Therefore, we had better investigate for what types
embeddings of this kind exist.

Consider a type TT of general trees, defined recursively as follows:

(7.19) datatype TT = fun_1 of $A_1 * \underbrace{\text{TT}*\ldots*\text{TT}}_{k_1}$

$\ldots$

| fun_n of $A_n * \underbrace{\text{TT}*\ldots*\text{TT}}_{k_n}$

where $A_1,\ldots,A_n$ are types and $k_1,\ldots,k_n$ are natural numbers. Some of these
numbers should better be 0, since otherwise the type recursion in (7.19) would
have no "bottom" and (7.19) would then define an empty type.

A function ff over TT is primitive recursive if (informally) either it has a
non-recursive definition, or it has a definition that uses recursion only in the
following restricted way:

(7.20) fun $\text{ff}(\text{fun}_1(a,tt_1,\ldots,tt_{k_1}),x) =$
         $h_1(\text{ff}(t_1,x),\ldots,\text{ff}(tt_{k_1},x),a,tt_1,\ldots,tt_{k_1},x)$
         $\ldots$
    | $\text{ff}(\text{fun}_n(a,tt_1,\ldots,tt_{k_n}),x) =$
         $h_n(\text{ff}(t_1,x),\ldots,\text{ff}(tt_{k_n},x),a,tt_1,\ldots,tt_{k_n},x)$

where functions $h_1,\ldots,h_n$ are known beforehand to be primitive recursive.

The definition pattern (7.20) of primitive recursion generalises similar patterns from Sections 7.1 and 7.2. Indeed, if the type of natural numbers were recursively defined as

(7.21) ```
datatype nat = zero of unit
             | succ of nat
```

then (7.20) boils down to

```
fun ff(zero(),x) = h₁(( ),x)
  | ff(succ(n),x) = h₂(ff(n,x),n,x)
```

which is basically the same as (7.2). For lists the corresponding definitions are

(7.22) ```
datatype ('a)list = nil of unit
                  | cons of 'a*('a)list
```

and

```
fun ff(nil(),x) = h₁(( ),x)
  | ff(cons(a,lis),x) =
       h₂(ff(lis,x),a,lis,x)
```

which is equivalent to (7.14). For trees the type definition (7.17) gives rise to the following specialisation of (7.20):

```
fun ff(leaf(b),x) = h₁(b,x)
  | ff(node(a,t₁,t₂),x) =
       h₂(ff(t₁,x),ff(t₂,x),a,t₁,t₂,x)
```

which is equivalent to (7.18).

Any type defined as in (7.19) has a primitive recursor

(7.23) ```
itTT : TT ->
         (A₁* 'a*...*'a -> 'a) ->
                 ⎵⎵⎵⎵⎵⎵
                   k₁
         ...
         (Aₙ* 'a*...*'a -> 'a) -> 'a
                 ⎵⎵⎵⎵⎵⎵
                   kₙ
```

('a is a type variable not occurring in $A_1$ through $A_n$) defined by

(7.24) ```
fun itTT(fun₁(a,tt₁,...,tt_{k₁})) g₁ ... gₙ =
        g₁(a,itTT tt₁ g₁ ... gₙ, ... ,itTT tt_{k₁} g₁ ... gₙ)
    ...
  | itTT(funₙ(a,tt₁,...,tt_{kₙ})) g₁ ... gₙ =
        gₙ(a,itTT tt₁ g₁ ... gₙ, ... ,itTT tt_{kₙ} g₁ ... gₙ)
```

When (7.24) is specialised to the definition (7.21) of natural numbers, one gets

```
fun itnat(zero()) g₁ g₂ = g₁()
  | itnat(succ(n)) g₁ g₂ = g₂(itnat n g₁ g₂)
```

which is equivalent to the definition of `iter` at the beginning of Sec.7.1. When (7.24) is specialised to the definition (7.22) of lists, one gets

```
fun itlist(nil()) g₁ g₂ = g₁()
  | itlist(cons(a,lis)) g₁ g₂ = g₂(a,itlist lis g₁ g₂)
```

which is equivalent to the definition of `itlist` in the beginning of Sec.7.2 (the order of arguments g_1 and g_2 is inessential). When (7.24) is specialised to the definition (7.17) of trees, one gets

```
fun ittree2(leaf(b)) g₁ g₂ = g₁(b)
  | ittree2(node(a,t₁,t₂)) g₁ g₂ =
       g₂(a,ittree2 t₁ g₁ g₂,ittree2 t₂ g₁ g₂)
```

which is the same as the definition of `ittree2` in Sec.7.2.

Assume a function `ff` is defined as in (7.20) and consider the non-recursive definition of another function `ff'`:

(7.25)
```
fun ff'(tt,x) =
      let fun ff₁(a,(y₁,tt₁),...,(y_{k₁},tt_{k₁})) =
             (h₁(y₁,...,y_{k₁},fun₁(a,tt₁,...,tt_{k₁}),x),
              fun₁(a,tt₁,...,tt_{k₁}))
          ...
      and fun ffₙ(a,(y₁,tt₁,tt₂),...,(y_{kₙ},tt_{kₙ})) =
             (hₙ(y₁,...,y_{kₙ},funₙ(a,tt₁,...,tt_{kₙ}),x),
              funₙ(a,tt₁,...,tt_{kₙ}))
      in let val (y₀,tt₀) = itTT tt ff₁ ... ffₙ
         in y₀
         end
      end
```

Theorem 8 (7.20) and (7.25) define the same function.

Proof: This follows from the following equality:

```
itTT tt ff₁ ... ffₙ = (ff(tt,x),tt)
```

that may be proved by induction on the height of the tree `tt`. The proof is rather tedious, but conceptually simple. □

The above considerations show how to introduce a primitive recursor for a very general tree type defined by (7.19). This can still be generalised — to mutually recursive polymorphic data types, but not to types defined differently, such as reals.

7.4 On the redundancy of the datatype construct

As the reader will remember, there are no arrays in Standard ML. One reason for this is that in a high order functional language arrays are redundant: a good approximation of a type

   array [k..n] of T

where k and n are integers, is the type

(7.26) int->T

From Sec.7.3 it follows that in a high order *polymorphic* functional language the types defined using the datatype construct are redundant too: a good approximation of

$$\text{datatype TT = fun}_1 \text{ of A}_1 * \underbrace{\text{TT}*\ldots*\text{TT}}_{k_1}$$

$$\ldots$$

$$|\ \text{fun}_n \text{ of A}_n * \underbrace{\text{TT}*\ldots*\text{TT}}_{k_n}$$

is

$$(\text{A}_1 * \underbrace{\text{'a}*\ldots*\text{'a}}_{k_1} \text{ -> 'a) ->}$$

$$\ldots$$

$$(\text{A}_n * \underbrace{\text{'a}*\ldots*\text{'a}}_{k_n} \text{ -> 'a) -> 'a}$$

(cf. (7.23)). Therefore, technically speaking, this type constructor could be eliminated from Standard ML, too.

The reasons for keeping it are mainly of a psychological nature and may appeal differently to different people. Very high order functions give the sensation of something "cosmic" and alien and one is inclined to treat them with undue respect. This is rather counterproductive when one's aim is to write programs.

I, personally, feel quite happy about the functional representation of arrays, as in (7.26), and do not need "true" arrays. On the other hand, lists are for me finite sequences of elements standing one behind another, and it costs me some effort to imagine them as functions of the type

   ('a*'b->'b)->'b->'b

I am, therefore, for keeping the redundant type of lists. Similarly, I am for keeping the redundant type constructor datatype, since it costs me even more effort to imagine trees as respective functions. As has been said before, these attitudes may vary from person to person and may, perhaps, be taught.

But even if we were never to identify data types with polymorphic functionals, it seems worth learning to define functions on data types using respective polymorphic recursors.

7.5   Exercises

Exercise 22

Write a non-recursive definition using iter of the function that finds the value of a given polynomial for a given argument:

$$\texttt{polval} : \texttt{int*(int->real)*real} \to \texttt{real}$$
$$\texttt{polval}(d, p, a) = \sum_{i=0}^{d} p(i) \cdot a^i$$

(d — degree, p — polynomial, a — argument).

Exercise 23

Define non-recursively but using recursors a function prodlis that, given two lists

$$[a_1, \ldots, a_n] \quad \text{and} \quad [b_1, \ldots, b_k]$$

of real numbers, produces an array of products $a_i \cdot b_j$, understood as a function

$$f : \texttt{int} \times \texttt{int} \to \texttt{real}$$

such that

$$f(i, j) = a_i \cdot b_j$$

Exercise 24

Define non-recursively but using itlist the following list processing functions:

•   flat : $(('a)\texttt{list})\texttt{list} \to ('a)\texttt{list}$

that concatenates all lists occurring in its argument. For instance,

flat [[1,2],[3],[4,5,6],[]] = [1,2,3,4,5,6]

-     split : ('a)list → (('a)list*('a)list)list

that, given a list `lis`, produces the list of all its decompositions into
pairs of lists that after concatenating yield again `lis`. For instance,

```
split [1,2,3]  =  [([1,2,3],[])
                   ([1,2],[3])
                   ([1],[2,3])
                   ([],[1,2,3])]
```

Exercise 25

Define non-recursively but using `itlist` the function

    permut : ('a)list → (('a)list)list

that, given a list, yields the list of all its permutations.

Chapter 8

Standard ML structures and signatures

With the discussion of polymorphism we have completed our description of the so called *core language* of Standard ML. The core language comprises the means to operate on:

- the universe of types; involving types unit, bool, int, real and string, and closed under Cartesian product, disjoint union, function space, polymorphism and type recursion;

- the universe of individual objects structured in types;

- the mechanisms to define new objects and new types.

A program in core Standard ML is basically a sequence of definitions that create an environment, followed by an expression that may be evaluated in this environment.

By an *environment* is meant an assignment of mathematical objects to a finite collection of identifiers. For instance, the following sequence of definitions:

```
val pi = 3.14159 ;
datatype nat = zero
            | succ of nat ;
fun double(zero) = zero
  | double(succ(n)) = succ(succ(double(n))) ;
```

creates the environment that assigns (or *binds*) the number 3.14159 to identifier pi, the type of natural numbers to identifier nat, and the function that doubles any natural number to identifier double. This environment also binds the standard meaning to Standard ML predefined identifiers such as int, 0 or div. In this sense, a programmer starts with a non-trivial environment that consists of predefined objects and types, and extends this environment with his own definitions.

When several programmers work on relatively independent sections of a large program, each of them creates an environment of his own. To put all these environments together into one program, may prove a complicated and error-prone task, since the programmers may have used the same identifiers to denote different things.

The problem is, of course, not confined to Standard ML nor to applicative programming. In many languages similar *modularisation* methods have been proposed, under various names such as *units, modules, packages, clusters* or *algebras*; the term *structures* is used in Standard ML. A structure is an environment closed into a manipulable object and given a name.

8.1   Simple examples of Standard ML structures

Assume a programmer is required to define the type of complex numbers together with basic operations on them. In fulfilment of this requirement he creates an environment in which identifiers compl (type of complex numbers), i (imaginary unit), add (addition of complex numbers) etc. acquire their usual meaning. The Standard ML structure concept is a way of "closing" such an environment and giving it a name so that it can be manipulated by other parts of the program:

```
- structure Compl =
    struct
      type compl = real*real ;
      fun compl(r:real) = (r , 0.0) ;
      val i = (0.0 , 1.0) ;
      fun add((xre,xim):compl,(yre,yim):compl) =
        (xre+yre , xim+yim) ;
      fun mul((xre,xim):compl,(yre,yim):compl) =
        (xre*yre-xim*yim , xre*yim+xim*yre)
    end ;
> structure Compl =
    struct
      type compl = real * real
      val add = fn : (compl * compl) -> (real * real)
      val compl = fn : real -> (real * real)
      val i = (0.0,1.0) : real * real
      val mul = fn : (compl * compl) -> (real * real)
```

```
        end
```

The keywords `struct...end` are the parentheses that delimit the environment and turn it into a manipulable object. The `structure Compl` declaration assigns this environment to the identifier `Compl`. Within this environment `compl` is the type of pairs of `reals`; `compl` is also the conversion function from real to complex numbers (this kind of overloading is harmless since in Standard ML the universes of types and of individual objects are disjoint); `i` is the imaginary unit; `add` and `mul` are respectively the addition and the multiplication of complex numbers. Note that the system's confirmation rearranges the component of the structure: types come before individual values and both are ordered alphabetically. This has no importance, since the components are identified by their name rather than by the order of their occurrence. More importantly, typing of components in the system's confirmation uses the old `real * real` rather than the new `compl` in all places where the programmer has not explicitly required `compl`.

Single component of structures may be accessed using the name of a component *qualified* by the name of the structure:

```
- Compl.mul (Compl.i , Compl.i)  =  Compl.compl (~1.0) ;
> true : bool
```

Structures are a distant relative of Pascal's records. In Pascal, only individual objects may make record components, while Standard ML structures may also involve types and other features which we shall discuss later. By analogy with Pascal's instruction `with...do...` one may avoid writing the qualifier `Compl` on every occurrence of a component by locally "opening" the structure to the external observer:

```
- let open Compl
  in mul(i,i) = compl(~1.0)
  end ;
> true : bool
```

As another simple example consider the following definition of rational numbers:

```
- structure Rat =
    struct
      type rat = int*int ;
      fun rat(k:int) = (k,1) ;
      fun rev((n,d):rat) = (d,n) ;
      fun add((n1,d1):rat,(n2,d2):rat) =
        (n1*d2+n2*d1 , d1*d2) ;
```

```
      fun mul((n1,d1):rat,(n2,d2):rat) =
        (n1*n2 , d1*d2) ;
      fun eq((n1,d1):rat,(n2,d2):rat) =
        (n1*d2 = n2*d1)
    end ;
> structure Rat =
    struct
      type rat = int * int
      val add = fn : (rat * rat) -> (int * int)
      val eq = fn : (rat * rat) -> bool
      val mul = fn : (rat * rat) -> (int * int)
      val rat = fn : int -> (int * int)
      val rev = fn : rat -> (int * int)
    end
```

This structure also contains functions `add` and `mul`, which are, however, not in conflict with those from structure `Compl`, since the access is always via the qualifiers, which makes their use unambiguous. Note that the programmer has to define his own equality, since the coordinate-wise equality provided by the system is unsatisfactory:

```
- let open Rat
  in let val half = rev(rat(2))
         and half' = mul(rat(2),rev(rat(4)))
     in half=half'
     end
  end ;
> false : bool
```

i.e. according to the interpreter: $\frac{1}{2} \neq \frac{2}{4}$; `Rat.eq` is definitely better:

```
- let open Rat
  in let val half = rev(rat(2))
         and half' = mul(rat(2),rev(rat(4)))
     in eq(half,half')
     end
  end ;
> true : bool
```

A need to define one's own equality arises often when introducing one's own types and operations.

As a third example consider the array implementation of stack, where by "array" is meant a function from `int`:

```
- structure Stack =
    struct
      exception no_entry ;
      type (''a)stack = int * (int->''a) ;
      val empty = (0 , (fn(k:int)=> raise no_entry)) ;
      fun push(a,(n,f)) =
        (n+1 ,
         fn(n')=> if n'=n+1 then a else f(n')
         ) ;
      fun top(n,f) = f(n) ;
      fun pop(n,f) =
        if n=0 then (n,f)
        else (n-1,f) ;
      fun eq((n1,f1),(n2,f2)) =
        if n1=0 andalso n2=0
        then true
        else if n1=n2
              then if f1(n1)=f2(n2)
                   then eq((n1-1,f1),(n2-1,f2))
                   else false
              else false
    end ;
> structure Stack =
    struct
      type 'a stack = int * (int -> 'a)
      con no_entry : exn
      val empty = (0,fn) : int * (int -> 'a)
      val eq = fn : ((int * (int -> ''a)) * (int * (int ->
''a))) -> bool
      val pop = fn : (int * 'a) -> (int * 'a)
      val push = fn : ('a * (int * (int -> 'a))) -> (int *
(int -> 'a))
      val top = fn : ('a * ('a -> 'b)) -> 'b
    end
```

The type of stacks, and all functions that operate on stacks, are polymorphic:

```
- let open Stack
  in top(push(5,empty))
  end ;
> 5 : int
- let open Stack
```

```
    in top(push(Compl.i,empty))
    end ;
> (0.0,1.0) : real * real
```

The programmer has again to define his own equality, this time because the
system cannot supply *any* equality: the definition of type (`'a`)`stack` involves
type `int->'a` and there is no equality on function types. It is the programmer's arbitrary decision to limit his concerns only to a finite number of function values:

```
- let open Stack
  in push(5,empty) = push(5,empty)
  end ;
Type clash  in:  ((push (5,empty)) = (push (5,empty)))
There is no equality defined on type int -> int
- let open Stack
  in eq(push(5,empty),push(5,empty))
  end ;
> true : bool
```

8.2   Nested structures

As appears in the examples from Sec.8.1, components of a structure may be
types, exceptions and individual values. Also structures may be components
of other structures, in which case one has to do with *nested* structures. In the
system's confirmation they come before types. For instance, `Compl` and `Rat`
may have been made internal parts of `Stack`:

```
- structure NestedStack =
    struct
      structure Compl = ... ;
      structure Rat = ... ;
      exception no_entry ;
      type (''a)stack = int * (int->''a) ;
      val empty = (0 , (fn(k:int)=> raise no_entry)) ;
      fun push(a,(n,f)) =
        (n+1 ,
         fn(n')=> if n'=n+1 then a else f(n')
        ) ;
      fun top(n,f) = f(n) ;
      fun pop(n,f) =
        if n=0 then (n,f)
```

```
                else (n-1,f) ;
              fun eq((n1,f1),(n2,f2)) =
                if n1=0 andalso n2=0
                then true
                else if n1=n2
                     then if f1(n1)=f2(n2)
                          then eq((n1-1,f1),(n2-1,f2))
                          else false
                     else false
          end ;
> structure NestedStack =
     struct
       structure Compl = ...
       structure Rat = ...
       type 'a stack = int * (int -> 'a)
       con no_entry : exn
       .val empty = (0,fn) : int * (int -> 'a)
       val eq = fn : ((int * (int -> ''a)) * (int * (int ->
''a))) -> bool
       val pop = fn : (int * 'a) -> (int * 'a)
       val push = fn : ('a * (int * (int -> 'a))) -> (int *
(int -> 'a))
       val top = fn : ('a * ('a -> 'b)) -> 'b
     end
```

(In fact, you must not replace structure definitions by dots in your input, as I have done above for the sake of readability; on the other hand, you do get dots in the system's confirmation).

Components of nested structures may be accessed as usual, by qualifying the name of a component by the name of the structure; but this time the name of the structure may itself be qualified. For instance, NestedStack.Compl is the qualified name of a nested structure, and it may serve as a qualifier to access the component i of this structure: NestedStack.Compl.i. Example of the use of this:

```
- NestedStack.top(
    NestedStack.push(
      NestedStack.Compl.i ,
      NestedStack.empty
                  ) ) ;
> (0.0,1.0) : real * real
- let open NestedStack
```

```
in eq (empty ,
        push (Rat.rev(Rat.rat(5)) ,
            empty
      )    )
end ;
> false : bool
```

The concept of nested structures is in line with the general idea that structures are local environments: since it is possible to define structures at the top level, i.e. in the global environment, it should also be possible to define them locally, within other structures.

Structures, as presented so far, solve the simple modularisation problem formulated at the beginning of this chapter. To put together environments created by separate programmers, one makes all these environments local by enclosing them in structures. This removes the conflict of identifiers since, in any case, only qualified identifiers may be used. If a collectively produced program is intended as a part of a still larger program, the environment may be enclosed into a higher level structure. This process may be iterated arbitrarily giving rise to an arbitrarily deep nesting of structures in other structures.

8.3 "Typing" the structures: signatures

It has been a leading idea of the core language that every value has a type. Structures are a way of turning environments into manipulable objects, by analogy with values in the core. By further analogy then, they should have types.

The "types" of structures are called *signatures*. In the simplest case, a signature is just a collection of identifiers meant to denote types, and a collection of identifiers meant to denote individual values together with the types of these values:

```
- signature COMPL =
    sig
      type compl ;
      val compl : real -> compl ;
      val i : compl ;
      val add : compl * compl -> compl ;
      val mul : compl * compl -> compl
    end ;
> signature COMPL =
    sig
```

```
            type compl
            val add : (compl * compl) -> compl
            val compl : real -> compl
            val i : compl
            val mul : (compl * compl) -> compl
         end
```

A signature serves as a list of contents, or an inventory of a structure: it gives an external user a very general knowledge of what comes into the structure and how it may be used. It reveals absolutely no implementation details; for instance, nothing in the signature COMPL above conveys the information that a complex number is a pair of reals. An analogous concept may be traced in other programming languages under the names of *interface*, or *package description*.

When designing a structure, a programmer may require that it conform to a certain signature. For instance

```
- structure Compl1 : COMPL  =
    struct
      type compl = real*real ;
      fun compl(r) = (r , 0.0) ;
      val i = (0.0 , 1.0) ;
      fun add((xre,xim):compl,(yre,yim):compl) =
        (xre+yre , xim+yim) ;
      fun mul((xre,xim):compl,(yre,yim):compl) =
        (xre*yre-xim*yim , xre*yim+xim*yre) ;
      fun eq((xre,xim):compl,(yre,yim):compl) =
        ((xre,xim)=(yre,yim))
    end ;
> structure Compl1 =
    struct
      type compl = real * real
      val add = fn : (compl * compl) -> compl
      val compl = fn : real -> compl
      val i = (0.0,1.0) : compl
      val mul = fn : (compl * compl) -> compl
    end
```

Note that the system's confirmation, in contrast to the case of structure Compl in Sec.8.1, refers explicitly to type compl rather than to type real * real; and that the superfluous component eq that does not occur in the signature has been trimmed off.

Of course, any signature may not be imposed on any structure:

```
- structure Rat1 : COMPL  =
    struct
      type rat = int*int ;
      fun rat(k:int) = (k,1) ;
      fun rev((n,d):rat) = (d,n) ;
      fun add((n1,d1):rat,(n2,d2):rat) =
        (n1*d2+n2*d1 , d1*d2) ;
      fun mul((n1,d1):rat,(n2,d2):rat) =
        (n1*n2 , d1*d2) ;
      fun eq((n1,d1):rat,(n2,d2):rat) =
        (n1*d2 = n2*d1)
    end ;
Signature match failure in: structure Rat1:COMPL =
struct {type rat = % enc {% enc %}} end
Type compl in signature not present in structure.
```

A structure *matches* a signature if, roughly speaking, it has all the components required by the signature (or more), and the types of these components are consistent with the typing given by the signature. In the presence of polymorphism for "consistent with" read "at least as general as". In other words, a signature may trim a structure down, both in the number and in the generality of components, but it must not extend it. For instance:

```
- structure Wrong : sig
                      val l : ('a)list
                    end
  =    struct
          val l = [1,2,3]
       end ;
Signature match failure in: structure Wrong:sig
val l:(('a) list) end = struct l = [%,%,%] end
Type of variable l in signature is not an instance of type
  in structure:
'a list is not an instance of int list
```

— the signature requires that l be of type ('a)list, therefore an l of the less general type (int)list will not do. This is different from the typing conditions for the core language, where

```
- [1,2,3] : ('a)list ;
> [1,2,3] : int list
```

works.

8.4 Signatures as rough specifications of structures

It is often argued that a *type* is more than a set: it is a set with a collection of *operations*. As long as one is not concerned with operations, sets differ only in their cardinalities. Thus, for instance, set `int` is isomorphic to set `string`. What makes them different, are the inventories of available operations.

A type comes equipped with a collection of characteristic operations defined over it; but some of these operations may involve other types. For instance, type `int` involves comparisons which yield values in type `bool`. Therefore, types do not come alone, but rather in systems known as *many-sorted algebras*. The Standard ML counterpart of algebras are structures.

When presenting an algebra of types and functions one is well advised to start by giving them explicit names and specifying the sources and the targets of the functions. Such a list of contents of an algebra is called its *signature*.

Signatures are often used as a rough description of algebras (structures). A common way of specifying library functions of a programming language to a user that does not need to know how they are implemented is by giving their headings and verbal descriptions of their operation. The headings are what go into the respective signatures. In this sense, signatures are incomplete specifications of algebras; incomplete — since they have to be completed with (informal) verbal explanations. The verbal explanations can be, at least in principle, replaced by *axioms* that a given algebra is obliged to satisfy, resulting in formal *specifications*.

A specification of a dictionary may be formulated as follows:

```
- signature DICT =
    sig
      exception not_found ;
      type key ;
      type cont ;
      type dict ;
      val initial : dict ;
      val ins : key * cont * dict -> dict ;
      val find : key * dict -> cont
    end ;
> signature DICT =
    sig
      type cont
      type dict
      type key
```

```
    val find : (key * dict) -> cont
    val initial : dict
    val ins : (key * cont * dict) -> dict
    con not_found : exn
end
```

On top of this one has to explain that finding any key in the initial dictionary always results in the exception not_found; furthermore finding a key
k in a dictionary ins(k,c,d) results in c; and that finding a key k1 in a
dictionary ins(k2,c,d) for k1 ≠ k2 is the same as finding k1 in d; etc. This
informal explanation may be made formal by the following axiom:

$$(\forall k, k_1, k_2 \in \text{key})(\forall c \in \text{cont})(\forall d \in \text{dict})$$
$$\text{find}(k, \text{initial}) = \text{raise not\_found } \&$$
$$\text{find}(k_1, \text{ins}(k_2, c, d)) =$$
$$\quad \text{if } k_1 = k_2 \text{ then } c$$
$$\quad \text{else find}(k_1, d)$$

Usually, such a specification may be realised in many different ways. Here
follow two different realisations of DICT. The first one by binary trees:

```
- structure Dict1 : DICT =
    struct
      exception not_found ;
      type key = int ;
      type cont = real ;
      datatype dict = empty
                    | node of (key*cont) * dict * dict ;
      val initial = empty ;
      fun ins(k,c,empty) = node((k,c),empty,empty)
        | ins(k,c,node((k',c'),l,r)) =
            if k<k'
            then node((k',c'),ins(k,c,l),r)
            else node((k',c'),l,ins(k,c,r)) ;
      fun find(k,empty) = raise not_found
        | find(k,node((k',c'),l,r)) =
            if k=k'
            then c'
            else if k<k'
                    then find(k,l)
                    else find(k,r)
    end ;
> structure Dict1 =
    struct
```

```
          type cont = real
          type dict = dict
          type key = int
          con not_found : exn
          val find = fn : (key * dict) -> cont
          val initial = empty : dict
          val ins = fn : (key * cont * dict) -> dict
        end
```

The second realisation of dictionaries is by functions:

```
- structure Dict2 : DICT =
    struct
      exception not_found ;
      type key = int ;
      type cont = real ;
      type dict = key -> cont ;
      val initial =  fn(k)=> raise not_found ;
      fun ins(k,c,d) =
        fn(k')=> if k'=k
                   then c
                   else d(k') ;
      fun find(k,d) = d(k)
    end ;
> structure Dict2 =
    struct
      type cont = real
      type dict = key -> cont
      type key = int
      con not_found : exn
      val find = fn : (key * dict) -> cont
      val initial = fn : dict
      val ins = fn : (key * cont * dict) -> dict
    end
```

An external user need not be aware which of these two realisations is applied
as long as they both conform to the signature and to the verbal, or axiomatic,
requirements.

It is worth noting, that specifications and structures are not an invention
of computer scientists. The mathematical definition of, say, *group*, is basically
the same as the specification consisting of the following signature:

```
signature GROUP =
```

```
sig
  type group ;
  val ope : group * group -> group ;
  val one : group ;
  val rev : group -> group
end
```

and of the following axiom:

$(\forall a, b, c \in \text{group})$
$\text{ope}(\text{ope}(a, b), c) = \text{ope}(a, \text{ope}(b, c))$ &
$\text{ope}(\text{one}, a) = a$ &
$\text{ope}(\text{rev}(a), a) = \text{one}$

As another example take the definition of *partial order*. Signature:

```
signature POSET =
  sig
    type set ;
    val le : set * set -> bool
  end
```

axiom:

$(\forall a, b, c \in \text{set})$
$\text{le}(a, a)$ &
$(\text{le}(a, b)\&\text{le}(b, a) \Rightarrow a = b)$ &
$(\text{le}(a, b)\&\text{le}(b, c) \Rightarrow \text{le}(a, c))$

Algebras that involve more than one type are also considered by mathematicians. For example, a *vector space* is a commutative group, a field and an external operation of the field over the group. The reader is encouraged to write the signature by himself (cf. Exercise 28 after this chapter).

8.5 Exercises

Exercise 26

The definition of structure Rat given in this chapter is incomplete, since it does not define all four arithmetic operations on rational numbers; and uneconomical, since, e.g. the addition $\frac{1}{3} + \frac{1}{3}$ yields $\frac{6}{9}$ rather than $\frac{2}{3}$. Design a new structure Rat to match the signature:

```
signature RAT =
  sig
    type rat ;
```

```
         exception denominator_is_zero ;
         val rat : int -> rat ;          (*conversion from int*)
         val add : rat * rat -> rat ;    (*addition*)
         val dif : rat * rat -> rat ;    (*subtraction*)
         val mul : rat * rat -> rat ;    (*multiplication*)
         val dvs : rat * rat -> rat ;    (*division*)
         val eq  : rat * rat -> bool     (*equality*)
      end
```

such that the result of any operation be in its simplest form.

Exercise 27

Design a structure containing everything necessary to deal with complex
numbers: the Cartesian and polar representations, conversions between the
representations, conversions from the type real, the imaginary unit in both
representations, the four arithmetic operations and the equality of complex
numbers in both representations.

Exercise 28

Write down the signature of vector space, and design a structure that
corresponds to the three-dimensional Euclidean space, and matches the signature.

Exercise 29

Explain why the following structure Aa does not match the following signature AA:

```
   signature AA =
     sig
       type aa ;
       val f : ('a)list -> ('a)list
     end ;

   structure  Aa : AA  =
     struct
       type aa = real*real ;
       fun map(f)[] = []
         | map(f)(x::lis) = f(x) :: map(f)lis ;
       val f  =  map (fn(x)=> x+1)
     end ;
```

Exercise 30

Assume somebody has defined 3D graphics as a Standard ML structure
ThreeDim that matches the signature:

```
signature THREEDIM =
  sig
    type screen ;
    val emptyscreen : screen ;
    val drawcurve :
        (real -> real*real*real) * screen -> screen ;
      (* drawcurve(f,s)  adds to screen  s  the image of
         the unit interval <0.0,1.0> via function  f *)
    val drawsurface :
        (real*real -> real*real*real) * screen -> screen;
      (* drawsurface(f,s)  adds to screen  s  the image of
         the unit square  <0.0,1.0> x <0.0,1.0>  via
         function  f *)
  end
```

Use this structure to produce a picture of a screw-line and of a sphere.

Chapter 9

Parametric structures: functors

Many mathematical constructions may be carried out uniformly over all algebras satisfying a given specification; for instance, over all groups, or over
all ordered sets. These constructions are *parameterised* by an algebra of a
given specification — which means, that a construction works properly if an
arbitrary concrete algebra that fulfils the specification is substituted for the
parameter.

   Such parametric constructions may be expressed in Standard ML by *functors*, which are functions from structures to structures.

9.1   Example: power structure on a monoid

A *monoid* is a structure consisting of one type, one binary operation on this
type and one distinguished element:

```
signature MONOID =
  sig
    type set ;
    val ope : set * set -> set ;
    val one : set
  end
```

with the requirement that the operation be associative and that the distinguished element be its neutral:

$(\forall a, b, c \in \mathsf{set})$
$\mathsf{ope}(\mathsf{ope}(a, b), c) = \mathsf{ope}(a, \mathsf{ope}(b, c))$ &
$\mathsf{ope}(\mathsf{one}, a) = a$ &
$\mathsf{ope}(a, \mathsf{one}) = a$

This differs from a group by the absence of the operation **rev**.

   When discussing monoids it is customary to write a^n for

$$\underbrace{\mathsf{ope}(a, \ldots \mathsf{ope}(a, \mathsf{one}) \ldots)}_{n}$$

Formally, this means one takes into consideration, besides the usual monoid operation ope, another operation of "powering" which, given an element of the monoid and a natural number, yields an element of the monoid. Let us call such a structure a *power monoid*[1]. The specification of a power monoid consists of the following signature:

```
signature POWMON =
  sig
    type set ;
    val ope : set * set -> set ;
    val one : set ;
    val pow : set * int -> set
  end
```

and the following axiom:

$$(\forall a, b, c \in \text{set})(\forall p, q \in \text{int})$$
$$\text{ope}(\text{ope}(a, b), c) = \text{ope}(a, \text{ope}(b, c)) \ \&$$
$$\text{ope}(\text{one}, a) = a \ \&$$
$$\text{ope}(a, \text{one}) = a \ \&$$
$$\text{pow}(a, 0) = \text{one} \ \&$$
$$\text{pow}(a, 1) = a \ \&$$
$$(p \geq 0 \& q \geq 0 \Rightarrow \text{pow}(a, p + q) = \text{ope}(\text{pow}(a, p), \text{pow}(a, q)))$$

The first three equalities above refer to the fact that a power monoid has to be a monoid, the remaining two become clear when rewritten in the standard power notation[2]:

$$a^0 = \text{one} \ \&$$
$$a^{p+q} = a^p \cdot a^q$$

The following Standard ML functor turns an arbitrary monoid into a power monoid:

```
- functor Pow (Monoid : MONOID) : POWMON  =
    struct
      type set = Monoid.set ;
      val ope = Monoid.ope ;
      val one = Monoid.one ;
      fun pow(a,n) =
        if n=0 then one
```

---

[1]When the monoid is a group, integers may be used instead of naturals, and the resulting structure is called a *Z-module*.

[2]We use here the type int of integers rather then the more appropriate type nat of natural numbers (defined via datatype, see Section 5.3). This is of no significance. Anyway, we are not concerned with the value of pow(a, p) for $p < 0$.

```
                  else ope(pow(a,n-1),a)
         end ;
  > functor Pow( Monoid : MONOID ) : POWMON
```

The heading of the functor definition looks very much like the heading of function definition in Pascal: Pow is the functor's name; Monoid is its formal parameter, ranging over the signature MONOID; POWMON is the required signature of the result. The body of the functor definition is a structure that may involve references to components of the formal parameter Monoid. The only non-trivial part of the body of this particular functor concerns pow, which is defined as "raising an element of the monoid to a natural power using the monoid operation for multiplication".

Consider now the monoid of real numbers with addition:

```
  - structure RealAdd =
      struct
        type set = real ;
        fun ope(r1:real,r2:real) = r1+r2 ;
        val one = 0.0
      end ;
  > structure RealAdd =
      struct
        type set = real
        val one = 0.0 : real
        fun ope = fn : (real * real) -> real
      end
```

and produce the power structure over this monoid using the functor Pow:

```
  - structure PowRA = Pow(RealAdd) ;
  > structure PowRA =
      struct
        type set = real
        val one = 0.0 : set
        val ope = fn : (set * set) -> set
        val pow = fn : (set * int) -> set
      end
  - PowRA.pow (17.1 , 0) ;
  > 0.0 : PowRA.set
  - PowRA.pow (2.0 , 10) ;
  > 20.0 : PowRA.set
```

The results are not surprising: power over addition is multiplication.

Consider now the monoid of real numbers with multiplication:

```
- structure RealMul =
    struct
      type set = real ;
      fun ope(r1:real,r2:real) = r1*r2 ;
      val one = 1.0
    end ;
> structure RealMul =
    struct
      type set = real
      val one = 1.0 : real
      val ope = fn : (real * real) -> real
    end
```

and the power monoid defined over this structure by the functor Pow:

```
- structure PowRM = Pow(RealMul) ;
> structure PowRM =
    struct
      type set = real
      val one = 1.0 : set
      val ope = fn : (set * set) -> set
      val pow = fn : (set * int) -> set
    end
- PowRM.pow (17.1 , 0) ;
> 1.0 : PowRM.set
- PowRM.pow (2.0 , 10) ;
> 1024.0 : PowRM.set
```

This time the result is the true power.

Consider a third monoid: functions with composition as the monoid operation:

```
- structure Fun =
    struct
      type set = int -> int ;
      fun ope(f,g) =
        fn(x)=> f(g(x)) ;
      val one =
        fn(x)=> x
    end ;
> structure Fun =
    struct
      type set = int -> int
      val one = fn : 'a -> 'a
      val ope = fn : (('a -> 'b) * ('c -> 'a)) -> ('c ->
```

```
    'b)
        end
  - structure PowF = Pow(Fun) ;
  > structure PowF =
        struct
           type set = int -> int
           val one = fn : set
           val ope = fn : (set * set) -> set
           val pow = fn : (set * int) -> set
        end
  - PowF.pow ((fn(n)=> ~n) , 7) (10) ;
  > ~10 : int
  - PowF.pow ((fn(n)=> n*n) , 3) (2) ;
  > 256 : int
```

Powering in the monoid of functions is the function iteration:

$$\texttt{power}(f,n)(x) = f^n(x) = \underbrace{f(\ldots(f(x))\ldots)}_{n}$$

Therefore, the 7-th power of the function that changes the sign of a natural number, is the function that performs a single change of the sign; and the third power of squaring is the function that raises its argument to the power eight:

$$(((x^2)^2)^2 = x^8$$

9.2   Example: dictionaries

Sec.8.4 presents an example specification of a programming task using signatures: signature DICT specifies dictionaries, and two structures Dict1 and Dict2 both solve this task. In both these structures component key is bound to type int and component cont is bound to type real. This, however, is not required either by the signature, or by the verbal explanation, or by the axioms. Here follows an example of a structure in which both key and cont are bound to unit, the specification still being satisfied:

```
    structure TrivDict : DICT =
       struct
          exception not_found ;
          type key = unit ;
          type cont = unit ;
          type dict = bool ;
          val initial = false ;
```

```
    fun ins(k,c,d) = true ;
    fun find(k,d) =
      if d then ()
      else raise not_found
  end ;
```

In this dictionary there is just one key: (); and only one contents: (). There exist two dictionaries: **false** which stands for "empty" and **true** which stands for "full":

```
find((),true) = ()
find((),false) = raise not_found
```

Insertion changes the dictionary to "full".

The satisfaction of axioms by such a collapsed structure is an unwelcome effect of using simple rather than parameterised structures. One would like the dictionary example to work properly for *any* choice of types **key** and **contents**, but this choice must not be decided by a realisation. Thus, what one really wants to specify is a functor that, given *arbitrary* types **key** and **contents**, yields a dictionary over these types.

To be more exact, only the type **contents** may be quite arbitrary; the keys have to be compared and therefore their structure is a bit more complex. This can be precisely stated as follows:

```
signature CONT =
  sig
    type set
  end ;
signature KEY =
  sig
    type set ;
    val eq : set * set -> bool ;
    val lt : set * set -> bool
  end ;
```

According to the signature, keys may be compared by equality (function **eq**) and by precedence (function **lt**) and appropriate axioms may easily be written. The dictionaries are understood as before:

```
signature DICT =
  sig
    exception not_found ;
    type key ;
    type cont ;
    type dict ;
```

```
      val initial : dict ;
      val ins : key * cont * dict -> dict ;
      val find : key * dict -> cont
   end ;
```

The programmer's task is to design an arbitrary functor

```
functor Dict (Key:KEY , Cont:CONT) : DICT
```

such that any Dict(Key,Cont) satisfies the axioms from the preceding chapter, and additionally:

```
Dict(Key,Cont).key = Key.set
Dict(Key,Cont).cont = Cont.set
```

These additional two axioms rule out the trivial solution.

Here is the functor counterpart of the structure Dict1, the counterpart of the other structure is left to the reader as an exercise.

```
- functor Dict (Key:KEY , Cont:CONT) : DICT  =
    struct
      exception not_found ;
      type key = Key.set ;
      type cont = Cont.set ;
      datatype dict = empty
                    | node of (key*cont) * dict * dict ;
      val initial = empty ;
      fun ins(k,c,empty) = node((k,c),empty,empty)
        | ins(k,c,node((k',c'),l,r)) =
            if Key.lt(k,k')
            then node((k',c'),ins(k,c,l),r)
            else node((k',c'),l,ins(k,c,r)) ;
      fun find(k,empty) = raise not_found
        | find(k,node((k',c'),l,r)) =
            if Key.eq(k,k')
            then c'
            else if Key.lt(k,k')
                 then find(k,l)
                 else find(k,r)
    end ;
> functor Dict( Key : KEY, Cont : CONT ) : DICT
```

This functor may now be applied to the algebras of integer keys and real contents, as follows:

```
- structure Real =
    struct
      type set = real
    end ;
> structure Real =
    struct
      type set = real
    end
- structure Integ =
    struct
      type set = int ;
      fun eq(n:int,k:int) = (n=k) ;
      fun lt(n:int,k:int) = (n<k)
    end ;
> structure Integ =
    struct
      type set = int
      val eq = fn : (int * int) -> bool
      val lt = fn : (int * int) -> bool
    end
- structure DictIR = Dict(Integ,Real) ;
> structure DictIR =
    struct
      type cont = real
      type dict = dict
      type key = int
      con not_found : exn
      val find = fn : (key * dict) -> cont
      val initial = empty : dict
      val ins = fn : (key * cont * dict) -> dict
    end
- let open DictIR
  in find (15 , ins(5 , 0.0 , ins(15 , 3.14 , initial)))
  end ;
> 3.14 : DictIR.cont
```

The last example illustrates an important fact about the specifications of programming tasks: in most cases the programmer is to design a functor rather than a single structure. The arguments of that functor are the structures he is making use of, without going into details of how they are constructed. Whatever the arguments, as long as they fulfil the appropriate specifications, the resulting structure of this functor must satisfy its requirements. When later somebody changes an argument structure to some other structure within the same specification, for instance by changing keys in our dictionary example from integers to strings, then the functor should still yield a correct solution to the original problem.

9.3 Functors vs. polymorphism

As has been said earlier, polymorphism is a type dependence of types and individual objects, while functors are structure-dependent structures. Since structures are made of types and functions, the areas of applicability of these two concepts overlap.

Standard ML types are, in a sense, a special case of Standard ML structures. To observe this, consider the following signature:

```
signature MONO =
  sig
    type elem
  end
```

It describes the family of algebras that consist of one type and no objects; in other words, it corresponds to the family of Standard ML mononomorphic types. A polymorphic type may therefore be identified with a functor whose parameters range over MONO, and whose value is again in MONO; for instance,

```
functor List(Mono:MONO) : MONO  =
  struct
    type elem = (Mono.elem)list
  end
```

corresponds to the polymorphic type ('a)list.

In translating polymorphic individual objects (constants and functions) to functors, simply note that they never come alone, and are always accompanied by their respective polymorphic types. For instance, the polymorphic function hd is accompanied by the types ('a)list (its source) and 'a (its target). Therefore, they may be considered as forming parts of structures. Here is the structure that describes the inventory of means used for lists:

```
- structure List1 =
    struct
      exception Hd ;
      exception Tl ;
      datatype ('a)list = empty
                        | cons of 'a * ('a)list ;
      fun hd(empty) = raise Hd
        | hd(cons(a,l)) = a ;
```

```
        fun tl(empty) = raise Tl
          | tl(cons(a,l)) = l
      end ;
  > structure List1 =
      struct
        datatype 'a list = cons of 'a * ('a list) | empty
        con Hd : exn
        con Tl : exn
        con cons = fn : ('a * ('a list)) -> ('a list)
        con empty = - : 'a list
        val hd = fn : ('a list) -> 'a
        val tl = fn : ('a list) -> ('a list)
      end
```

The type and individual objects of List1 are polymorphic and depend on type variable 'a. Compare this with the following functor:

```
  - functor List2(Mono:MONO) =
      struct
        exception Hd ;
        exception Tl ;
        type aa = Mono.elem ;
        datatype ll = empty
                    | cons of aa * ll ;
        fun hd(empty) = raise Hd
          | hd(cons(a,l)) = a ;
        fun tl(empty) = raise Tl
          | tl(cons(a,l)) = l
      end ;
  > functor List2( Mono : MONO) :
      sig
        type aa
        type ll
        con Hd : exn
        con Tl : exn
        con cons : (aa * ll) -> ll
        con empty : ll
        val hd : ll -> aa
        val tl : ll -> ll
      end
```

(there is no obligation in Standard ML to specify the resulting signature of a functor).

The polymorphic structure List1 and the functor List2 are basically the same thing, only for syntactic reasons List1 is easier to use. Polymorphism may therefore be considered syntactic sugar for functors whose parameters range over Mono.

Both polymorphism and functors in Standard ML are shallow: generic parameters of polymorphic types and objects may only range over monomorphic types and functors may not depend on other functors. Yet, there exists a way of simulating some deeply polymorphic operations by a combination of the two. Let MONO denote, as usual, the family of all monomorphic types. The function

$$\Phi : (\text{MONO} \rightarrow \text{MONO}) \rightarrow \text{MONO}$$
$$\Phi(F) \stackrel{\text{def}}{=} F_{\text{int}}$$

that to any polymorphic function F assigns F instantiated to int, is deeply polymorphic. Nevertheless it may be programmed in Standard ML if we allow ourselves to represent the family

$$\text{POLY} = \text{MONO} \rightarrow \text{MONO}$$

by a signature with one polymorphic type:

```
- signature POLY =
    sig
      type ('a)elem
    end ;
> signature POLY =
    sig
      type 'a elem
    end
```

Indeed, any structure F that matches this signature, takes a monomorphic type for the generic argument 'a upon which it becomes a monomorphic type. Now, Φ may be defined as follows:

```
- functor Fi(F:POLY) : MONO  =
    struct
      type elem = (int)F.elem
    end ;
> functor Fi( F : POLY ) : MONO
```

For instance, given a polymorphic structure

```
- structure SimpList:POLY  =
    struct
      type ('a)elem = ('a)list
    end ;
> structure SimpList =
    struct
      type 'a elem = 'a list
    end
```

the functor Φ instantiates it with int:

```
- structure FiSimpList = Fi(SimpList) ;
> structure FiSimpList =
    struct
      type elem = int list
    end
```

This really simulates deep polymorphism, but in spite of this fact, Standard ML may not be called deeply polymorphic. The above example runs contrary to the whole line of Standard ML's philosophy and should be considered a trick.

9.4 Exercises

Exercise 31

The task of a programmer has been to design a parser for a given grammar making use of somebody else's implementation of stacks. That implementation is assumed to match the following signature:

```
signature STACKS =
  sig
    type ('a)stacks ;
    exception empty_stack ;
    val empty : ('a)stacks ;
    val push : 'a * ('a)stacks -> ('a)stacks ;
    val pop : ('a)stacks -> ('a)stacks ;
    val top : ('a)stacks -> 'a
  end ;
```

The programmer has designed the following functor:

```
functor Parser(Stacks:STACKS) =
  struct
    type lexunit = ... ;
    exception empty_stack ;
    fun  parser (x:string , st:(lexunit)Stacks.stacks) =
      ... pop(st) handle empty_stack => ...
  end ;
```

where the arrow => is followed by a certain recovery action for the case when the stack st is empty.

Find and correct the error in this design.

Exercise 32

A large program consists of the structure

```
    structure Plane =
      struct
        type point = real * real ;
        ...
      end ;
```

and of the functor

```
    functor Graphic(Curves:CURVES) =
      struct
        fun draw(curv) = ... ;
        ...
      end ;
```

where CURVES is the following signature:

```
    signature CURVES =
      sig
        type curve ;
        val selfintersecting : curve -> bool ;
        val maxcurvature : curve -> (point)list ;
        ...
      end ;
```

The idea is that in order to draw a curve one needs some information about its behaviour; e.g. whether it is self-intersecting, and where its points of (locally) maximal curvature are.

However this does not work. Find and correct the error.

Exercise 33

This is a project manager's exercise. A team of programmers is supposed to design an interpreter that would read in either an expression constructed accordingly to the following grammar:

Expr	::=	*Summ*
	|	*Summ* + *Expr*
Summ	::=	*Fact*
	|	*Fact* * *Summ*
Fact	::=	*Numb*
	|	*Iden*
	|	(*Expr*)

or a definition matching the following grammar:

Defn	::=	DEF *Iden* = *Expr*

and would either print the value of the expression (or an error message), or store the new value of the identifier respectively. The interpreter should consist of scanner, parser, symbol table and evaluator, to be programmed independently by distinct programmers.

Specify the tasks for each programmer using appropriate Standard ML signatures and functor headings.

Part III

Implementation Issues

Chapter 10

Type inference

Applicative programming languages require different implementation techniques from their imperative counterparts. On the one hand, their syntax is usually simpler, which allows for the use of unsophisticated parsers. On the other hand, one of the main rationales for applicative programming is the freeing of the programmer from the responsibility for implementation details, such as memory management, internal representation of data, order of evaluation etc. This responsibility now has to be taken over by an automatic translator, and this makes hard demands on an implementor.

The scope of this lecture does not allow for the discussion of all, or even of all the main, problems encountered by an implementor of a high order functional language, such as ML. We are going to address only a couple of sample issues.

This chapter is devoted to type checking. Most of the errors a programmer is likely to make in an applicative program are type inconsistencies. To quote Robin Milner's slogan: "well typed expressions cannot go wrong". Therefore, a sufficiently competent type checker is an invaluable help. The automatic type inference for ML expressions works surprisingly well even in quite complex situations. Often it looks as if the type checker has performed a long process of intelligent reasoning before it has found the appropriate typing of an expression.

The basis for type checking is the algorithm worked out by Milner in the mid-1970s. It is based on a powerful technique of *term unification*. This chapter explains how the term unification works and also how it is applied in the typing of expressions. Since all algorithms are written in Standard ML itself, this chapter may also be considered an example of a large Standard ML program.

10.1 Hand typing of Standard ML expressions

The aim of this section is to make the reader aware of problems encountered while trying to determine the type of an expression in the presence of polymorphism; and also to suggest some ways of carrying out typing. The detailed typing algorithm will follow in further sections.

Consider the following Standard ML definition:

```
fun len(lis) =
  if lis=[] then 0
  else 1+len(tl(lis)) ;
```

In order to determine the type of `len`, one should first get rid of "syntactic sugar" present in the function definition to make it more easily digestible for the human reader. Assume the type checker can only deal with constants, variables, functional abstraction and function application to a single argument. Assume also, it *cannot* deal with recursion.

This modest inventory is sufficient to write the definition of `len`, and also of other recursive functions, provided the set of constants is rich enough. For instance, there should be a general recursor constant

```
FIX : (('a->'b) -> ('a->'b)) -> ('a->'b)
```

that assigns to every functional

```
ff : ('a->'b) -> ('a->'b)
```

the function

```
f = FIX(ff) : 'a->'b
```

defined recursively by

```
fun f(a) = ff(f)(a)
```

Of course, the type checker needs only the type of `FIX` and not its full definition.

Other constants necessary to "unsugar" the definition of `len` are:

```
IF : bool -> 'c -> 'c -> 'c
EQ : 'd -> 'd -> bool
[] : ('e)list
tl : ('f)list -> ('f)list
0 : int
1 : int
PLUS : int -> int -> int
```

The unsugared version of the definition of `len` is:

```
val len =
  FIX (fn(len1)=> fn(lis)=>
        IF (EQ lis []) 0 (PLUS 1 (len1(tl(lis))))) ;
```

Note that the type variables in types of various constants have been made distinct, e.g. `'c` occurs only in the type of `IF` and `'d` only in the type of `EQ`. Variables occurring in the expression defining `len1` under the functional abstraction `fn(...)=>` have to be typed to type variables that are different again:

```
len1 : 'g
lis : 'h
```

Now, the type of the expression defining `len` may be found incrementally, which sometimes requires the introduction of new type variables, or equalities on existing type expressions:

```
EQ lis : 'd->bool      'h = 'd
```

— since the only possibility of applying `EQ` of type `'d->'d->bool` to `lis` of type `'h` is to make types `'h` and `'d` equal; and then the result has type `'d->bool`.

```
EQ lis [] : bool      'd = ('e)list
```

— since the only possibility of applying `EQ lis` of type `'d->bool` to `[]` of type `('e)list` is to make types `'d` and `('e)list` equal; and then the result has type `bool`. Let us go on:

```
IF (EQ lis []) : 'c->'c->'c    no new equalities
IF (...) 0 : int->int           'c = int
tl(lis) : ('f)list              'h = ('f)list
len1(tl(lis)) : 'i              'g = ('f)list->'i
```

The last line may be justified as follows: since `len` is applied to an argument of type `('f)list`, its type `'g` has to be equal to a type `('f)list->'i`, where `'i` is a newly introduced type variable.

```
PLUS 1 : int->int                    no new equalities
PLUS 1 (len1(tl(lis))) : int         'i = int
IF (...) 0 (PLUS...) : int           no new equalities
fn(lis)=> IF... : 'h->int            no new equalities
```

This is so because `fn(lis)=> IF...` takes an argument of type `'h` and yields a result of type `int`.

```
fn(len1)=> fn(lis)=> IF... :
  'g -> ('h->int)                    no new equalities

FIX(...) : 'a->'b                    { 'g = 'a->'b
                                     { 'h->int = 'a->'b
```

It is easy to see that the system of equalities above is equivalent to:

```
'e = 'f
'b = 'c = 'i = int
'a = 'h = 'd = ('f)list
'g = ('f)list->int
```

and it has many solutions: each replacement of a type for the type variable 'f generates one solution. The derived type of len is therefore polymorphic:

```
('f)list -> int
```

Consider another example definition:

```
fun wrong(f)(lis) =
  if lis=[] then []
  else f(hd(lis))::f(tl(lis)) ;
```

This may be unsugared to

```
val wrong =
  fn(f)=> fn(lis)=>
    IF (EQ lis EMPT1) EMPT2
    (CONS (f(hd(lis))) (f(tl(lis)))) ;
```

with the base typing:

```
IF : bool -> 'a -> 'a -> 'a
EQ : 'b -> 'b -> bool
EMPT1 : ('c)list
EMPT2 : ('d)list
CONS : 'e -> ('e)list -> ('e)list
hd : ('f)list -> 'f
tl : ('g)list -> ('g)list
f : 'h
lis : 'i
```

The incremental typing proceeds as follows:

EQ lis : 'b->bool	'i = 'b
EQ lis EMPT1 : bool	'b = ('c)list
IF (EQ...) : 'a->'a->'a	no new equalities
IF (EQ...) EMPT2 : ('d)list->('d)list	'a = ('d)list
hd(lis) : 'f	'i = ('f)list
f(hd(lis)) : 'j	'h = 'f->'j
CONS(...) : ('e)list->('e)list	'j = 'e
tl(lis) : ('g)list	'i = ('g)list
f(tl(lis)) : 'k	'h = ('g)list->'k
CONS(...)(...) : ('e)list	'k = ('e)list

At this point our system of equations becomes inconsistent, since it implies that

'h = 'f->'e   and
'h = ('g)list->('e)list

which can only be satisfied by

'f = ('g)list   and
'e = ('e)list

The last equality cannot be made true by any type for 'e, therefore the definition of function **wrong** should be rejected as type-incorrect.

This is, more or less, how the type checker works. Note, however, that we have so far not said *how* it decides whether or not a given system of type equations is consistent.

10.2   Term unification

Assume, we are given a collection *Ops* of *operators* and a collection *Vars* of *variables*. The family *Terms* of *terms* is then defined by

(10.1) *Terms* ::= *Vars*
                 | (*Ops*, [*Terms*, ..., *Terms*])

i.e. variable is a term, and operator followed by a list (possibly empty) of terms is a term. For instance,

(+ , [(1,[]) , (*,[x,y])])

is a term that may be considered an unsugared version of

1 + x*y

Any function that assigns terms to variables is referred to as a *substitution*. Every such function may be extended to act on terms by the obvious recursive definition: if σ is a substitution, then $\tilde{\sigma} : Terms \rightarrow Terms$ is defined as

$$\tilde{\sigma}(v) = \sigma(v) \quad \text{for } v \in Vars$$
$$\tilde{\sigma}(o, [t_1, \ldots, t_n]) = (o, [\tilde{\sigma}(t_1), \ldots, \tilde{\sigma}(t_n)])$$

For instance, if σ assigns x+y to x and 0 to y, then

$$\tilde{\sigma}(1+x*y) = 1+(x+y)*0$$

Any two substitutions σ and τ may be composed yielding a new substitution $\tau; \sigma$ defined as

$$\tau; \sigma(v) = (\tilde{\sigma} \circ \tau)(v) = \tilde{\sigma}(\tau(v)) \quad \text{for } v \in Vars$$

Given two terms t and t', any substitution σ such that $\tilde{\sigma}(t) = \tilde{\sigma}(t')$ is called a *unifier* of these two terms. For instance, the substitution

$$\sigma_0 = \cdots \begin{array}{|c|c|c|} \hline \mathtt{x} & \mathtt{y} & \mathtt{z} \\ \hline \mathtt{x} & \mathtt{1} & \mathtt{x+1} \\ \hline \end{array} \cdots$$

is a unifier of terms

    (x+y)*z   and
    z*(x+1)

because it transforms both terms to

    (x+1)*(x+1)

This is not the only unifier of these two terms: if τ is any other substitution then $\sigma_0; \tau$ is also a unifier, because once two terms get *unified*, or made equal by applying a unifier σ_0, no other substitution τ may make them distinct again.

The *most general unifier* of two terms is the unifier σ_0 of these terms such that for any other unifier σ_1 there exists a substitution τ such that

$$\sigma_1 = \sigma_0; \tau$$

It may be proved that for any pair of *unifiable* terms, i.e. the ones that have a unifier, there exists also the most general unifier. The most general unifier of two terms is unique up to the renaming of variables. By *term unification* is meant the process of finding the most general unifier of two given terms.

Term unification may be thought of as syntactic equation solving. To solve an equation

$$t = t'$$

means producing a substitution of terms for variables which makes terms t and t' syntactically identical, in other words, finding their unifier.

Here follows a rough description of how the most general unifier

    unify(t, t')

of two given terms t and t' may be found.

If t is a variable that does not occur in t' then unify(t, t') is the substitution $[t'/t]$ of term t' for variable t. For instance,

$$\mathtt{unify}(\mathtt{y}, \mathtt{x+z}) = \cdots \begin{array}{|c|c|c|} \hline \mathtt{x} & \mathtt{y} & \mathtt{z} \\ \hline \mathtt{x} & \mathtt{x+z} & \mathtt{z} \\ \hline \end{array} \cdots$$

If t is a variable that does occur in t' then the two terms have no unifier, unless they are equal. For instance,

    unify$(\mathtt{y}, \mathtt{x+y})$ does not exist

$$\mathtt{unify}(\mathtt{y}, \mathtt{y}) = \cdots \begin{array}{|c|c|c|} \hline \mathtt{x} & \mathtt{y} & \mathtt{z} \\ \hline \mathtt{x} & \mathtt{y} & \mathtt{z} \\ \hline \end{array} \cdots$$

Of course, the situation is the same if t' is a variable.

Assume now that both t and t' are operator terms:

$$t = (o, [t_1, \ldots, t_n])$$
$$t' = (o', [t'_1, \ldots, t'_k])$$

If $o \neq o'$ then the terms have no unifier, for instance

    unify(x+y, (y+1)*z)   does not exist

If $o = o'$ then a necessary and sufficient requirement for the existence of a unifier is the equality of the lengths n and k of the respective argument lists and the pairwise unifiability of terms t_i and t'_i, for $i = 1, \ldots, n$, by the same substitution. Let then

$$\sigma_1 = \mathtt{unify}(t_1, t'_1)$$
$$\sigma_2 = \mathtt{unify}(\tilde{\sigma}_1 t_2, \tilde{\sigma}_1 t'_2)$$
$$\sigma_3 = \mathtt{unify}(\tilde{\sigma}_2(\tilde{\sigma}_1 t_3), \tilde{\sigma}_2(\tilde{\sigma}_1 t'_3))$$
$$\ldots$$

$$\sigma_n = \mathtt{unify}(\tilde{\sigma}_{n-1}(\ldots(\tilde{\sigma}_1 t_n)\ldots), \tilde{\sigma}_{n-1}(\ldots(\tilde{\sigma}_1 t'_n)\ldots))$$

If either of the unifiers above fails to exist, then t and t' are not unifiable. If all the unifiers do exist, then

$$\mathtt{unify}(t, t') = \sigma_1; \sigma_2; \ldots; \sigma_n$$

In the remainder of this section we give the Standard ML code for term unification.

First of all, the definition (10.1) of terms has to be rewritten into Standard ML:

```
signature TERMS =
  sig
    type ops
    and vars
    and terms ;
    val eqo : ops * ops -> bool
    and eqv : vars * vars -> bool
    and eqt : terms * terms -> bool ;
    val arity : ops -> int ;
    exception arity
          and destr ;
    val vtm : vars -> terms
    and otm : ops * (terms)list -> terms
    and tmv : terms -> vars
    and tmo : terms -> ops * (terms)list
  end (* signature TERMS *) ;
```

With respect to the abstract definition (10.1) this signature is enriched by the
equality functions eqo, eqv and eqt; by the function arity over operators; by
the constructors vtm and otm of terms; and by the destructors tmv and tmo
of terms. It is assumed that the constructor function otm raises the exception
arity when applied to a pair (oo,tlis) such that the arity of oo does not
coincide with the length of tlis. It is also assumed that both the destructors
raise the exception destr whenever they are non-applicable, i.e. if destructor
tmv is used over a term that involves an operator, or if destructor tmo is used
over a term that does not.

The following signature describes our aim:

```
signature UNIFICATION =
  sig
    type terms ;
    exception non_unifiable ;
    val unify : terms * terms -> terms -> terms
  end (* signature UNIFICATION *) ;
```

Given two terms, the function unify is supposed to yield their most general
unifier, or to raise the exception non_unifiable. A substitution σ is here
identified with the term-transforming function $\tilde{\sigma}$ that extends it.

The functor that follows realises the unification as required; some explanations are given after the definition:

```
functor Unification (Terms : TERMS) : UNIFICATION  =
  struct
    type terms = Terms.terms ;
    exception non_unifiable ;
    fun occurs(v) t =
        (* does variable  v   occur in term  t *)
        ... ;
    fun subst(t,v) tt =
        (* term  tt  with  t  replaced for all
           occurrences of variable  v *)
        ... ;

    fun idsubst(t) = t ;

    fun unify(t,t') =
      let val v = Terms.tmv(t)
      in if occurs(v) t'
         then if Terms.eqt(t,t')
              then idsubst
              else raise non_unifiable
```

```
                else subst(t',v)
            end
              handle Terms.destr =>
            let val v' = Terms.tmv(t')
            in  (* likewise, symmetrically *)
              ...
            end
              handle Terms.destr =>
            let val (ope,tlis) = Terms.tmo(t)
                and (ope',tlis') = Terms.tmo(t')
            in if Terms.eqo(ope,ope')
               then unifylist(idsubst)(tlis,tlis')
               else raise non_unifiable
            end (* fun unify *)

        and unifylist(s)([],[]) = s
          | unifylist(s)(t::tlis,[]) = raise non_unifiable
          | unifylist(s)([],t'::tlis') = raise non_unifiable
          | unifylist(s)(t::tlis,t'::tlis') =
              let val s1 = unify(s(t),s(t'))
              in unifylist(s1 o s)(tlis,tlis')
              end (* fun unifylist *) ;

      end (* functor Unification *) ;
```

The dotted parts of this functor are two auxiliary functions that operate on
terms, and an obvious symmetrical case of unification with a variable. The
functions that operate on terms have to be defined using term destructors
and exception handling:

```
    fun subst(t,v) tt =
      let val vv = Terms.tmv(tt)
      in if Terms.eqv(v,vv)
         then t
         else tt
      end
        handle Terms.destr =>
      let val (oo,tlis) = Terms.tmo(tt)
      in Terms.otm (oo , map(subst(t,v)) tlis)
      end ;
```

where map is the functional that performs a function over all elements of a
list; its definition is

```
    fun map(f) []  =  []
```

```
| map(f) (x::lis)  =  f(x):: map(f) lis ;
```

The definition of occurs is left as an exercise. The above definition of the auxiliary function unifylist uses the predefined Standard ML functional o for function composition:

```
f o g  =  fn(x)=> f(g(x))
```

10.3   Typing the expressions

Expression typing is an incremental process.

The (polymorphic) types of constants are known beforehand. One must only rename the type variables in types of distinct constants in an expression so as to make them all different. Also different occurrences of *the same* constant in an expression need to have disjoint sets of type variables. For instance, in the definition

```
fun map(f) lis =
  if lis=[] then []
  else f(hd(lis))::map(f)(tl(lis)) ;
```

the two occurrences of [] have to be treated as distinct constants:

```
[]₁  :  ('a)list
[]₂  :  ('b)list
EQ   :  'c->'c->bool
IF   :  bool->'d->'d->'d
...
etc.
```

Variables found under functional abstraction fn(...)=> are typed to type variables not occurring in the types of constants of the expression. Other variables are free in the expression and have to be reported as errors (exception unknown_var in the functor below). Unlike constants, different occurrences of the same variables are typed alike[1]. E.g.

```
f : 'e
lis : 'f
...
etc.
```

---

[1]Before this is done, bound variables in the expression have to be renamed so that they are all distinct.

The type of functional abstraction `fn(x)=>e` is `t1->t2`, where `t1` is the type of `x` and `t2` is the type of `e`.

The crucial point in the whole process of expression typing is the application `e1 e2`. To start with, the types `t1` and `t2` respectively of `e1` and `e2` have to be found. Then, in order for the application to be type correct, `t1` has to be unifiable with `t2->tv` where `tv` is an entirely new type variable. The type of the `e1 e2` is the one assigned to `tv` by the resulting unifier.

The unification algorithm is, therefore, used at the level of type expressions rather than at the level of individual expressions. In order to apply the functor `Unification` from the previous section, one has first to interpret type expressions as terms.

We shall call a *type system* any structure matching the following signature:

```
signature TYPE_SYS =
  sig
    type cons
    and vars
    and exprs
    and typops
    and tyvars
    and types ;
    val eqv : vars * vars -> bool
    and eqto : typops * typops -> bool
    and eqtv : tyvars * tyvars -> bool
    and eqt : types * types -> bool ;
    exception typarity
          and destr ;
    (* Constructors and selectors for  expr : *)
    val cex : cons -> exprs
    and vex : vars -> exprs
    and fnc : vars * exprs -> exprs
    and app : exprs * exprs -> exprs
    and exc : exprs -> cons
    and exv : exprs -> vars
    and cnf : exprs -> vars * exprs
    and ppa : exprs -> exprs * exprs ;
    (* Constructors and selectors for  types : *)
    val tvtp : tyvars -> types
    and totp : typops * (types)list -> types
    and tptv : types -> tyvars
    and tpto : types -> typops * (types)list ;
    (* Special objects: *)
```

```
        val arrow : typops ;
        val typarity : typops -> int ;
        val typcon : cons -> types ;
        val newtv : (tyvars)list -> tyvars
      end (* signature TYPE_SYS *) ;
```

One should uderstand this signature as declaring:

- a universe of expressions constructed of constants and variables using constructors cex, vex, fnc and app, and destructors exc, exv, cnf and ppa; this corresponds to the grammar

$$
\begin{aligned}
Expr \quad ::= \quad & Cons \\
| \quad & Vars \\
| \quad & \texttt{fn}(Vars)\texttt{=>}Expr \\
| \quad & Expr\ Expr
\end{aligned}
$$

- a universe of types constructed of type operators and type variables using constructors tvtp and totp, and destructors tptv and tpto; this corresponds to the grammar

$$
\begin{aligned}
Types \quad ::= \quad & Tyvars \\
| \quad & (Typops, [Types, \ldots, Types])
\end{aligned}
$$

- a special type operator arrow, function typarity giving the arity of type operators[2] and function newtv that generates a new type variable, not present on the list that makes its argument;

- a function typcon that gives the initial typing of constants; this function is the only link between the two universes.

Our task is to extend the typing of constants to the typing of all expressions, i.e. to construct a structure matching the signature:

```
      signature TYPING =
        sig
          type exprs
           and types ;
          exception type_clash ;
          val typing : exprs -> types
        end (* signature TYPING *) ;
```

This is done by the following functor:

---

[2]If we were allowed to write axioms, we would certainly state that typarity(arrow) = 2.

```
functor Typing (TypeSys : TYPE_SYS) : TYPING =
  struct
    type exprs = TypeSys.exprs
     and types = TypeSys.types ;
    structure TypesAsTerms =
      struct
        type ops = TypeSys.typops
         and vars = TypeSys.tyvars
         and terms = TypeSys.types ;
        val eqo = TypeSys.eqto
        and eqv = TypeSys.eqtv
        and eqt = TypeSys.eqt ;
        val arity = TypeSys.typarity ;
        exception arity = TypeSys.typarity
              and destr = TypeSys.destr ;
        val vtm = TypeSys.tvtp
        and otm = TypeSys.totp
        and tmv = TypeSys.tptv
        and tmo = TypeSys.tpto
      end (* structure TypesAsTerms *) ;
    structure Unif = Unification(TypesAsTerms) ;
    exception type_clash
          and unknown_var ;
    fun rentv(t,usedtv) = ... ;

    fun typexpr(ex,typenv,usedtv) =
      let val c = TypeSys.exc(ex)
      in let val (t,usedtv') =
             rentv(TypeSys.typcon(c),usedtv)
         in (t , typenv , usedtv')
         end
      end
        handle TypeSys.destr =>
      let val v = TypeSys.exv(ex)
      in (typenv(v) , typenv , usedtv)
      end
        handle TypeSys.destr =>
      let val (v1,ex1) = TypeSys.cnf(ex)
      in let val tv = TypeSys.newtv(usedtv)
         in let val t1 = TypeSys.tvtp(tv)
            in let val typenv1 = upd(t1,v) typenv
                   and usedtv1 = tv::usedtv
               in let val (t2,typenv2,usedtv2) =
```

```
                                 typexpr(ex1,typenv1,usedtv1)
                    in let val typenv2' =
                            fn(v')=> if v'=v1
                                     then typenv(v1)
                                     else typenv2(v')
                       in (TypeSys.totp(TypeSys.arrow,
                                        [typenv2(v1),t2]) ,
                            typenv2 ,
                            usedtv2
                            )
                       end
                   end
                end
             end
          end
        end
          handle TypeSys.destr =>
        let val (ex1,ex2) = TypeSys.ppa(ex)
        in let val (t1,typenv1,usedtv1) =
                   typexpr(ex1,typenv,usedtv)
             in let val (t2,typenv2,usedtv2) =
                    typexpr(ex2,typenv1,usedtv1)
                in let val tv = TypeSys.newtv(usedtv2)
                   in let val t =
                          TypeSys.totp(TypeSys.arrow ,
                                       [t2,TypeSys.tvtp(tv)]
                                       )
                      in let val unif = Unif.unify(t1,t)
                         in (unif(tv) ,
                             unif o typenv2 ,
                             tv::usedtv2
                             )
                         end
                            handle Unif.non_unifiable =>
                            raise type_clash
                      end
                   end
                end
             end
          end (* fun typexpr *) ;

fun typenv0(v) =
  raise untyped_var ;
```

```
        fun typing(ex) =
          let val (t,typenv,usedtv) =
            typexpr(ex , typenv0 , [])
          in t
          end
      end (* functor Typing *) ;
```

A few comments about the above piece of code. Firstly, the components of the functor's argument structure TypeSys are so renamed as to match the signature TERMS, which enables us to apply the functor Unification. The resulting structure Unif provides a function Unif.unify to be used for the unification of type expressions. Fuction rentv is very technical: given a type expression t and a list of used type variables usedtv, it produces a new type expression t1 that differs from t in that all its type variables are renamed to make them distinct from the ones from list usedtv, and then a new list of used type variables which is usedtv plus all the newly introduced type variables of t1. The definition of this function is the only reason for the requirement that there be function newtv in TypeSys.

Function typexpr provides the main typing mechanism of our functor. It takes an expression, and a type environment, i.e. an assignment of type expressions to variables, and a list of used type variables; upon which it yields the type of the expression, a new type environment, and a new list of used type variables. The function typing is defined by using typexpr with the trivial environment and with the empty list of used type variables.

10.4 Typing in a simple ML-like language

One may view the unsugared version of Standard ML as the language involving the universe of types and the universe of individual objects. The universe of types is defined as follows:

$$(10.2) \quad \textit{Types} \quad ::= \quad \textit{Tyvars}$$
$$| \quad (\textit{Typops}, [\textit{Types}, \ldots, \textit{Types}])$$

where

$$(10.3) \quad \textit{TypOps} \quad ::= \quad \texttt{log} \mid \texttt{integ} \quad — \text{ arity } 0$$
$$| \quad \texttt{seq} \qquad\qquad — \text{ arity } 1$$
$$| \quad \texttt{star} \mid \texttt{arrow} \quad — \text{ arity } 2$$

Legal type expressions are the ones that conform to (10.2) with the additional restriction that in any type of form $(to, [t_1, \ldots, t_n])$, the arity of to has to be equal to n.

The universe of individual objects is:

(10.4) $Expr$ ::= $Vars$
                | $Cons$
                | fn($Vars$)=>$Expr$
                | $Expr$ $Expr$

In the definition of $Cons$ that follows the natural abbreviations are used to denote types: log for (log,[]), integ for (integ,[]), (T)seq for (seq,[T]), T_1*T_2 for (star,[T_1,T_2]), T_1->T_2 for (arrow,[T_1,T_2]):

(10.5) $Cons$ ::= yes | no   — of type log
                | ortest   — of type log->log->log
                | iftest   — of type log->'a->'a->'a
                | eq   — of type 'a->'a->log
                | Int — of type integ
                | add | sbt | mul — of type integ->integ->integ
                | pair   — of type 'a->'b->'a*'b
                | fst   — of type 'a*'b->'a
                | snd   — of type 'a*'b->'b
                | empt   — of type ('a)seq
                | cons   — of type 'a->('a)seq->('a)seq
                | isempt   — of type ('a)seq->log
                | head   — of type ('a)seq->'a
                | tail   — of type ('a)seq->('a)seq
                | fix   — of type
                                     ((('a->'b)->('a->'b))->('a->'b)

(all identifiers have been renamed in order not to be in conflict with Standard ML identifiers in the Standard ML program that follows). The collection of constants may, of course, be enlarged or changed. All constants have to be assigned legal types as described by (10.2).

Type inference for this language consists of extending the typing of constants to the typing of expressions in the way given in Sec.10.3. In order to use the functor Typing from that section one has to define a type system corresponding to (10.2)–(10.5):

```
structure ExTypSys =
  struct
    datatype cons = yes | no | ortest | iftest | eq
                  | numb of int | add | sbt | mul
                  | pair | fst | snd
                  | empt | cons | isempt | head | tail
                  | fix ;
    type vars = string ;
```

```
datatype exprs = vex of vars
               | cex of cons
               | fnc of vars*exprs
               | app of exprs*exprs ;
datatype typops = log | integ
                | seq
                | star | arrow ;
fun typarity(log) = 0
  | typarity(integ) = 0
  | typarity(seq) = 1
  | typarity(star) = 2
  | typarity(arrow) = 2 ;
type tyvars = string ;
type types = tvtp of tyvars
           | totp' of typops * (types)list ;
val eqv = (op =)
and eqto = (op =)
and eqtv = (op =)
and eqt = (op =) ;
exception typ_arity : unit
     and destr : unit ;
fun exv(vex(v)) = v
  | exv(_)= raise destr ;
fun exc(cex(c)) = c
  | exc(_)= raise destr ;
fun cnf(fnc(v,ex)) = (v,ex)
  | cnf(_)= raise destr ;
fun ppa(app(ex1,ex2)) = (ex1,ex2)
  | ppa(_)= raise destr ;
fun totp(to,tlis) =
  if typarity(to)=len(tlis)
  then totp'(to,tlis)
  else raise typ_arity ;
fun tptv(tvtp(tv)) = tv
  | tptv(_) = raise destr ;
fun tpto(totp'(to,tlis)) = (to,tlis)
  | tpto(_) = raise destr ;
local
  val xx = tvtp"xx"
  and yy = tvtp"yy"
  and log = totp(log,[])
  and integ = totp(integ,[]) ;
  fun seq(t) = totp(seq,[t])
```

```
 ·and star(t1,t2) = totp(star,[t1,t2])
  and arr(t1,t2) = totp(arrow,[t1,t2])
in fun typcon(yes) = log
    | typcon(no) = log
    | typcon(ortest) = arr(log,arr(log,log))
    | typcon(iftest) = arr(log,arr(xx,arr(xx,xx)))
    | typcon(eq) = arr(xx,arr(xx,log))
    | typcon(numb(n)) = integ
    | typcon(add) = arr(integ,arr(integ,integ))
    | typcon(sbt) = arr(integ,arr(integ,integ))
    | typcon(mul) = arr(integ,arr(integ,integ))
    | typcon(pair) = arr(xx,arr(yy,star(xx,yy)))
    | typcon(fst) = arr(star(xx,yy),xx)
    | typcon(snd) = arr(star(xx,yy),yy)
    | typcon(empt) = seq(xx)
    | typcon(cons) = arr(xx,arr(sqn(xx),sqn(xx)))
    | typcon(isempt) = arr(sqn(xx),log)
    | typcon(head) = arr(sqn(xx),xx)
    | typcon(tail) = arr(sqn(xx),sqn(xx))
    | typcon(fix) =
         arr(arr(arr(xx,yy),arr(xx,yy)),arr(xx,yy))
  end ;
  fun newtv(usedtv) = ...
end (* structure ExTypSys *) ;

structure ExTyping = Typing(ExTypSys) ;
```

This defines the function `ExTyping.typing` responsible for typing expressions in our small language.

10.5   Exercises

Exercise 34

In the calculus of combinators one considers an operator S that, given two expressions

$$e_1 \quad \text{of type} \quad t_1 \to t_2 \to t_3 \quad \text{and}$$
$$e_2 \quad \text{of type} \quad t_1 \to t_2$$

yields an expression

$$S[e_1, e_2] \quad \text{of type} \quad t_1 \to t_3$$

Assume tt_1 and tt_2 are polymorphic types of certain expressions e_1 and e_2 respectively. Find a method of inferring the type of $S[e_1, e_2]$ using the unification algorithm.

Exercise 35

Define the function `occurs` that has not been defined in the text of functor `Unification` in this chapter.

Exercise 36

A simple language of expressions is given by the following grammar:

$$
\begin{aligned}
Expr \quad ::= \quad & Var \\
| \quad & 0 \\
| \quad & 1 \\
| \quad & Expr \; + \; Expr \\
| \quad & Expr \; * \; Expr
\end{aligned}
$$

A *system of equations* is any list of pairs of expressions:

$$ex_1' = ex_1''$$
$$\cdots$$
$$ex_n' = ex_n''$$

A *solution* of such a system is any substitution σ of expressions for variables such that

$$\tilde{\sigma}(ex_1') \equiv \tilde{\sigma}(ex_1'')$$
$$\cdots$$
$$\tilde{\sigma}(ex_n') \equiv \tilde{\sigma}(ex_n'')$$

where $\equiv$ is the syntactic equality of expressions.

Define all necessary types and the function that, given a system of equations, yields its most general solution.

Chapter 11

Interpretation

When an expression is fed into Standard ML, it is first type-checked using the methods described in Chapter 10; then either an error is reported, or the expression is *evaluated*. This chapter gives a bird's eye view of the techniques used for the evaluation of expressions in an applicative language.

11.1 Interpretation by graph reduction

The simplest way of implementing a functional language is to provide a number of simplification rules for the parse trees of expressions of this language. This method is called *graph reduction*, since the simplification process may lead to graphs that are not trees any more.

Unsugared versions of expressions make trees of a rather simple shape as described in Sec.10.4. For instance, the unsugared version of definition

```
fun parity(n) =
   if n=0 then 1
   else ~parity(n-1)
```

is

```
val parity =
   FIX (fn(parity)=> fn(n)=>
         IF (EQ n 0) 1 (SBT 0 (parity(SBT n 1)))
       )
```

which corresponds to the following tree in which the leaves are constants and variables, and the internal nodes are applications @ and functional abstractions fn(...)=>:

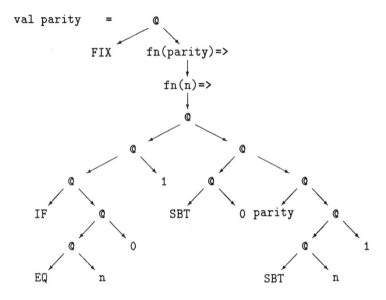

Giving an argument to function `parity` means putting together this tree and the argument's tree by creating a new node; for instance `parity 2` is

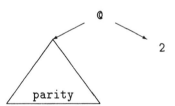

In order to evaluate `parity 2` one has to reduce that latter tree.

Trees (and other graphs) are represented in the obvious way by *nodes* and *pointers*. Reductions usually consist of creating a new root node and making pointers in this new node equal to some pointers from the old graph; this corresponds to the inclusion of portions of the old graph into the new one. The old root becomes inaccessible and will be dealt with by the garbage collector discussed in Sec.11.4.

The main reduction rules are:

- β-reduction

$$(\text{fn}(v)\texttt{=>}ex)\,ex_1 \quad \longmapsto \quad ex[ex_1/v]$$

- specific rules for constants, e.g.

$$\text{FIX } ex \;\longmapsto\; ex(\text{FIX } ex)$$

Besides the rules, the evaluation mechanism has to be committed to some *reduction strategy*, that prescribes a certain order in which the reductions are to be carried out. By the *normal order reduction* is meant the strategy, by which the leftmost subexpressions are dealt with first. This results in *lazy* evaluation (cf. Sec.2.1).

In terms of tree operations this means the following proceeding. Firstly, the evaluator descends the leftmost branch of the tree from its root either to an `fn(...)=>`-node, or to a constant-leaf, whichever comes first[1]. If the expression has been successfully type-checked, then the leaf may not be a variable, because this variable would then be unbound. Then, if the node encountered is a functional abstraction node, the evaluator performs β-reduction; if it is a constant, it performs an appropriate reduction specific to that constant.

11.2 A simple evaluator of expressions

It is important to realise that after successful type checking these reductions can certainly be performed since they have as many arguments (*vertebrae*) as they need. Had the user typed a correct expression with too few arguments, such as

```
- sbt 5;
```

where `sbt` is the (curried) subtraction operator for integers, then the evaluator would not be called at all, and the system's answer

```
> fn : int -> int
```

would come from the type checker rather than from the evaluator.

By normal order reduction, the expression `parity 2` reduces as follows:

```
parity 2  =
=  FIX (fn(parity)=> ...) 2  ->
```

apply the rule for `FIX`:

```
->  (fn(parity)=> ...) (FIX (fn(parity)=> ...)) 2 ->
```

apply β-reduction; note that `FIX (fn(parity)=> ...)` is again equal to `parity`:

---

[1]The leftmost branch of the tree is sometimes called its *spine*, and the subtrees left aside when descending are called *vertebrae*.

```
-> (fn(n)=> IF ...) 2 ->
```

apply the β-reduction:

```
-> IF (EQ 2 0) 1 (SBT 0 (parity (SBT 2 1))) ->
```

The rule for IF prescribes first the evaluation of the first *vertebra*, i.e. EQ 2
0 in this case; then the second or the third *vertebra* is selected depending on
the result of this evaluation:

```
-> SBT 0 (parity (SBT 2 1)) ->
```

The rule for SBT and all other rules for arithmetic operators prescribe first the
evaluation of the arguments, and therefore the expression parity (SBT 2 1)
is now treated:

```
-> ... ->

-> MIN (IF (EQ (SBT 2 1) 0) 1
           (SBT 0 (parity (SBT (SBT 2 1) 1)))
       ) ->

-> SBT 0 (SBT 0 (parity (SBT (SBT 2 1)))) -> ... ->

-> SBT 0 (SBT 0 (IF (EQ (SBT (SBT 2 1) 1) 0) 1
                    (SBT 0 (parity (SBT (SBT (SBT 2 1) 1) 1)))
       )   ) -> ... ->

-> SBT 0 (SBT 0 1) -> ... ->

-> 1
```

While a lot may be said both in favour and against normal order reduction,
it is certainly the easiest strategy to implement. The Standard ML function

```
eval : expr -> cons
```

defined below may serve as a normal order evaluator for expressions from the
simple language defined in Sec.10.4. The definition of eval uses the auxiliary
functions

```
subst : expr * vars -> expr -> expr
evcon : const * (expr)list -> expr
ev : expr * (expr)list -> const
```

`subst(ex1,v)ex` is the result of substituting expression `ex1` for free occurrences of variable `v` in expression `ex`. The definition of `subst` is left to the reader; note that after the type checking phase the expression `ex1` may be assumed not to involve any free variables, which considerably simplifies the definition of `subst` (cf. Exercise 37). `evcon(c,[ex1,...,exn])` is the expression resulting from the application of reductions specific for constant `c` to argument expressions. The last function is simply a generalisation of `eval`:

$$ev(ex,[ex1,\ldots,exn]) \;=\; eval(app(\ldots app(ex,ex1)\ldots,exn))$$

but its Standard ML definition is of course different, since we have to define `eval` using `ev`, rather than the other way round:

```
fun ev(con(c),exlis) =
        if arity(c)=0 then c
        else let val (exlis1,exlis2) =
                 chop(arity(c))exlis
             in ev(evcon(c,exlis1),exlis2)
             end
    | ...
```

— `chop n` is the function that splits its argument list into two lists of which the first has length `n`:

$$chop \; n \; [a_1,\ldots,a_k] = ([a_1,\ldots,a_n],[a_{n+1},\ldots,a_k])$$

The precise definition of `chop` is left to the reader.

```
    | ev(app(ex1,ex2),exlis) = ev(ex1,ex2::exlis)
    | ...
```

— this means going down the spine.

```
    | ev(fnc(v,ex),ex1::exlis) =
        ev(subst(ex1,v)ex,exlis)
    | ...
```

— this is the β-reduction.

```
    | ev _ => raise error_in_type_checker
```

— this exception should never be raised if the type checker is properly implemented.

The definition of `evcon` may read as follows:

```
and evcon(iftest,[ex1,ex2,ex3]) =
        case ev(ex1,[]) of
            yes => ex2
        | no => ex3
        | _ => raise error_in_type_checker
    | ...
```

— this means that the rule for `iftest` prescribes the evaluation of the first argument and the yielding of either the second or the third unevaluated, depending on the value of `ex1`. An analogous definition of `ortest` is left to the reader.

```
| evcon(add,[ex1,ex2]) =
   case (ev(ex1,[]),ev(ex2,[])) of
   (numb(n),numb(k)) => con(numb(n+k))
 | _ => raise error_in_type_checker
```

— the addition requires evaluating both arguments, then the integers n and k that correspond to the resulting constants are added to each other. The remaining arithmetic operations: `eq`, `sbt` and `mul` are defined in the same way. The definitions of operations on Cartesian products and on lists are left to the reader. Finally:

```
| evcon(fix,[ex]) =
   app(ex,app(con(fix),ex))
```

— this is the fixpoint rule. The case of arity 0 constants has been already considered in the definition of `ev`.

Finally, the definition of `eval` reads:

```
eval(ex) = ev(ex,[])
```

11.3   Sharing and cycles

In the evaluation process described above there seems to be no room for non-trees to come around. Actually, graphs that are not trees are introduced as a means of optimisation when transcribing the evaluator given in the preceding section to a program directly dealing with pointers.

Consider the expression

```
(fn(x)=>~SBT~x~x)(PLUS~1~2)
```

and its corresponding tree:

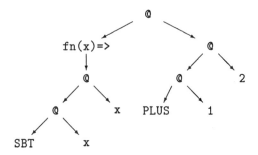

For this case the normal order reduction algorithm prescribes carrying out
β-reduction, which results in two distinct occurrences of the argument subexpression PLUS 1 2:

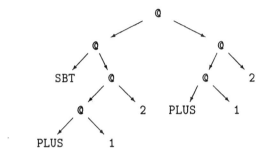

As it stands, this subexpression will have to be evaluated twice. This may be
optimised in terms both of time and of space by allowing several nodes to
share a subtree. Then the β-reduction above could yield the following graph:

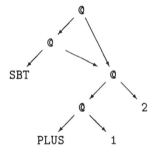

The structures resulting from sharing subtrees are the *directed acyclic graphs*
(DAG-s).

Another optimisation will produce cycles in graphs. This has to do with
recursion. The fixpoint rule with sharing takes the following form:

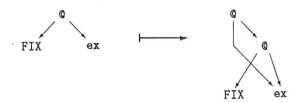

Instead, one may use the following reduction rule:

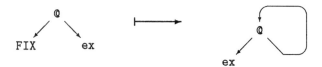

This saves both space and time.

Some other problems encountered when implementing a graph reduction evaluator are hinted at in the exercises to this chapter.

11.4   An overview of techniques for garbage collection

Any machine-level implementation of graph reduction involves operations on pointers. Carrying out a reduction consists in most cases in creating a new node pointing to fragments of an old graph. This results eventually in the exhaustion of the whole available storage while the memory is littered with inaccessible parts of old graphs. Some effort has to be made then to recuperate this inaccessible storage and to use it for further node allocations.

This is called *garbage collection*. There is one fundamental difference between the garbage collection as used in implementations of applicative languages and the corresponding activity concerning operations on pointers in, say, Pascal. While in Pascal a programmer may occupy or release arbitrary heap locations according to his will, it is unthinkable to burden a Standard ML programmer with *any* concern about storage management. The garbage collection has to be performed by an automatic system that does not know which parts of information are still important for the user. It will treat as garbage only the fragments already inaccessible to the running program.

There are basically three different methods of garbage collection, and many variations of these methods. An overview of the methods follows.

Mark and scan

When the store is already completely filled up with graphs and a need arises to allocate a new node, then the normal operation of the system is interrupted for garbage collection. Only after completing this phase will the system resume its tasks.

The graph at this point is presumably quite entangled and has a number of *entrance points*. These entrance points are pointers from the host program, such as the root of the expression to be evaluated, entries in the library of function names, or entries in the program stack. The *mark* phase of garbage collection consists of going through all possible paths in the graph, that start from either entry point, and marking all nodes in the path[2]. Nodes have a special bit reserved for this marking.

After all accessible nodes in the graph have been marked, the *scan* phase follows. The memory is searched linearly (by physical addresses) and all unmarked nodes are collected as garbage, i.e. put on a special list of available locations. At the same time the marked nodes become unmarked. Then the normal operation of the system is resumed.

There are two main drawbacks of this method. One is the *memory fragmentation*. After several rounds of allocating and garbage collecting nodes of varying sizes, the available space tends to be scattered in many, physically separated, small sections. It may then happen that a new node cannot be allocated because it is too large for any single section even though the total free storage is large enough. Therefore, this garbage collection method can only be used with implementations in which all nodes are of equal size.

The second disadvantage is the requirement that the normal operation of the system be stopped for garbage collectioon. This precludes any real time applications. Imagine, for instance, the behaviour of a robot driven by an applicative program with the mark and scan algorithm. It would periodically freeze for garbage collection, while events would still happen in the real world, that require its response.

Copying and compacting

This is *the* method used in the running implementations of Standard ML.

The available store is divided into two halves of which one is active and the other is idle. The active half is in turn divided into the occupied region and the free region — both regions are contiguous parts of memory. Every new node is allocated at the beginning of the free region until there is no more place. At this point the normal operation of the system is stopped and the garbage collector takes over. It follows all accessible paths in the graph, as in the mark and scan algorithm, but instead of marking the nodes it rewrites them to the idle half of the store. Of course, the garbage is not rewritten, thus the whole process results in the whole graph being compacted into a contiguous region within the idle half, leaving another contiguous region for succeeding allocations. Now, the idle half becomes active and *vice versa*, and the operation of the system is resumed.

Unlike the mark and scan algorithm, *copying and compacting* does not suffer from memory fragmentation. But it shares with the latter the disadvantage of being inapplicable to real time operations.

At first sight it may seem that keeping 50% of memory permanently idle is a rather high cost to pay. But in large implementations of applicative languages one uses virtual memory anyway, so the fast storage will only be occupied by pages belonging to the active half.

---

[2]There is of course no need to traverse a shared subgraph more than once.

Reference counting

This requires a counter at every node that keeps track of the number of pointers to this node. Whenever a new node is allocated, it is made accessible to the system by a pointer, and its counter is set to 1. Any duplication of the pointer has to be accompanied by a stepping up of the counter; any redirection of the pointer and any killing of the pointer has to be accompanied by stepping down of the counter. When the value of the counter hits zero, the node is returned to the list of free locations and the counters of all nodes it points to are stepped down.

A great advantage of this method is that the cost of garbage collection is spread evenly over the life time of the system rather than being condensed in separate garbage collection phases. This makes the method eligible for real time applications. The reference counting algorithm suffers, however, from memory fragmentation.

It is also helpless with cyclic graphs, such as the one used in the preceding section to optimise recursion. It costs space to have an integer counter at every node. On the other hand, the method may be more time-efficient than the others, since it does not require that all accessible nodes of the graph be visited, but only the ones currently in use.

11.5   Exercises

Exercise 37

When performing the substitution of expressions for free variables in an expression, one faces the so called *name capturing* problem. For instance, the non-discriminating replacement of y+1 for x in fn(y)=>x results in fn(y)=>y+1 in which the free variable y from y+1 has been "captured" by the accidental coincidence with the variable under the binding operator fn(y). For most applications this method of substituting is wrong; such collisions of identifiers should be avoided by renaming bound variables before substituting. In our case y in fn(y)=>x should be renamed to, say, y' resulting in fn(y')=>y+1 which leaves y free.

Design a Standard ML function that performs substitution with appropriate renaming. Assume expressions are defined by

```
type vars = string ;
datatype expr = var of vars ;
              | app of expr*expr
              | fnc of vars*expr
```

and fnc(...,...) is the variable binding operator. Make the definition economic in the sense that it make as few renamings as possible.

Exercise 38

Design a Pascal definition of expressions, that corresponds to the definition of **expr** in Ex.37. Of course, this definition has to use explicit pointers. Define constructors **var**, **app** and **fnc** (**var** has to be given a different name).

Exercise 39

While implementing tree reduction a need often arises to traverse a tree. For instance, when performing a β-reduction one has to find *all* free occurrences of a certain variable in an expression. For the sake of space efficiency it is advantageous to perform such tree traversal non-recursively.

Design a non-recursive Pascal function that would count the number of leaves in a binary tree corresponding to the following Standard ML data type:

```
datatype tree = leaf on real
              | fork of tree*tree
```

You may need to introduce a special tag in every **fork**-node to assist tree traversal.

Chapter 12

Compilation

One way to speed up the evaluation of an expression in an applicative language is to precede the evaluation phase by translating the expression into a more machine oriented language. In most cases the expression involves recursion, by which some parts of it are evaluated many times. These parts are translated only once; therefore, the gain of their running faster is likely to offset the cost of translation.

Typically, expressions are translated to programs of an *abstract machine* rather than directly to the machine code of some VAX or SUN. This intermediate step contributes to the ease of implementation and to the portability of the resulting compilers. The program for the abstract machine is then either interpreted, or translated to a program of a true computer.

The abstract machine described below is a distant relative of the so called SECD-machine, the acronym standing for Stack-Environment-Control-Dump. The machine presented below is not nearly as efficient as the original SECD, since it involves many high order features, but for the same reason its operation should be easier to understand.

12.1 Required properties of the compiled code

In Chapter 11 the evaluator

$$\texttt{eval} : \texttt{expr} \to \texttt{cons}$$

was defined. In this chapter the reader will find the definitions of a compiler

$$\texttt{compile} : \texttt{expr} \to \texttt{program}$$

and of a program executor

$$\texttt{run} : \ldots \times \texttt{program} \to \texttt{cons}$$

the dots stand for configurations of the abstract machine, yet to be defined. The basic property that one has to keep in mind while designing these two functions is

$$\text{eval}(\text{ex}) = \text{run}(\dots, \text{compile}(\text{ex}))$$

(the dots now stand for the initial configuration), i.e. the value assigned to an expression by the interpreter must be equal to the value assigned by the executor to the code corresponding to that expression.

When the code corresponding to a certain expression is executed, the net effect of this execution is to add the value of the expression to the *stack of arguments* of the abstract machine. If cd1 and cd2 are codes corresponding respectively to expressions ex1 and ex2, then the concatenation cd1@cd2 (codes are lists of commands and thus may be concatenated) causes both the values of ex1 and ex2 to be added to the stack. An obvious translation of, say, app(ex2,ex1) (application of ex2 to ex1) is therefore

    cd1@cd2@cd

where cd accounts for the general function application; i.e. it causes the replacement of the two top stack values c_2 and c_1 by the value $c_2(c_1)$. Our compiler is *referentially transparent*, which means it translates syntactic components of expressions independently of each other and then puts together the resulting pieces of code without further changes[1].

This means that expressions denoting functions must also have values that may be put on the stack. It is therefore important to understand precisely what objects representable in the abstract machine are values of functions.

The most obvious choice for the storable value of a function would be the address of the subprogram that corresponds to this function, but, unfortunately, during the translation process one may encounter functions that may not be assigned subprograms. Consider the expression

    fn(x)=> fn(y)=> x

In order that the compiler be referentially transparent, it must put together the code for this expression from the codes of its components; thus it first has to translate

    fn(y)=> x

However, since this subexpression is not closed, i.e. it has a free variable, it has no unique value, and may not be assigned a unique subprogram.

As storable values of function expressions serve so called *closures*, i.e. pairs

(12.1) $\langle \text{lb}, env \rangle$

---

[1]In fact, this is not quite true. In Sec.12.4 the reader will find out that labels are generated in a way which is not quite referentially transparent.

where lb is an address (label) of a subprogram, and *env* is an *environment*, i.e. an assignment of values to variables:

    env : vars $\rightarrow$ args

In the above, args is the set of all possible storable values, i.e. constants and closures such as (12.1). Obviously, the definition of args has to be recursive, since it involves environments, which again involve args. Environments may be partial functions, but they have to be defined at least for any free variables of the subprogram they accompany in a closure.

12.2 An abstract stack machine

Our abstract machine has a *stack of arguments*, and a *stack of return labels*, and a stack of *environments*. Since, however, the stack of return labels has always the same depth as the stack of environments, we will glue these two stacks together into one stack of pairs consisting of a label and an environment. Besides these, the machine has space for a *program*, which consists of *commands*.

Arguments are defined as follows:

```
datatype args = arg1 of cons
              | arg2 of label*(vars->args);
type envir = vars -> args ;
```

This means the arguments of the first kind are constants, and the arguments of the second kind are closures. Constants and expressions are defined as in Sec.10.4. Labels are natural numbers.

In the presentation below stacks are always lists, but of course, in any true running compiler they can, and should, be implemented more efficiently.

The commands of the abstract machine are as follows:

```
datatype command =
    push of cons          — constant to stack
  | get of vars           — value of var under env to stack
  | closure of label      — label and env to stack
  | assign of vars        — update env with top of stack for var
  | lab of label          — label
  | jump of label         — unconditional jump
  | cjp of cons*label     — conditional jump
  | apply                 — activate the closure from stack
  | return                — return from subprogram
```

Command push(c) puts the argument arg1(c) at the top of the argument stack. Command get(v) does likewise with the value of v under the environment from the top of the other stack. We will refer to that environment as the *current* environment; analogously: the current argument and the current return label sit at the tops of respective stacks. Command closure(lb) forms a new closure argument out of two things: firstly, the label lb that it expects to denote a subprogram corresponding to some functional expression and secondly, the current environment; this argument is put at the top of the argument stack. Command assign(v) updates the current environment with the current argument for variable v while the current argument is removed from the stack. Command lab(n) does not perform any action, it simply serves as a place holder for use by control commands. Command jump(lb) searches the program for label lab(lb) and transmits control there. Command cjp(c,lb) executes the jump to lab(lb) if the top of the current argument is c; whether or not the jump is effective, the current argument is removed from the stack. In a correct program command apply is always followed by a lab(lb) and it expects to find a closure ⟨lb', *env*⟩ on the argument stack. Its effect is than to remove the closure from the argument stack, to store the pair ⟨lb, *env*⟩ on the stack of return labels, and to jump to the label lb'; in other words, to activate the subprogram from the top of the argument stack with the proper environment. Command return removes the top pair ⟨lb, *env*⟩ from the stack of return labels and jumps to lb. This means resuming the operation of the host program.

For a simple illustration of the operations that the machine may perform, consider the following expression:

```
(fn(x)=> fn(y)=> x) 22 33
```

This may be translated to the following code of the abstract machine:

```
lab(3)           — Subprogram fn(y)=>...
assign(y)
get(x)
return
lab(0)           — Subprogram fn(x)=>...
assign(x)
closure(3)
return

push(33)         — Starting point of the execution
push(22)
closure(0)
apply lab(1)
apply lab(2)
```

The first three commands of the main program cause the three arguments to be put on the stack: numbers 33 and 22 and the closure ⟨0, *env₀*⟩, where *env₀* is the empty environment. The stacks of arguments and of return labels now look as follows:

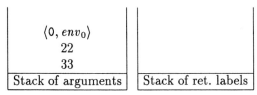

$\langle 0, env_0 \rangle$	
22	
33	
Stack of arguments	Stack of ret. labels

The first `apply` executes the program from the top of the stack, i.e. the one under label 0. The command removes the top argument from the stack, places the return label 1 and the environment env_0 on the stack of return labels, resulting in the following configuration of the machine:

22	
33	$\langle 1, env_0 \rangle$
Stack of arguments	Stack of ret. labels

and jumps to subprogram 0. Now, the current argument 22 is assigned to x in the current environment:

and jumps to subprogram 0. Now, the current argument 22 is assigned to x in the current environment:

Next, the new closure with label 3 (meaning the function `fn(y)=>...`) is put on the stack, and the subprogram is exited back to label 1:

The reader should convince himself, that the first `apply` has returned the functional value of `fn(x)=> fn(y)=> x` applied to 22, i.e. `fn(y)=> 22`. In the same way, the second `apply` will return this last value applied to 33.

12.3   Standard ML executor for the abstract machine

The informal explanation of commands of the abstract machine given in Sec.12.2 can be made quite formal by presenting a Standard ML program that would simulate the behaviour of the machine. First, define the *configuration* of the machine as consisting of two stacks and a program:

```
type argstack = (args)list ;
type rlbstack = (label*envir)list ;
type prog = (command)list * (command)list ;
type config = argstack * rlbstack * prog ;
```

The two components of prog correspond to the list of commands that have
already been executed and the list of commands still to come. The operation
of the abstract machine is given by the function

```
run : config -> args
```

defined below, after the definition of an auxiliary function:

```
fun find(lb)(cd',cd'') =
  let fun f(lb)(cd',[]) = raise nonexistent_lab
        | f(lb)(cd',cmd::cd'') =
            if cmd=lab(lb)
            then (cd'@[cmd],cd'')
            else f(lb)(cd'@[cmd],cd'')
  in f(lb)([],cd'@cd'')
  end ;
```

Function find will be used to find a label in a program.

The interpreter run of the abstract machine is defined as follows:

```
fun run([a] , [] , (cd',[])) = a
  | ...
```

This is the proper termination of the program: there are no more commands
to execute, an empty stack of return labels and on the argument stack a single
argument which is the result of the whole evaluation.

```
  | run(ast , rst , (cd',push(c)::cd'')) =
      run(arg1(c)::ast , rst , (cd'@[push(c)],cd''))
  | ...
```

This puts a constant on the top of the stack, and the command joins the list
of commands that have already been executed.

```
  | run(ast , (lb,env)::rst , (cd',get(v)::cd'')) =
      run(env(v)::ast, (lb,env)::rst, (cd'@[get(v)],cd''))
  | ...
```

The value of variable v under the current environment env goes to the stack.

```
| run(ast , rst , (cd',closure(lb)::cd'')) =
    (case rst of
       [] => run(arg2(lb,env0)::ast ,
                 rst ,
                 (cd'@[closure(lb)],cd'')
                 )
     | (lb',env)::rst' => run(arg2(lb,env)::ast ,
                             rst ,
                             (cd'@[closure(lb)],cd'')
    )                        )
  | ...
```

The closure consisting of label lb and the current environment goes to the
stack. The env0 above is the empty environment.

```
| run(a::ast , (lb,env)::rst , (cd',assign(v)::cd'')) =
    run(ast,(lb,upd(a,v)env)::rst,(cd'@[assign(v)],cd''))
  | ...
```

The current environment is updated with the current argument for v. Note
that the current argument is removed from the stack.

```
| run(ast , rst , (cd',lab(lb)::cd'')) =
    run(ast , rst , (cd'@[lab(lb)],cd''))
| run(ast , rst , (cd',jump(lb)::cd'')) =
    run(ast , rst , find(lb)(cd',jump(lb)::cd''))
| run(arg1(c1)::ast , rst , (cd',cjp(c2,lb)::cd'')) =
    if c1=c2
    then run(ast , rst , find(lb)(cd',cjp(c2,lb)::cd''))
    else run(ast , rst , (cd'@[cjp(c2,lb)],cd''))
  | ...
```

These are the label and the jumps. Note the way find is used to perform a
jump. Note also that the conditional jump removes the discriminating constant from the stack.

```
| run(arg2(lb1,env)::ast , rst ,
      (cd',apply::lab(lb2)::cd'')
      ) =
    run(ast ,
        (lb2,env)::rst ,
        find(lb1)(cd'@[apply],lab(lb2)::cd'')
        )
| run(ast , (lb,env)::rst , (cd',return::cd'')) =
    run(ast , rst , find(lb)(cd',return::cd''))
  | ...
```

These are the entrance to a subprogram and the return from a subprogram.
This works correctly only if the current argument is a closure because functions only may be applied. But another case where an application should also
work correctly is when the current argument is a constant denoting a built-in
function. This is taken care of below:

```
| run(arg1(c)::arg1(c1)::arg1(c2)::ast ,
     rst ,
     (cd',apply::lab(lb1)::apply::lab(lb2)::cd'')
   ) =
  (case c of
     ortest =>
       let val c' = case (c1,c2) of
                       (no,no) => no
                     | _ => yes
       in
        run(arg1(c')::ast ,
            rst ,
            (cd'@[apply,lab(lb1),apply,lab(lb2)],cd'')
           )
       end
   | eq =>
       let val c' = if c1=c2
                    then yes
                    else no
       in
        run(arg1(c')::ast ,
            rst ,
            (cd'@[apply,lab(lb1),apply,lab(lb2)],cd'')
           )
       end
   | add =>
       let val c' =
         case (c1,c2) of
           (numb(n1),numb(n2)) => numb(n1+n2)
         | _ => raise wrong_arithm_args
       in
        run(arg1(c')::ast ,
            rst ,
            (cd'@[apply,lab(lb1),apply,lab(lb2)],cd'')
           )
       end
   | ...
```

```
                      )
```

Note that a 2-argument function, such as ortest, eq and add above, needs two apply-s. The list of built-in constants may, of course, be arbitrarily extended.

12.4 Code generation for the abstract machine

The compiler is defined by

```
fun compile(ex) =
  let fun cp(ex)(cd',cd'',lb) =
        . . .
  in let val (cd',cd'',lb) = cp(ex)([],[],0)
     in (cd',cd'')
     end
  end ;
```

with the auxiliary function

```
cp : expr ->
        (command)list*(command)list*label ->
        (command)list*(command)list*label
```

still to be defined. Function cp is supposed to take an expression, a program (pair of command lists) and the least label which has not been used so far; its result is supposed to be a new program which consists of the old one updated by the piece taken from the expression and the new least label which has not been used. Function compile, given an expression, produces a program.

When defining cp(ex) for any particular expression ex, one has to produce both the running code corresponding to ex and the subprograms that this compilation may generate. The subprograms are concatenated to the first command list in the program, and the running code to the second.

Here follows the definition of cp:

```
fun cp(vex(v))(cd',cd'',lb) =
        (cd' , cd'' @ [get(v)] , lb)
  | cp(cex(c))(cd',cd'',lb) =
        (cd' , cd'' @ [push(c)] , lb)
  | ...
```

Simple expressions, i.e. variables and constants, generate respectively push and get commands. This is in line with our conventions, since the execution of such a command puts on the stack the value of the variable under a current environment or the constant.

```
| cp(fnc(v,ex))(cd',cd'',lb) =
    let val (cd1',cd1'',lb1) = cp(ex)(cd',[],lb+1)
    in (cd1' @ [lab(lb),assign(v)] @ cd1'' @ [return] ,
        cd'' @ [closure(lb)] ,
        lb1
        )
    end
| ...
```

Functional abstraction is translated in the way hinted at in the simple example ending Sec.12.2. The running code consists only of the `closure` command which puts on the stack the closure which makes the value of `fnc(v,ex)`; to make this statement true it must also generate a subprogram corresponding to this function. Such a subprogram begins with the `assign` command that initialises the function's parameter `v` in the current environment with the current stack argument; it ends with the `return` command and its body is the running code of `ex`. Note the binding role of the label `lb` and the need to generate a new least unused label `lb+1`.

```
| cp(app(app(app(cex(iftest),ex1),ex2),ex3))
      (cd',cd'',lb) =
    let val (cd1',cd1'',lb1) = cp(ex1)(cd',[],lb+2)
    in let val (cd2',cd2'',lb2) = cp(ex2)(cd1',[],lb1)
       in let val (cd3',cd3'',lb3) =
              cp(ex3)(cd2',[],lb2)
          in (cd3' ,
              cd'' @
                cd1'' @ [cjp(no,lb)] @
                cd2'' @ [jump(lb+1)] @
                lab(lb)] @ cd3'' @
                [lab(lb+1)] ,
              lb3
              )
          end
       end
    end
| ...
```

A conditional expression is translated using the usual conditional and unconditional jump to go around the then or around the else case, depending on the value of the if expression.

```
| cp(app(cex(fix),fnc(v,ex)))(cd',cd'',lb) =
    let val (cd1',cd1'',lb1) = cp(ex)(cd',[],lb+2)
```

```
        in (cd1' @ [lab(lb),closure(lb),assign(v)] @ cd1'' @
                    [apply,lab(lb+1),return] ,
            cd'' @ [closure(lb)] ,
            lb1
            )
    end
| ...
```

The fixpoint operator is responsible for recursion. Expression

```
app(cex(fix),fnc(v,ex))
```

means something like

```
let fun v(x) = ex(x)
in v
end
```

i.e. v is the recursively defined function. Its corresponding subprogram must first bind its name v to the closure which makes its value: this is done by commands

```
[closure(lb),assign(v)]
```

Executing the function v is now equivalent to executing its body ex; the translation of ex follows on from this. If the subprogram has been entered at all, then the corresponding function has to be applied to the current stack argument; instead our translation applies the equivalent ex.

```
| cp(app(ex2,ex1))(cd',cd'',lb) =
    let val (cd1',cd1'',lb1) = cp(ex1)(cd',[],lb+1)
    in let val (cd2',cd2'',lb2) = cp(ex2)(cd1',[],lb1)
        in (cd2' ,
            cd'' @ cd1'' @ cd2'' @ [apply,lab(lb)] ,
            lb2
            )
        end
    end
```

This last case is the translation of the general function aplication. It consists of the code to compute the argument, the code to compute the function and the apply command.

12.5   Making it less abstract

The Standard ML code given in this chapter has been tested to yield correct translations, and to execute them correctly. The reader may, however, consider the exercise useless, since it relies on powerful means available in Standard ML and not directly available on anything that approaches real computers. Recall the very high order and recursive definition of the type of arguments in Sec.12.2.

It would run against the spirit of this book, to go into the actual implementation details of existing compilers of functional languages for existing computers. But a number of points should be clarified.

It is easy to note that environments are never defined by functional abstraction: the process starts with the empty environment env0 and then follows a finite number of updates. Therefore, the full force of Standard ML functions is not really required to handle environments properly; and the operations on environments need not be high-order.

The simplest way of implementing any partial functions with finite domains, such as our environments, is by *association lists* — lists of argument-value pairs. On the other hand, there is no need for variables to be true strings; during the lexical analysis of input they may be translated to natural numbers. This enables the next simplification: every association list

          [(1,arg1),(2,arg2),...,(n,argn)]

may be simplified to

          [arg1,arg2,...,argn]

at the small cost of keeping the lists properly ordered. There are also better techniques.

Type recursion can be rendered by pointers. A closure consists then of a label and a pointer to an association list. The elements of such a list, the arguments, are either constants or closures, so again these are label-pointer pairs.

There is no reason to create an entirely new environment with every **assign**. The algorithm that builds environments is non-destructive, hence substructures may be safely shared.

And of course true stacks are more efficient than lists.

12.6   Exercises

Exercise 40

Give a Standard ML definition of the operation of the machine, the architecture of which is described below.

The machine has a memory of n *cells* numbered from 0 to n − 1; these numbers are referred to as the *addresses* of the cells. Each cell can hold a natural number ranging from 0 to k − 1 (assume k is even); these numbers are referred to as *values*. The machine also has the following special registers that contain values from the following ranges:

Acc — accumulator, from 0 to k − 1
PC   — program counter, from 0 to n − 1
Z   — zero test, either true or false
N   — negative test, either true or false

The next command to be executed is the one whose address is stored in PC. Unless it is a jump or a halt, upon completion of its execution the value of PC is stepped up modulo n, i.e. after n − 1 comes again 0. The commands are as follows (v is a value, a is an adress):

LDC v — load v to Acc
LD a   — load the contents of a-th cell to Acc
ST a   — store the contents of Acc to a-th cell
ADD a — add to Acc the contents of a-th cell modulo k
SBT a — subtract from Acc the contents of a-th cell modulo k
JMP a — jump to address a
JPZ a — jump to address a if Z is true
JPN a — jump to address a if N is true
STOP   — halt the operation of the machine

A side effect of the arithmetic commands ADD and SBT is to set the test registers Z and N to logical values of $(r = 0)$ and $(r \geq \frac{k}{2})$ respectively, where r is the result of the operation (in the completion arithmetic the natural numbers greater or equal to the half of the range count as negative integers).

Exercise 41

Assume the expressions of our functional language may involve, besides the usual variables, constants, abstractions and applications, also case expressions:

```
datatype exprs = ...
               | cas of exprs * (cons*exprs)list * exprs
               | ...
```

Informally, cas(ex,[(c1,ex1),...,(cn,exn)],ex0) stands for

```
case ex of
  c1 => ex1
    ...
| cn => exn
| _ => ex0
```

Extend the definition of the compiler function cp to handle this case also:

```
   ...
| cp(cas(ex,cexlis,ex0))(cd',cd'',lb) = ...
   ...
```

Part IV

Appendices

Appendix A

Solutions of exercises

A.1 Applicative vs. imperative programming

Exercise 1

Operations `div 10` and `mod 10` may be used to chop off the last digit of a natural number. This last digit is to become the first digit of the result. The function **rev** below is defined using an auxiliary function **rev'** with two arguments n and k; its value is the natural number obtained by attaching the digits of its first argument in the reverse order to the "tail" of its second argument; for instance,

```
rev'(123,45) = 45321
```

(leading 0-s of the first argument are disregarded).

```
- fun rev(n) =
    let fun rev'(n,k) =
            if n=0 then k
            else rev'(n div 10 , k * 10 + n mod 10)
    in rev'(n,0)
    end ;
> val rev = fn : int -> int
- rev(1988);
> 8891 : int
- rev(1000);
> 1 : int
```

Exercise 2

The precision requirement (1.1) is met by any number $\frac{n}{2^k}$ for c such that

$$a^{\frac{n}{2^k}} \leq b < a^{\frac{n+1}{2^k}} \;\&\; \frac{1}{2^k} < \varepsilon$$

or equivalently

$$a^n \le b^{2^k} < a^{n+1} \& \frac{1}{2^k} < \varepsilon$$

which is further equivalent to

$$(A.1) \quad x = a^n \ \& \ y = b^{2^k} \ \& \ \frac{1}{2^k} < \varepsilon \ \& \ x \le y < x \cdot a$$

If for the time being we drop the requirement that $\frac{1}{2^k} < \varepsilon$ then (A.1) may be met by $k = 0$ and $(n, x, y) = \mathtt{rlg}(a, b)$ where $\mathtt{rlg}$ is the "rough" logarithm given by:

```
fun rlg(a,b) =
  if 1.0<=b andalso b<a then (0.0, 1.0, b)
  else if b<1.0 then
          let (n,x,y)=rlg(a,a*b)
          in (n-1.0,x/a,y/a)
          end
       else
          let (n,x,y)=rlg(a,a/b)
          in (n+1.0,x*a,y*a)
          end ;
```

Condition (A.1) is equivalent to

$$(A.2) \quad x^2 = a^{2 \cdot n} \ \& \ y^2 = b^{2^{k+1}} \ \& \ \frac{1}{2^{k+1}} < \frac{\varepsilon}{2} \ \& \ x^2 \le y^2 < x^2 \cdot a \cdot a$$

which provides a way of increasing the accuracy of our logarithm:

```
fun lg(a,b,eps) =
  let fun lg'(n,x,y,eps') =
          if eps'<=eps then n*eps'
          else let val x = x*x
                   and y = y*y
                   and n = n+n
               in if y<x*a then lg'(n,x,y,eps'/2.0)
                  else lg'(n+1.0,x*a,y,eps'/2.0)
               end
  in let val (n,x,y) = rlg(a,b)
     in lg'(n,x,y,1.0)
     end
  end
```

A.2   The art of applicative programming

Exercise 3

```
f(2) =
= f(1)+g(1,1) =
= f(0)+g(0,0)+g(1,1) =
= 1+g(0,0)+g(1,1) =
= 1+g(1,1) =
= 1+f(1)+g(1,0) =
= 1+f(0)+g(0,0)+g(1,0) =
= 2+g(0,0)+g(1,0) =
= 2+g(1,0) =
= 2
```

Exercise 4

Eager:

```
apply(ident,raise wrong) =
```

(first evaluate the arguments, the second argument raises the exception **wrong** which is not handled anywhere in the expression)

```
= Failure: wrong
```

Lazy:

```
apply(ident,raise wrong)  =
```

(replace the function **apply**)

```
=  ident(raise wrong)  =
```

(replace the function **ident**)

```
=  raise wrong
      handle wrong =>
   raise right         =
```

(the exception is handled)

```
=  Failure: right
```

Exercise 5

The command

```
repeat c until b
```

is the same as

```
c; while ¬b do c
```

Therefore, in force of Theorem 1 from Sec.2.2, the required counterpart of the
repeat-loop is:

```
fun repeat(x) =
  let fun loop(y) =
          if b(y) then y
          else loop(g(y))
  in h(repeat(g(f(x))))
  end ;
```

Exercise 6

```
fun bubblesort(a,n) =
  let fun bubble(a,i) =
          if i=0 then a
          else let val a' =
                      if a(i)>a(i+1) then swap(a,j,j+1)
                      else a
               in bubble(a',i-1)
               end
  in if n=1 then a
     else bubblesort(bubble(a,n),n-1) ;
  end ;
```

A.3 Proving properties of recursive functions

Exercise 7

Once it is proved that $P(l)$ holds for any $l \in Nat$, $P(n + 1)$ may be
instantiated with n for n, 0 for 0, 0 for k, 0 for a and 1 for b to get

$$n - 0 < n + 1 \ \& \ 0 = 0^2 \ \& \ 1 = 2 \cdot 0 + 1 \ \& \ 0 \geq 0 \ \& \ 0 \leq \sqrt{n} + 1 \Rightarrow$$
$$g(n,0,0,1) \leq \sqrt{n} < g(n,0,0,1) + 1$$

and this is equivalent to the hypothesis (3.27).

Assume

(A.3) $\forall_{l' \in Nat}\ l' < l \Rightarrow P(l')$

and infer $P(l)$. Let n, k, a and b be natural numbers that satisfy

(A.4) $n - a < l$

(A.5) $a = k^2$

(A.6) $b = 2 \cdot k + 1$

(A.7) $k \geq 0$

(A.8) $k \leq \sqrt{n} + 1$

CASE $a > n$:
Then $g(n, k, a, b) = k - 1 \leq \sqrt{n}$ (the inequality follows from (A.8)); on the other hand, in the presence of (A.5) the entrance condition to this case implies $k^2 > n$ which by (A.7) is equivalent to $\sqrt{n} < k = g(n, k, a, b) + 1$, which proves $P(l)$.

CASE $a \leq n$:
Since

(A.9) $\begin{aligned} n - (a + b) =\ & \quad\quad \text{(by (A.6))} \\ n - a - 2 \cdot k - 1 \leq\ & \quad\quad \text{(by (A.7))} \\ n - a - 1 <\ & \quad\quad \text{(by (A.4))} \\ l - 1 \end{aligned}$

the "measure" $n - a$ of our problem decreases from the arguments of g to the arguments of its recursive call within the body of its definition. The instantiation of $P(l - 1)$, which is true by (A.3), with n for n, $k + 1$ for k, $a + b$ for a and $b + 2$ for b results in

(A.10) $\begin{aligned} & n - (a + b) < l - 1\ \& \\ & (a + b) = (k + 1)^2\ \& \\ & b + 2 = 2 \cdot (k + 1) + 1\ \& \\ & k + 1 \geq 0\ \& \\ & k + 1 \leq \sqrt{n} + 1\ \Longrightarrow \\ & g(n, k + 1, a + b, b + 2) \leq \sqrt{n} < g(n, k + 1, a + b, b + 2) + 1 \end{aligned}$

and the precedent of this implication is satisfied, because:

$$n - (a + b) < l - 1 \qquad \qquad \text{(by (A.9))}$$
$$a + b = k^2 + 2 \cdot k + 1 = (k + 1)^2 \qquad \text{(by (A.5) and (A.6))}$$
$$b + 2 = 2 \cdot k + 1 + 2 = 2 \cdot (k + 1) + 1 \quad \text{(by (A.6))}$$
$$k + 1 \geq 0 \qquad \qquad \text{(obvious)}$$
$$k + 1 = \sqrt{a} + 1 \leq \sqrt{n} + 1 \qquad \text{(by (A.5) and by the entrance}$$
$$\text{condition for this case)}$$

Therefore, the consequent of the implication (A.10) is also satisfied, hence

$$g(n, k, a, b) = g(n, k + 1, a + b, b + 2) \leq$$
$$\sqrt{n} <$$
$$g(n, k + 1, a + b, b + 2) < g(n, k, a, b) + 1$$

Exercise 8

The definition should look analogously:

```
fun f(n)=
  let fun g(n,k,a,...) =
    if a>n then k-1
    else g(n,k+1,...)
  in g(n,0,...)
  end
```

and one has to find a way of filling the dots with appropriate auxiliary variables.

In Exercise 7 a was the square of k; this time we want it to be k^3. Therefore, upon initialisation it should be 0, since k is then 0. The recursive call has to take $a + b$ for a corresponding argument, where b is the difference between $(k+1)^3$ and k^3, hence b has to be equal $(k+1)^3 - k^3 = 3 \cdot k^2 + 3 \cdot k + 1$, initially 1. The argument corresponding to b in the recursive call should be $b+c$ where c is the difference between $3 \cdot (k + 1)^2 + 3 \cdot (k + 1) + 1$ and $3 \cdot k^2 + 3 \cdot k + 1$, i.e. it has to be $6 \cdot k + 6$, initially 6. Finally, c increases by 6 with every call. Therefore, the function is:

```
fun f(n) =
  let fun g(n,k,a,b,c) =
    if a>n then k-1
    else g(n,k+1,a+b,b+c,c+6)
  in g(n,0,0,1,6)
  end
```

The inductive property:

$$P(l) \Longleftrightarrow$$
$$\forall_{n,k,a,b,c \in Nat}$$
$$n - a < l \ \& \ a = k^3 \ \& \ b = 3 \cdot k^2 + 3 \cdot k + 1 \ \&$$
$$c = 6 \cdot k + 6 \ \& \ k \geq 0 \ \& \ k \leq \sqrt[3]{n} + 1 \ \Rightarrow$$
$$g(n, k, a, b) \leq \sqrt[3]{n} < g(n, k, a, b) + 1$$

The proof is analogous to that in Exercise 7.

Exercise 9

The sequence will be represented as a function a from integer numbers to real numbers. The following function finds the maximal element of $a(1), a(2), \ldots, a(n)$:

```
fun m(a,n) =
    if n=1 then a(1)
    else let val r = m(a,n-1)
         in if r<a(n)
             then a(n)
             else r
         end ;
```

To prove this assume that for some natural n:

(A.11) $\forall_{k \in Nat} \ 1 \leq k < n \Rightarrow m(a, k) = max\{a(1), a(2), \ldots, a(k)\}$

where max of a finite non-empty set of reals is the largest element of this set.

CASE $n = 1$:
Then by the definition of m: $m(a, 1) = a(1)$; on the other hand: $max\{a(1)\} = a(1)$.

CASE $n > 1$:
When $n - 1$ is replaced in (A.11) for k, we get

$$1 \leq n - 1 < n \Rightarrow m(a, n - 1) = max\{a(1), a(2), \ldots, a(n - 1)\}$$

and the precedent of this implication is obviously satisfied, hence

$$m(a, n - 1) = max\{a(1), a(2), \ldots, a(n - 1)\}$$

Let $r = max\{a(1), a(2), \ldots, a(n - 1)\}$. This means that

- $r \in \{a(1), a(2), \ldots, a(n - 1)\}$

- $a(1) \leq r \ \& \ a(2) \leq r \ \& \ \ldots \ \& \ a(n - 1) \leq r$

SUBCASE $r < a(n)$:
Then

- $a(n) \in \{a(1), a(2), \ldots, a(n-1), a(n)\}$

- $a(1) \le r < a(n) \ \& \ \ldots \ \& \ a(n-1) \le r < a(n) \ \& \ a(n) \le a(n)$

hence $a(n) = max\{a(1), a(2), \ldots, a(n)\}$.
SUBCASE $r \ge a(n)$:
Then

- $a(n-1) \in \{a(1), a(2), \ldots, a(n-1), a(n)\}$

- $a(1) \le r \ \& \ a(2) \le r \ \& \ \ldots \ \& \ a(n-1) \le r \ \& \ a(n) \le r$

hence $a(r) = max\{a(1), a(2), \ldots, a(n)\}$.

Exercise 10
The picture suggests that the common part of the two subgroups is always
nonempty, which is actually not true for $n = 2$. The error results from lack
of care at start.

A.4 High order functions

Exercise 11
By *sequence* we will obviously mean a function from int to int. Therefore
we have to design a high order function

$$power : int \rightarrow (int \rightarrow int)$$
$$power(n)(k) \stackrel{def}{=} \text{maximal } i \text{ s.t. } k^i \mid n$$

hence the requirement that the function yield a sequence does not cause any
additional complications:

```
- fun power(n)(k) =
    if n mod k = 0 then power(n div k)(k) + 1
    else 0 ;
> val power = fn : int -> (int -> int)
- power(24)(2);
> 3 : int
- power(24)(3);
> 1 : int
- power(24)(4);
> 1 : int
```

Exercise 12
A continuous function that changes sign over an interval is guaranteed
to have a zero within this interval. Using the binary divisions we may select
shorter and shorter intervals which we know contain a zero, until the length
of intervals becomes less than ε:

```
fun solve(a,b,f,eps) =
  if b-a<eps then a
  else let val c=(a+b)/2
       in if f(c)=0.0 then c
          else if f(a)*f(b)<0.0
               then solve(a,c,f,eps)
               else solve(c,b,f,eps)
       end ;
```

Exercise 13

A sequence is of course a function from int to real. Let us start with a definition of a sequence updating function:

```
fun upd(x,n)seq =
  fn(n')=> if n'=n then x
           else seq(n') ;
```

The following function merges a sorted sequence seq1 of length n1 with a sorted sequence seq2 of length n2 into one sorted sequence of length n1 + n2. If one of the sequences is empty this comes down to returning the other sequence. Otherwise the last, i.e. the biggest elements of the two sequences are compared and the bigger, which is the maximal element of the whole set, is left aside; the recursive merge is applied to the two sequences without this maximal element, and then this element is added in the last (n1 + n2)-th position.

```
fun merge(seq1:int->real ,n1, seq2:int->real ,n2) =
  if n1=0 then seq2
  else if n2=0 then seq1
       else if seq1(n1)<seq2(n2)
            then let val seq = merge(seq1,n1,seq2,n2-1)
                 in upd(seq2(n2),n1+n2)seq
                 end
            else let val seq = merge(seq1,n1-1,seq2,n2)
                 in upd(seq1(n1),n1+n2)seq,
                 end ;
```

Note the explicit types int->real attached to the parameters seq1 and seq2 of merge. Without them, the type checker of the translator has no way of knowing whether the comparison < concerns integers or reals and it *must* know that. The programmer has to make this unambiguous; writing explicit types is one way of doing this.

Now, to sort a sequence, split it in two, shift the second half so that it too begins with the index 1, sort both halves and merge the results:

```
fun sort(seq,n) =
  if n<=1 then seq
  else let val k = n div 2  (* splitting  seq  in two *)
       in let val seq' =    (* shifting the second half *)
            fn(m)=> seq(m-k)
          in merge(sort(seq,k),k,sort(seq',n-k),n-k)
          end
       end ;
```

Exercise 14

Crossing a natural number out of a sequence may be programmed as
changing its original tag in the sequence from true to false:

```
- fun crossout(f,n:int) =
    fn k => if k=n then false
            else f(k) ;
> val crossout = fn : ((int -> bool) * int) -> (int ->
bool)
```

Note that the :int typing attribute has to accompany the function's argument n since otherwise the type-checker has no way of finding out the type
of crossout. The following function crosses out the multiples of p, i.e. the
numbers $i + j*p$ up to n, for all $j = 0, 1, 2, \ldots$:

```
- fun crossmult(f,p,i,n) =
    if i>n then f
    else crossmult(crossout(f,i),p,i+p,n) ;
> val crossmult = fn : ((int -> bool) * int * int * int)
-> (int -> bool)
```

The following function searches f for the least present (not crossed out) natural number above p:

```
- fun next(f,p) =
    if f(p) then p
    else next(f,p+1) ;
> val next = fn : ((int -> bool) * int) -> int
```

The following function performs Eratosthenes' algorithm on sequence f up to
natural n starting from prime p:

```
- fun sie(f,p,n) =
    if p>n then f
    else sie(crossmult(f,p,p+p,n),next(f,p+1),n) ;
> val sie = fn : ((int -> bool) * int * int) -> (int ->
bool)
```

The final sieve function is the following:

```
- fun sieve(n) =
    sie((fn k => true),2,n) ;
> val sieve = fn : int -> (int -> bool)
```

This is a small test of its operation:

```
- val f = sieve(10);
> val f = fn : int -> bool
- f(2);
> true : bool
- f(3);
> true : bool
- f(4);
> false : bool
- f(5);
> true : bool
- f(6);
> false : bool
- f(7);
> true : bool
- f(8);
> false : bool
- f(9);
> false : bool
- f(10);
> false : bool
```

Exercise 15

The fundamental operation for the Gaussian elimination algorithm is the addition of a multiple of a given row of the matrix to another row of the matrix:

```
- fun addrow(mat: int*int->real ,source,destin,factor) =
    fn (i,j) => if i=destin
                then mat(i,j)+factor*mat(source,j)
                else mat(i,j) ;
> val addrow = fn :
    (((int * int) -> real) * int * int * real) ->
    ((int * int) -> real)
```

Assuming $mat(i,i) \neq 0.0$ for a certain natural i, the elements $mat(j,i)$ for $i < j \leq n$ (i.e. the ones below the diagonal in the i-th column) may be made equal to 0.0 by adding the i-th row multiplied by $-\dfrac{\mathtt{mat(j,i)}}{\mathtt{mat(i,i)}}$ to each j-th row. The following function makes the elements of the i-th column below the diagonal down to n, equal to 0.0, assuming $\mathtt{mat(i,i)} \neq 0.0$:

```
- fun zerocol(mat: int*int->real ,i,n) =
    if n=i then mat
    else
      zerocol(addrow(mat,i,n,~(mat(n,i)/mat(i,i))),i,n-1);
> val zerocol = fn :
    (((int * int) -> real) * int * int) ->
    ((int * int) -> real)
```

Before the function zerocol may be applied we have to make sure that $\mathtt{mat(i,i)} \neq 0.0$. If it is not, a non-zero element in the i-th column has to be found and the appropriate rows swapped:

```
- fun zerocolumn(mat,i,n) =
    let fun swaprows(mat,k,l) =
          fn (i,j) => if i=k then mat(l,j)
                      else if i=l then mat(k,j)
                      else mat(i,j)
    in if n=i then mat
       else if mat(i,i)=0.0
            then zerocolumn(swaprows(mat,i,n),i,n-1)
            else zerocol(mat,i,n)
    end ;
> val zerocolumn = fn :
    (((int * int) -> real) * int * int) ->
    ((int * int) -> real)
```

In order to diagonalise a matrix up to size n apply the following function:

```
- fun diagonalise(mat,n) =
    let fun diag(mat,i,n) =
          if i>n then mat
          else diag(zerocolumn(mat,i,n),i+1,n)
    in diag(mat,1,n)
    end ;
> val diagonalise = fn :
    (((int * int) -> real) * int) ->
    ((int * int) -> real)

- fun mat0(i,j) =
    if i=0 then 1.0
```

```
              else real(j)*mat0(i-1,j) ;
> val mat0 = fn : (int * int) -> real

- val mat1 = diagonalise(mat0,3) ;
> val mat1 = fn : (int * int) -> real
```

The rows of the matrix mat1 may be displayed using the following function
that makes a list out of the i-th row up to the length n:

```
- fun seerow(mat: int*int->real ,i,n) =
    let fun see(mat,i,j,n) =
          if j>n then nil
          else mat(i,j)::see(mat,i,j+1,n)
    in see(mat,i,1,n)
    end ;
> val seerow = fn :
    (((int * int) -> real) * int * int) -> (real list)

- seerow(mat1,1,3) ;
> [1.0,2.0,3.0] : real list
- seerow(mat1,2,3) ;
> [0.0,2.0,6.0] : real list
- seerow(mat1,3,3) ;
> [0.0,0.0,6.0] : real list
```

A.5   Data types

Exercise 16

The type of binary trees of reals should be defined as follows:

```
datatype realtree = empty
                  | mktree of real * realtree * realtree ;
```

The following function insert inserts a single real number into an ordered
tree of reals preserving the order. The new element is compared with the root
of the tree and sent either to the left or to the right subtree depending on the
result of this comparison:

```
fun insert(x,empty) = mktree(x,empty,empty)
  | insert(x,mktree(root,left,right)) =
      if x<root
      then mktree(root,insert(x,left),right)
      else mktree(root,left,insert(x,right)) ;
```

Function `seqtotree` produces an ordered tree given a sequence. It does so by inserting one by one the elements of the sequence into the initially empty tree:

```
fun seqtotree([]) = empty
  | seqtotree(x::lis) = insert(x,seqtotree(lis)) ;
```

Once the tree is constructed the following function `treetoseq` traverses it and constructs a list of all real numbers sitting in the nodes of this tree (the auxiliary function `adjoin` could be avoided by making use of the Standard ML list concatenation operator `@`):

```
fun treetoseq(tree) =   (* inorder *)
  let  (* Auxiliary function that adjoins all the elements
          from its argument tree to the front of  lis  *)
      fun adjoin(empty,lis) = lis
        | adjoin(mktree(root,left,right),lis) =
            adjoin(left,(root::adjoin(right,lis)))
  in adjoin(tree,[])
  end ;
```

Finally, the two functions are put together to produce the list sorting function:

```
fun sort(lis) =
  treetoseq(seqtotree(lis)) ;
```

Exercise 17

One way is to define this tree as consisting of a person and a list (possibly empty) of the family trees of his sons:

```
type person = string * int * int ;
datatype family = genealogy of person * (family)list ;
```

The reason for using the `datatype` construct above is the presence of type recursion. To find the average length of life we need an auxiliary function that calculates the sum of the lengths of lives of the whole family, and the number of family members that are already dead; and another auxiliary function that does the same to a list of families:

```
fun sumandnumb(fam) =
  let fun sumandnumblist([]) = (0,0)
        | sumandnumblist(fam::lis) =
            let val (sum1,numb1) = sumandnumb(fam)
                and (sum2,numb2) = sumandnumblist(lis)
            in (sum1+sum2 , numb1+numb2)
            end
```

```
 in let val ((name,birth,death),sons) = fam
    in let val (sum,numb) = sumandnumblist(sons)
       in if death=0 then (sum,numb)
          else (sum+(death-birth),numb+1)
       end
    end
 end ;
fun average(fam) =
  let val (sum,numb) = sumandnumb(fam)
  in real(sum)/real(numb)
  end ;
```

A simpler solution may be obtained if one realises that the family tree is
just a binary tree of persons: move left to access the eldest son, and move
right to access the next younger brother. This results in the following code:

```
type person = string * int * int ;
datatype family = none
                  | mkfam of person * family * family ;
fun sumandnumb(none) = (0,0)
  | sumandnumb(mkfam((name,birth,death),sons,brothers)) =
      let val (sum1,numb1) = sumandnumb(sons)
          and (sum2,numb2) = sumandnumb(brothers)
      in if death=0 then (sum1+sum2,numb1+numb2)
         else ((death-birth)+sum1+sum2,1+numb1+numb2)
      end ;
fun average(fam) =
  let val (sum,numb) = sumandnumb(fam)
  in real(sum)/real(numb)
  end ;
```

Exercise 18
The definition of the tree is standard.

```
datatype realtree = empty
                  | mktree of real * realtree * realtree ;
```

Now the function:

```
fun isotree(empty,empty) = true
  | isotree(empty,mktree(root,left,right)) = false
  | isotree(mktree(root,left,right),empty) = false
  | isotree( mktree(root1,left1,right1) ,
             mktree(root2,left2,right2)
           ) =
```

```
(root1=root2) andalso
( ( isotree(left1,left2)
      andalso
    isotree(right1,right2)
  )
        orelse
  ( isotree(left1,right2)
      andalso
    isotree(right1,left2)
) ) ;
```

A.6 Polymorphism

Exercise 19

Lexicographic order for lists is defined using an order `comp` on single elements of lists:

```
fun lexic(comp)(empty,lis2) = true
  | lexic(comp)(a::lis1,empty) = false
  | lexic(comp)(a1::lis1,a2::lis2) =
      if a1=a2
      then lexic(comp)(lis1,lis2)
      else comp(a1,a2) ;
```

Function `lexic` has the polymorphic type

```
(''a*''a -> bool) -> (''a)list*(''a)list -> bool
```

and therefore it may be applied to the standard order on strings (i.e. the alphabetic order), and to the standard order on reals:

```
val f = lexic(fn(s1,s2:string)=> s1<=s2) ;
val g = lexic(fn(r1,r2:real)=> r1<=r2) ;
```

Exercise 20

The definition of polymorphic tree is standard:

```
datatype ('a)tree = empty
                  | node of 'a*('a)tree*('a)tree ;
```

The polymorphic function `maptree` is:

```
fun maptree(f)(empty) = empty
  | maptree(f)(node(a,left,right)) =
      node(f(a),maptree(f)(left),maptree(f)(right)) ;
```

By this definition the type of `maptree` is:

```
('a->'b) -> ('a)tree -> ('b)tree
```

Function `f` is defined using the auxiliary function `f'` that finds the sum of integers on a given list:

```
val f =
  let fun f'([]) = 0
        | f'(n::l) = n + f'(l)
  in maptree(f')
  end ;
```

Function `g` is defined using the auxiliary function `g'` that finds the list of digits of a natural number:

```
val g =
  let fun g'(n) =
        if n=0 then []
        else (n mod 10) :: g'(n div 10)
  in maptree(g')
  end ;
```

Exercise 21

A result of a dictionary query may be `no_entry`, where a given key is not assigned any entry; thus we have to enlarge the type `'c` of possible contents by this special symbol:

```
datatype ('c)entry = no_entry
                   | cont of 'c ;
```

(alternatively, we might use exception for `no_entry`). A dictionary is either empty, or it has a node and a function that assigns a new dictionary to any element of type `'a`:

```
datatype ('a,'c)dict =
    empty
  | node of ('c)entry * ('a -> ('a,'c)dict) ;
```

These are the access functions:

```
fun find(l,empty) = no_entry
  | find([],node(c,f)) = c
  | find(a::l,node(c,f)) = find(l,f(a)) ;

fun insert(([],c),empty) = node(cont(c), fn(a)=> empty)
  | insert((a::l,c),empty) =
```

```
      node(no_entry,
          fn(a')=> if a'=a
                   then insert((l,c),empty)
                   else empty
      )
 | insert(([],c),node(cc,f)) = node(cont(c),f)
 | insert((a::l,c),node(cc,f)) =
     node(cc,
         fn(a')=> if a'=a
                  then insert((l,c),f(a'))
                  else f(a')
     ) ;
```

These functions may now be used to create, for instance, a dictionary with strings of characters as keys and real numbers as contents:

```
- val d = empty ;
> val d = empty : ('a,'b) dict
- val d = insert((explode"cap",5.8),d) ;
> val d = node (no_entry,fn) : (string,real) dict
- val d = insert((explode"cab",~3.14),d) ;
> val d = node (no_entry,fn) : (string,real) dict
- val d = insert((explode"cop",0.0),d) ;
> val d = node (no_entry,fn) : (string,real) dict
- val d = insert((explode"cob",6.13),d) ;
> val d = node (no_entry,fn) : (string,real) dict
- val d = insert((explode"cup",~15.0),d) ;
> val d = node (no_entry,fn) : (string,real) dict
- val d = insert((explode"cub",8.7),d) ;
> val d = node (no_entry,fn) : (string,real) dict
- find(explode"cob",d) ;
> cont 6.13 : real entry
```

A.7   Recursors for data types

Exercise 22

```
fun polval(d,p,a) =
  let fun pv(v:real,i:int) = (p(i)+a*v,i-1)
  in let val (value,i) = iter d pv (p(d),d-1)
     in value
     end
  end
```

To make sure this is a good solution one has to prove by induction on k that

$$\text{iter } k \text{ pv } (p(d), d-1) = (\sum_{i=d-k}^{d} p(i) \cdot a^{i-d+k}, d - k - 1)$$

Indeed, for $k = 0$ both sides are equal to $(p(d), d-1)$. When $k+1$ is replaced for k then the left hand side becomes

$$\text{iter } (k+1) \text{ pv } (p(d), d-1) =$$
$$= \text{pv(iter } k \text{ pv } (p(d), d-1)) = \quad \text{(ind. assump.)}$$
$$= \text{pv}(\Sigma_{i=d-k}^{d} p(i) \cdot a^{i-d+k}, d-k-1) =$$
$$= (p(d-k-1) + a \cdot \Sigma_{i=d-k}^{d} p(i) \cdot a^{i-d+k}, d-k-2) =$$
$$= (\Sigma_{i=d-k-1}^{d} p(i) \cdot a^{i-d+k+1}, d-k-2) =$$
$$= (\Sigma_{i=d-(k+1)}^{d} p(i) \cdot a^{i-d+(k+1)}, d-(k+1)-1)$$

which is precisely the right hand side with $k+1$ replaced for k.

Exercise 23
The easiest way is first to turn the argument lists into functions using the following functional:

```
fun listtofun(lis) =
  let fun upd(value,arg) ff arg' =
          if arg'=arg then value
          else ff(arg')
      and shift(g)(n) = g(n-1)
  in itlist lis (fn(a,g)=>shift(upd(a,0)g)) (fn(k)=>0.0)
  end
```

and then to define the product function in the obvious way:

```
fun prodlis(lis1,lis2)(i,j) =
  listtofun(lis1)i * listtofun(lis2)j
```

Exercise 24
Function flat:

```
fun flat lislis =
  itlist lislis concat []
```

where concat is the function defined by (7.15).
Function split:

```
fun split lis =
  itlist lis
         (fn(a,(lis1,lis2)::pairlis)=>
            ( concat(lis1,[hd(lis2)]),tl(lis2)) ::
```

```
              (lis1,lis2) ::
              pairlis
          )
      [([],lis)]
```

Exercise 25

The following auxiliary function

```
insert1 : 'a → ('a)list → (('a)list)list
```

given an element a and a list lis inserts a into lis in all possible positions
and produces the list of resulting lists:

```
fun insert1 a lis =
  itlist
    (split lis)
    (fn((lis1,lis2),lislis)=>concat(lis1,a::lis2)::lislis)
    []
```

where concat is the function defined by (7.15) and split comes from Exercise 24. For instance,

```
insert1 0 [1,2,3] = [[1,2,3,0] ,
                     [1,2,0,3] ,
                     [1,0,2,3] ,
                     [0,1,2,3]
                    ]
```

The following auxiliary function

```
insert2 : 'a × (('a)list)list → (('a)list)list
```

given an element a and a list of lists lislis, inserts a into all possible positions
of all lists in lislis and produces the list of resulting lists:

```
fun insert2(a,lislis) =
  flat (map (insert1 a) lislis) ;
```

where map is the function defined by (7.16) and flat comes from Exercise 24.
For instance,

```
insert2(0,[[1],[2,3],[]]) = [[1,0] ,
                             [0,1] ,
                             [2,3,0] ,
                             [2,0,3] ,
                             [0,2,3] ,
                             [0]
                            ]
```

Finally, **permut** is defined as follows:

```
fun permut lis = itlist lis insert2 [[]]
```

For instance,

```
permut [1,2,3] = [[3,2,1] ,
                  [3,1,2] ,
                  [1,3,2] ,
                  [2,3,1] ,
                  [2,1,3] ,
                  [1,2,3]
                  ]
```

A.8 Standard ML structures and signatures

Exercise 26

The simplest (canonical) form of a fraction $\frac{n}{d}$ is characterised by

$$(n = 0 \ \& \ d = 1) \ \vee$$
$$(n \neq 0 \ \& \ d > 0 \ \& \ \gcd(n, d) = 1)$$

i.e. either the numerator is zero and then the denominator is one; or else the numerator is non-zero and then the denominator is positive and there are no common divisors of n and d greater than 1 ($\gcd$ is the greatest common divisor).

The following function brings a fraction to its canonical form:

```
fun simplify(n,d) =
  let fun gcd(a:int,b:int) =
    if a=b then a
    else if a<b then gcd(a,b-a)
         else gcd(a-b,b)
  in if d=0 then (* n/0 *) raise denominator_is_zero else
     if d<0 then (* n/~d1 *) simplify(~n,~d) else
     if n=0 then (* 0/d *) (0,1) else
     if n<0 then (* ~n1/d *)
       let val (n',d') = simplify(~n,d)
       in (~n',d')
       end
     else let val g = gcd(n,d)
          in (n div g , d div g)
          end
  end
```

According to the given signature, this function must not be one of the components of structure Rat. One way to hide it is to make its definition local:

```
structure Rat =
  struct
    type rat = int*int ;
    exception denominator_is_zero ;
    fun rat(n:int) = (n,1) ;
    local
      fun simplify(n,d) = ...
    in
      fun add((n1,d1):rat,(n2,d2):rat) =
        simplify (n1*d2+n2*d1 , d1*d2) ;
      fun dif((n1,d1):rat,(n2,d2):rat) =
        simplify (n1*d2-n2*d1 , d1*d2) ;
      fun mul((n1,d1):rat,(n2,d2):rat) =
        simplify (n1*n2 , d1*d2) ;
      fun dvs((n1,d1):rat,(n2,d2):rat) =
        simplify (n1*d2 , n2*d1)
      fun eq((n1,d1):rat,(n2,d2):rat) =
        (simplify(n1,d1) = simplify(n2,d2))
    end
  end
```

Another way to hide the function simplify is to make it one of the components of the structure and then to cut it off using signature RAT:

```
structure Rat : RAT  =
  struct
    type rat = int*int ;
    exception denominator_is_zero ;
    fun simplify(n,d) = ...
    fun rat... ;
    fun add... ;
    fun dif... ;
    fun mul... ;
    fun dvs... ;
    fun eq...
  end
```

Exercise 27

The most complicated part of this structure is the definition of the *argument* of a complex number, i.e. of the angle between the x-axis and the vector leading from the origin to this number. To find the argument we use

Standard ML's predefined function arctan that yields its values within the range $(-\frac{\pi}{2}, \frac{\pi}{2})$. The reader should verify that the function arg defined below properly calculates the argument of a given complex number (re, im) with the results in the range $\langle-\pi, \pi\rangle$. We will also need the function anglerange that brings any angle to this range.

```
val pi = 4.0 * arctan(1.0) ;
fun arg(re,im) =
  if re=0.0 then  (* y-axis *)
    if im=0.0 then  (* origin *)  0.0 else
    if im>0.0 then  (* upper half of y-axis *)  pi/2.0
    else (* lower half of y-axis *)  ~p/2.0
  else if re>0.0 then  (* right from y-axis *)
          arctan(im/re)  else
      if im>0.0 then  (* left-upper quarter *)
          arctan(im/re)+pi
      else  (* left-lower quarter *)
          arctan(im/re)-pi ;
fun anglerange(fi) =
  if fi < ~pi then anglerange(fi+2.0*pi)  else
  if fi < pi then fi
  else anglerange(fi-2.0*pi)
```

The definition of the structure Compl is as follows:

```
structure Compl =
  struct
    type cart =real*real ;
    type polar = real*real ;
    local
      val pi... ;
      fun arg... ;
      fun anglerange...
    in
      fun pcconv((r,fi):polar) = (r*cos(fi),r*sin(fi)) ;
      fun cpconv((re,im):cart) =
        (sqrt(re*re+im*im) , arg(re,im)) ;
      fun rcconv(r:real) = (r , 0.0) ;
      fun rpconv(r:real) =
        if r>=0.0 then (r , 0.0)
        else (~r , ~pi) ;
      val carti = (0.0 , 1.0) ;
      val polari = (1.0 , pi/2.0) ;
      fun cartadd((re1,im1):cart,(re2,im2):cart) =
```

```
          (re1+re2 , im1+im2) ;
        fun polaradd(x:polar,y:polar) =
          cpconv(cartadd(pcconv(x),pcconv(y))) ;
        fun cartsub((re1,im1):cart,(re2,im2):cart) =
          (re1-re2 , im1-im2) ;
        fun polarsub(x:polar,y:polar) =
          cpconv(cartsub(pcconv(x),pcconv(y))) ;
        fun polarmul((r1,fi1):polar,(r2,fi2):polar) =
          (r1*r2 , anglerange(fi1+fi2)) ;
        fun cartmul(x:cart,y:cart) =
          pcconv(polarmul(cpconv(x),cpconv(y))) ;
        fun polardiv((r1,fi1):polar,(r2,fi2):polar) =
          (r1/r2 , anglerange(fi1-fi2)) ;
        fun cartdiv(x:cart,y:cart) =
          pcconv(polardiv(cpconv(x),cpconv(y))) ;
        fun carteq(x:cart,y:cart) = (x=y) ;
        fun polareq((r1,fi1):polar,(r2,fi2):polar) =
          (r1=0.0 andalso r2=0.0) orelse (r1,fi1)=(r2,fi2)
    end
  end
```

Exercise 28

```
    signature VECSPACE =
      sig
        (* commutative group: *)
        type group ;
        val gradd : group * group -> group ;
        val grzero : group ;
        val grminus : group -> group ;
        (* field: *)
        type field ;
        val fiadd : field * field -> field ;
        val fizero : field ;
        val fiminus : field -> field ;
        val fimul : field * field -> field ;
        val fione : field ;
        val firev : field -> field ;
        (* operation of the field over the group: *)
        val extermul : field * group -> group
      end ;

    structure Euclid : VECSPACE =
```

```
struct
  type group = real * real * real ;
  fun gradd((x1,x2,x3):group,(y1,y2,y3):group) =
    (x1+y1 , x2+y2 , x3+y3) ;
  val grzero = (0.0 , 0.0 , 0.0) ;
  fun grminus((x1,x2,x3):group) = (~x1,~x2,~x3) ;
  type field = real ;
  fun fiadd(r1:field,r2:field) = r1+r2 ;
  val fizero = 0.0 ;
  fun fiminus(r:field) = ~r ;
  fun fimul(r1:field,r2:field) = r1*r2 ;
  val fione = 1.0 ;
  fun firev(r:field) = 1.0/r ;
  fun extermul(r:field,(x1,x2,x3):group) =
    (r*x1 , r*x2 , r*x3)
end
```

Exercise 29

In order to match a signature, a structure must have all the required components, and their types have to be *at least as general* as the ones in the signature. Signature AA requires from a structure a type aa and a value f, and Aa meets these requirements. The required type of f is supposed to be at least general as ('a)list -> ('a)list . Let us find the type of Aa.f:

```
map  : ('a->'b) -> (('a)list->('a)list)
fn(x)=> x+1  :  int -> int
```

(the ambiguity concerning the type of + is resolved by the occurrence of the integer 1)

```
f  :  (int)list -> (int)list
```

and this type is strictly less general than ('a)list -> ('a)list .

Exercise 30

The motion of a pencil when drawing a screw-line is the superposition of the motion that draws a circle, with the additional linear motion along the third coordinate:

$$screwline(t) = (r\cos(2\pi st), r\sin(2\pi st), qt)$$

where r is the required radius of the screw-line, s is the number of "loops" of the line that will show at the picture and q is the vertical size of the picture.

```
val pi = 4.0 * arctan(1.0) ;
val r = ... ;
```

```
val s = ... ;
val q = ... ;
fun screwline(t) =
  (r*cos(2.0*pi*s*t),r*sin(2.0*pi*s*t),q*t) ;
let open ThreeDim
in  drawcurve(screwline,emptyscreen)
end
```

To produce a ball, imagine the unit square as consisting of an infinite number of parallel horizontal intervals:

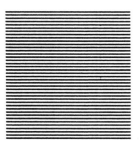

Each of these intervals may be transformed into a parallel of the sphere (the transformation going the other way is known as *Mercator's projection*). More precisely, the interval $\langle (0,y),(1,y) \rangle$ of the square is transformed into the parallel at height $h(y) = 2y - 1$; the radius of this parallel at height h is:

$$r(h) = \sqrt{R^2 - h^2} =$$
$$= \sqrt{R^2 - (2y-1)^2}$$

where R is the radius of the whole sphere. The parameterisation of the sphere is therefore:

$$sphere(x,y) = (\sqrt{R^2 - (2y-1)^2}\cos 2\pi x ,\ \sqrt{R^2 - (2y-1)^2}\sin 2\pi x ,\ y)$$

This suggests the following code in Standard ML:

```
val pi = 4.0 * arctan(1.0) ;
val R = ... ;
fun sphere(x,y) =
  let val r = sqrt(R*R-(2.0*y-1.0)*(2.0*y-1.0))
  in (r*cos(2.0*pi*x) , r*sin(2.0*pi*x) , y)
  end ;
let open ThreeDim
in drawsurface(sphere,emptyscreen)
end
```

A.9   Parametric structures: functors

Exercise 31

The **handle** clause in the body of the functor will not be activated by
the exception **empty_stack** raised by pop(st) because that exception is now
"shielded" by the newly declared exception of the same name, local to the
functor's body. Therefore, the error raised by pop(st) will go undetected
until the top level.

Skipping the local declaration of the exception within the body of functor
Parser will only result in making the error statically detectable: the type
checker will now be able to identify the unknown exception **empty_stack**.

A way out is to replace the **handle** clause so that it reads:

```
... pop(st) handle Stacks.empty_stack => ...
```

Exercise 32

Identifiers referred to in a signature have to be either locally declared
in this signature, or predefined in Standard ML (such as **bool** or **list**).
Signature CURVES refers to the non-local type **point**.

The solution is to declare type **point** within CURVES:

```
...
type curve
 and point ;
...
```

but then something within the definition of functor **Graphic** must ascertain
that the two **point**-types are identical. This may be achieved by the **sharing**
declaration within the parameters of the functor, but then **Plane** has to be
made one of the parameters:

```
signature PLANE =
  sig
    type point ;
    ...
  end ;
```

```
functor Graphic'(Curves:CURVES , Plane':PLANE
                sharing type Curves.point=Plane'.point) =
  struct
    fun draw(curv) = ... ;
    ...
  end ;
```

Finally, the old functor `Graphic` with only one parameter that matches `CURVES` may be defined as

```
functor Graphic(Curves:CURVES) =
  Graphic'(Curves,Plane) ;
```

This is clumsy, but I have no other idea.

Exercise 33

Let us start with a specification of the symbol table. This has to be a dictionary that translates strings of characters to identifiers (e.g. string `"x"` to identifier `x`), and identifiers to numbers:

```
signature SYMB_TAB =
  sig
    type iden     (* identifiers *)
     and symbols  (* dictionaries *) ;
    exception unknown_iden
      (* to be raised upon enquiry using  findstr
          about an unknown identifier *) ;
    val newsymbols : symbols ;
    val updstrsymb : symbols*iden*string -> symbols ;
    val findstr : symbols*string -> iden ;
    val updidsymb : symbols*int*iden -> symbols ;
    val findid : symbols*iden -> int
  end ;
```

The above signature serves as a specification for the programmer charged with the symbol table, and also as an interface between the symbol table and other program units.

The scanner has to divide the input string into lexical units (tokens); but whenever it encounters an identifier, it translates it to the internal form using the symbol table; and whenever it encounters a number, it yields an appropriate integer. Therefore, every scanning function takes in a string, and a dictionary, and yields the scanned lexical unit, the remaining portion of the input string, and the updated dictionary. It may also raise an exception if the input is empty, or if a wrong scanner function has been applied:

```
signature SCANNER =
  sig
    type iden
     and symbols ;
    exception empty_input
          and lex_error
          and unknown_iden ;
```

```
val cross : string*symbols -> unit*string*symbols ;
  (* if  str = "+"^str1  then
       cross(str,sym) = (() , str1 , sym)
     otherwise exception lex_error  *)
val star : string*symbols -> unit*string*symbols ;
  (* if  str = "*"^str1  then
       star(str,sym) = (() , str1 , sym)
     otherwise exception lex_error  *)
val lpar : string*symbols -> unit*string*symbols ;
  (* if  str = "("^str1  then
       lpar(str,sym) = (() , str1 , sym)
     otherwise exception lex_error  *)
val rpar : string*symbols -> unit*string*symbols ;
  (* if  str = ")"^str1  then
       rpar(str,sym) = (() , str1 , sym)
     otherwise exception lex_error  *)
val def : string*symbols -> unit*string*symbols ;
  (* if  str = "DEF"^str1  then
       def(str,sym) = (() , str1 , sym)
     otherwise exception lex_error  *)
val equ : string*symbols -> unit*string*symbols ;
  (* if  str = "="^str1  then
       equ(str,sym) = (() , str1 , sym)
     otherwise exception lex_error  *)
val ident : string*symbols -> iden*string*symbols ;
  (* if  str = str1^str2  where  str1  only consists
       of letters
     then  ident(str,sym) = (id1 , str2 , sym1)
     where  sym1  is the new symbol table after
     introducing  str1 , and  id1  is the
     corresponding internal representation
     otherwise exception lex_error  *)
val number : string*symbols -> int*string*symbols
  (* if  str = str1^str2  where  str1  only consists
       of digits
     then  number(str,sym) = (n , str2 , sym)
     where  n  is the numerical value of  str1
     otherwise exception lex_error  *)
end ;
```

The scanner itself is supposed to be a functor with the following heading:

```
functor Scanner(SymbTab:SYMB_TAB):SCANNER =
  struct
```

```
type iden = SymbTab.Iden
 and symbols = SymbTab.symbols ;
 exception unknown_iden = SymbTab.unknown_iden ;
 ...
end ;
```

The programmer in charge of the scanner gets this functor heading together
with signatures SYMB_TAB and SCANNER as the specification of his task.

The parser has to define the types corresponding to the non-terminals
of the grammar and also their respective selector functions; on top of this
it has to define peculiar constructors for the types corresponding to Expr
and Defn. The former constructor takes in an input string and a symbol
dictionary, and yields an expression, and the remaining portion of the input
string, and an updated dictionary; the latter constructor does the same to
definitions. Either constructor may raise the exception parse_error and also
any exceptions generated by the scanner; selectors may raise the exception
wrong_selector:

```
signature PARSER =
  sig
    type expr
    and summ
    and fact
    and defn
    and symbols ;
    exception empty_input
            and lex_error
            and parse_error
            and wrong_selector
            and unknown_iden ;
    (* Selectors: *)
    val exsumm : expr -> summ
    and explus : expr -> summ*expr
    and sumfc : summ -> fact
    and sumtim : summ -> fact*summ
    and fcnmb : fact -> int
    and fcid : fact -> iden
    and fcex : fact -> expr
    and df : defn -> iden*expr ;
    (* Constructors: *)
    val parsexpr : string*symbols -> expr*string*symbols
    and parsdefn : string*symbols -> defn*string*symbols
  end ;
```

The parser is intended as a functor with the following heading:

```
functor Parser(Scanner:SCANNER):PARSER =
  struct
    type iden = Scanner.iden
     and symbols = Scanner.symbols ;
    exception empty_input = Scanner.empty_input
          and lex_error = Scanner.lex_error
          and unknown_iden = Scanner.Unknown_iden ;
    ...
  end ;
```

Note that no explicit reference to the symbol table is necessary here. The programmer in charge of the parser gets this functor heading together with signatures SCANNER and PARSER as the specification of his task.

Finally, the evaluator has to define the function that evaluates an expression, and another function that elaborates an identifier definition:

```
signature EVALUATOR =
  sig
    type symbols ;
    exception empty_input
          and lex_error
          and parse_error
          and unknown_iden ;
    val evexpr : string*symbols -> int ;
    val evdefn : string*symbols -> symbols
  end ;


functor Evaluator(SymbTab:SYMB_TAB ,
                  Parser:PARSER
                    sharing type SymbTab.iden = Parser.iden
                        and type
                            SymbTab.symbols = Parser.symbols)
          : EVALUATOR  =
  struct
    type symbols = SymbTab.symbols ;
    exception empty_input = Parser.empty_input
          and lex_error = Parser.lex_error
          and parse_error = Parser.parse_error
          and unknown_iden = Parser.unknown_iden ;
    ...
  end ;
```

Once the project manager gets from his staff

- a particular structure SymbTab

- a particular functor `Scanner`

- a particular functor `Parser`

- a particular functor `Evaluator`

that satisfy the requirements, he produces the following structure as the required interpreter:

```
structure Interpreter =
  Evaluator (SymbTab , Parser(Scanner(SymbTab))) ;
```

A.10   Type inference

Exercise 34

Select three type variables tv_1, tv_2 and tv_3 that do not occur either in tt_1 or in tt_2. Find the most general unifier σ_1 of types

$$tt_1 \quad \text{and}$$
$$tv_1 \rightarrow tv_2 \rightarrow tv_3$$

If that unification fails then $S[e_1, e_2]$ is ill-typed. If it goes through then find the most general unifier σ_2 of types

$$tt_2 \quad \text{and}$$
$$\sigma_1(tv_1) \rightarrow \sigma_1(tv_2)$$

If that unification fails then $S[e_1, e_2]$ is ill-typed. If it goes through then the type of $S[e_1, e_2]$ is

$$\sigma_2(tv_1) \rightarrow \sigma_2(tv_3)$$

Exercise 35

```
fun occurs(v) t =
  let val v1 = Terms.tmv(t)
  in Terms.eqv(v,v1)
  end ·
    handle Terms.destr =>
    let val (oo,tlis) = Terms.tmo(t)
    in iter(fn(p,q)=> p orelse q) false (map(occurs(v))tlis)
    end ;
```

where auxiliary functions `iter` and `map` have the following definitions:

```
fun iter(f) a [] = a
  | iter(f) a (x::lis) =
      f(x , iter(f) a lis) ;

fun map(f) =
  iter (fn(x,y)=>f(x)::y) [] ;
```

Exercise 36

The definition of types:

```
type vars = string ;
datatype expr = var of vars
                | zer
                | one
                | plus of expr*expr
                | mult of expr*expr ;
type eqsys = (expr*expr)list ;
type solut = vars -> expr ;
```

The right vehicle to solve such equations is, of course, unification. Here follows the unification algorithm in the form specific to this problem rather than by applying the general pattern from the text of the chapter.

```
exception unbound_var
      and no_solution ;

fun un(s,var(v1),ex2) =
      if occurs(v1) ex2
      then if var(v1)=ex2 then s
          else raise no_solution
      else let val s' = un(s,s(v1),ex2)
          in let val ex2' = substitute(s') ex2
              in subst(ex2',v1) o s'
              end
          end
            handle unbound_var =>
            upd(ex2,v1)(subst(ex2,v1) o s)
  | un(s,ex1,var(v2)) = ...(* symmetrically *)
  | un(s,zer,zer) = s
  | un(s,one,one) = s
  | un(s,plus(ex1,ex2),plus(ex1',ex2')) =
      un(un(s,ex1,ex1'),ex2,ex2')
  | un(s,mult(ex1,ex2),mult(ex1',ex2')) =
      un(un(s,ex1,ex1'),ex2,ex2')
  | un(s,_,_) = raise no_solution ;
```

The definition of the function that solves systems of equations starts with
the trivial solution

```
fun s0(v) = raise unbound_var ;
```

and uses the above defined function un:

```
fun solve([]) = s0
  | solve((ex1,ex2)::lis) =
      un(solve(lis),ex1,ex2) ;
```

A.11   Interpretation

Exercise 37

Variables will always be renamed to ones that do not occur freely in a given
expression. The following function checks whether or not a given variable
occurs freely in a given expression:

```
fun free(v,var(v1)) = (v=v1)
  | free(v,app(ex1,ex2)) =
      (free(v,ex1) orelse free(v,ex2))
  | free(v,fnc(v1,ex1)) = (v<>v1 andalso free(v,ex1)) ;
```

Variables are renamed by concatenating to them an appropriate number of
primes (variables are strings!). The following function renames a variable so
as to "omit" an expression:

```
fun rename(v,ex) =
  if free(v,ex)
  then rename (v ^ "'" , ex)
  else v ;
```

Substitution of an expression ex for free occurrences of a variable v in an
expression that consists either of a variable, or of an application, is easy:

```
fun subst(ex,v)(var(v1)) =
      if v=v1 then ex
      else var(v1)
  | subst(ex,v)(app(ex1,ex2)) =
      app(subst(ex,v)ex1,subst(ex,v)ex2)
  | subst(ex,v)(fnc(v1,ex1)) =
      ...
```

Substitution in a functional abstraction over the same variable v is trivial,
since the functional abstraction kills all free occurrences of variable v:

```
                 if v=v1 then fnc(v1,ex1)
                 else ...
```

If variable v1 does not occur freely in ex then there is no danger of it being
captured:

```
                 if not free(v1,ex)
                 then fnc(v1,subst(ex,v)ex1)
                 else ...
```

In the last remaining case, the bound variable v1 in fnc(v1,ex1) has to be
renamed to some other variable v2 not free either in ex or in ex1; then we
are back to the then-case:

```
                 let val v2 = rename(v1,app(ex,ex1))
                 in let val ex2 = subst(var(v2),v1)ex1
                     in subst(ex,v)(fnc(v2,ex2))
                     end
                 end ;
```

Exercise 38

```
    cons varlength = ... ;
    type vars = packed array[1..varlen] of char;
         expr = record case k:(v,a,f) of
                    v : (vrb1:vars) ;
                    a : (app1,app2:^expr) ;
                    f : (fnc1:vars; fnc2:^expr)
                  end ;

    procedure vrb(vr:vars; var ex:expr) ;
    begin
      ex.k:=v ; ex.vrb1 := vr
    end {vrb} ;

    procedure app(ex1,ex2:expr; var ex:expr) ;
    begin
      ex.k:=a ; ex.app1 := ex1 ; ex.app2 := ex2
    end {app} ;

    procedure fnc(vr1:vars; ex1:expr; var ex:expr) ;
    begin
      ex.k:=f ; ex.fnc1 := vr1 ; ex.fnc2 := ex1
    end {fnc} ;
```

Exercise 39

The nodes of a tree will be visited in the following order: start at the root; then go down to the left; after traversing the whole left subtree come back to the root; then go down to the right; after traversing the whole right subtree come back to the root; then leave the tree. A tag will indeed be necessary at every **fork**-node to say how many times this node has already been visited: if 0 then go down left, if 1 then go down right, if 2 then go up to the father node.

The Pascal definition of trees reads:

```
type expr = record case k:(lf,fk) of
             lf : (leaf:real) ;
             fk : (fork1,fork2:^tree; tag:0..2)
           end
```

and all tags in a newly constructed tree are initialised to 0.

Actual tree traversal will be done by the so called *pointer reversal* method. At all times a pointer l (for *lower*) will point to the currently visited node and a pointer u (for *upper*) will point to its father. Since pointer l prevents the subtree it points to from being "lost", the pointer in the father node may safely be reversed from its son to point to its father. This concerns all pointers on the path from the currently visited node up to the root of the tree. In this way, u points to a path upwards that may be used to withdraw from nodes already visited.

Descent to the left is performed by the cyclic permutation of pointers l, u and l^.fork1:

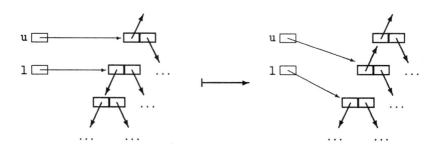

Analogously, descent to the right requires the cyclic permutation of pointers l, u and l^.fork2; and to go up to the father requires the cyclic permutation of pointers u, l and u^.fork1 if u^.tag is 1, and the cyclic permutation of pointers u, l and u^.fork2 if u^.tag is 2.

This leads to the following Pascal code:

```
procedure cyclic(var a,b,c:^expr) ;
  var d:^expr ;
begin
  d:=a ; a:=c ; c:=b ; b:=d
end{cyclic} ;

function leafcount(l:^expr):integer ;
  var u:^expr ;
      lc : integer ;
begin
  if l^.k = lf
  then leafcount:=1
  else
    begin
      u:=nil ; lc:=0 ;
      repeat
        if l^.k = lf
        then begin  { l^  is a leaf}
               lc:=lc+1 ;
               if u^.tag = 1
               then cyclic(u,l,u^.fork1)
               else cyclic(u,l,u^.fork2)
             end
        else begin  { l^  is a fork}
               case l^.tag of
                 0 : begin  { go down left }
                       l^.tag := 1 ;
                       cyclic(l,u,l^.fork1)
                     end ;
                 1 : begin  { go down right }
                       l^.tag := 2 ;
                       cyclic(l,u,l^.fork2)
                     end ;
                 2 : begin  { go up to father }
                       l^.tag := 0 ;
                       if u^.tag = 1
                       then cyclic(u,l,u^.fork1)
                       else cyclic(u,l,u^.fork2)
                     end
               end
             end
      until u=nil ;
      leafcount:=lc
    end
end{leafcount} ;
```

A.12   Compilation

Exercise 40

The configuration of the machine is determined by the state of its memory and of its registers:

```
type address = int ;   (* between 0 and  n  *)
type value = int ;     (* between 0 and  k  *)
type memory = address -> value ;
type config = memory * value * address * bool * bool ;
```

— the components of `config` are memory, accumulator, program counter, Z-register and N-register. The commands are:

```
datatype command = LDC of value
                 | LD of address
                 | ST of address
                 | ADD of address
                 | SBT of address
                 | JMP of address
                 | JPZ of address
                 | JPN of address
                 | STOP
```

For simplicity, assume that each command occupies two consecutive machine cells, and that a decoding function

```
exception decode ;
decode : value * value -> command
```

is given. This function yields a command stored in two given consecutive cells; it may raise an exception if the two values do not correspond to any command.

The command executor is defined as follows:

```
fun run(Mem,Acc,PC,Z,N) =
  case decode(Mem(PC),Mem((PC+1)mod n)) of
    LDC(v) => run(Mem,v,(PC+2)mod n,Z,N)
  | LD(a) => run(Mem,Mem(a),(PC+2)mod n,Z,N)
  | ST(a) => run(upd(Acc,a)Mem,Acc,(PC+2)mod n,Z,N)
  | ADD(a) =>
      let val Acc' = (Acc+Mem(a))mod k
      in
        run(Mem,Acc',(PC+2)mod n,(Acc'=0),(Acc'>=k div 2))
      end
```

```
| SBT(a) =>
    let val Acc' = (Acc-Mem(a))mod k
    in
      run(Mem,Acc',(PC+2)mod n,(Acc'=0),(Acc'>=k div 2))
    end
| JMP(a) => run(Mem,Acc,a,Z,N)
| JPZ(a) => if Z
              then run(Mem,Acc,a,Z,N)
              else run(Mem,Acc,(PC+2)mod n,Z,N)
| JPN(a) => if N
              then run(Mem,Acc,a,Z,N)
              else run(Mem,Acc,(PC+2)mod n,Z,N)
| STOP => (Mem,Acc,PC,Z,N)
```

Exercise 41

Informally, the code for `cas(ex,[(c1,ex1),...,(cn,exn)],ex0)` may look as follows:

```
code for ex
assign(xx)            — var xx does not occur in the expression
get(xx), cjp(c1,lb+1)
...
get(xx), cjp(cn,lb+n)
code for ex0
jump(lb)
lab(lb+1), code for ex1, jump(lb)
...
lab(lb+n), code for exn, jump(lb)
lab(lb)
```

The role of the `assign` command above is to protect the value of `ex` from disappearing from the stack — remember that conditional jumps remove the current argument.

The main part of the above code are two blocks of commands of length n each. They are generated by the auxiliary functions `block1` and `block2` in the Standard ML definition below. While reading this definition keep the informal example above in front of you.

```
| cp(cas(ex,cexlis,ex0))(cd',cd'',lb) =
    let val n = length(cexlis)
    in let fun block1(k,[]) = []
           | block1(k,(c,ex)::cexlis) =
               [get(xx),cjp(c,lb+k)] @ block1(k+1,cexlis)
         and block2(k,[])(cd',cd'',lb') = (cd',cd'',lb')
```

```
                    | block2(k,(c,ex)::cexlis)(cd',cd'',lb') =
                        let val (cd1',cd1'',lb1) =
                              cp(ex)(cd',[],lb')
                        in let val (cd2',cd2'',lb2) =
                                  block2(k+1,cexlis)(cd1',[],lb1)
                            in (cd2' ,
                                [lab(lb+k)] @ cd1'' @
                                [jump(lb)] @ cd2'' ,
                                lb2
                                )
                            end
                        end
            in let val (cd1',cd1'',lb1) = cp(ex)(cd',[],lb+n+1)
               in let val (cd2',cd2'',lb2) =
                       cp(ex0)(cd1',[],lb1)
                  in let val (cd3',cd3'',lb3) =
                          block2(1,cexlis)(cd2',[],lb2)
                     in (cd3' ,
                         cd'' @cd1'' @ [assign(xx)] @
                         block1(1,cexlis) @ cd2'' @
                         [jump(lb)] @ cd3'' @ [lab(lb)] ,
                         lb3
                         )
                     end
                  end
               end
            end
         end
```

Appendix B

Guide to the literature

Applicative, or functional, programming has been advocated as a serious alternative to imperative programming since the mid-seventies. Backus' manifesto [2] may be considered as a milestone but the main concepts have been around much longer. Both Landin [18] and Burge [5] directly discuss issues characteristic of this programming style.

Applicative programming may shortly be characterised as programming based on the λ-calculus of Church. Actually, the λ-calculus is *the* theoretical basis for functional programs in much the same way as Turing machines are the theoretical basis for imperative programming. A systematic study of λ-calculus may be found in [16] by Hindley and Seldin; Barendregt [3] serves, however, as the main reference in this area, although this work may be difficult to read. A reader with a more casual interest in the theoretical foundations is referred to short chapters on λ-calculus in almost any textbook dealing with the theory or with the implementation of programming languages; two examples of such books are Gordon [10] and Peyton Jones [22].

Today, designing functional programs requires as little familiarity with theoretical foundations, as does driving a car with combustion engines. Many beginner courses do not mention λ-calculus at all, e.g. Bird and Wadler [4], or only casually, e.g. Henderson [15]. Clearly, this approach will not do at the expert level.

A reader who finds these notes too difficult may start with the above mentioned [4], [15] or [9]. Courses on functional programming are also to be found in many textbooks describing particular functional programming languages. A reader interested in methods of verifying properties of functional programs is referred to [17].

The best known, and the oldest, functional language is LISP 1.5, see [19]. Purists, however, refuse to call LISP a functional language since it fails to realize correctly the λ-calculus. The most criticised features of LISP are the dynamic binding of identifiers and the low order (there are no functionals). There are many versions and dialects of LISP designed to overcome these shortcomings; and also to make the general appearance of programs more programmer-friendly. LISP and its sister languages have been the programming languages of Artificial Intelligence for a long time, before they gave way to Prolog. Notwithstanding these successes, many professionals share Dijkstra's view, that LISP is the most refined way of improperly using a computer.

Nowadays, there exist many other applicative programming languages. Gedanken [23], Miranda [25] and Hope [6] are probably the most widely known.

ML was first designed as a metalanguage (hence the acronym) for a general purpose theorem prover LCF (see Gordon, Milner and Wadsworth [11]). Only in the eighties did it develop into an independent programming language Standard ML. The complete definition of its most recent version, as for Winter 1988/1989, may be found in Harper, Milner and Tofte [14]. That report is, however, extremely hard to read. A professional, intending to start writing Standard ML programs as soon as possible, would probably be best advised to try Harper [12]. Wikström [26] is a textbook for a novice whose first programming language is to be Standard ML.

Academic literature concerning Standard ML abounds. A comprehensive set of references may be found in the above mentioned [14], I will only cite three papers that have, I feel, directly influenced my way of thinking. These are: Mitchell and Harper [21] on type systems; Harper, Milner and Tofte [13] on structures and signatures; and Sannella and Tarlecki [24] on extending signatures to specifications by adding axioms. Of course, I am solely responsible for the views expressed here.

The implementation of applicative languages is a separate issue. A comprehensive monograph on implementation is Field and Harrison [8]. Peyton Jones [22] is a large do-it-yourself manual. Specific problems arising while implementing ML are described in Milner [20] on polymorphic type inference; and in Cardelli [7], and in Appel and MacQueen [1] on compilation.

[1] Appel A., MacQueen D. *A Standard ML Compiler* Proc. 1987 Symposium on Functional Languages and Computer Architecture, 301–324, 1987

[2] Backus J. *Can Programming be Liberated from the von Neumann Style? A Functional Style and its Algebra of Programs* Comm. ACM 21, 8, 1978

[3] Barendregt H. *The Lambda Calculus* North-Holland, 1984

[4] Bird R., Wadler P. *An Introduction to Functional Programming* Prentice Hall, 1988

[5] Burge W. *Recursive Programming Techniques* Addison-Wesley, Reading, Mass., 1975

[6] Burstall R., MacQueen D., Sannella D. *HOPE: An Experimental Applicative Language* University of Edinburgh, Computer Science Dept., Report CSR-62-80, 1980

[7] Cardelli L. *Compiling a Functional Language* Proc. 1984 ACM Symposium on LISP and Functional Programming, 208–217, 1984

[8] Field A.J., Harrison P.G. *Functional Programming* Addison-Wesley, 1988

[9] *Functional Programming and its Application: An Advanced Course* (ed. J. Darlington) Cambridge University Press, 1982

[10] Gordon M. *Programming Language Theory and its Implementation* Prentice Hall, 1988

[11] Gordon M., Milner R., Wadsworth C. *Edinburgh LCF* Lecture Notes in Computer Science No. 78, Springer-Verlag, 1979

[12] Harper R. *Introduction to Standard ML* University of Edinburgh, Laboratory for Foundations of Computer Science, Report ECS-LFCS-86-14, 1986

[13] Harper R., Milner R., Tofte M. *A Type Discipline for Program Modules* University of Edinburgh, Laboratory for Foundations of Computer Science, Report ECS-LFCS-87-28, 1987

[14] Harper R., Milner R., Tofte M. *The Definition of Standard ML. Version 2* University of Edinburgh, Laboratory for Foundations of Computer Science, Report ECS-LFCS-88-62, 1988

[15] Henderson P. *Functional Programming: Application and Implementation* Prentice Hall International, 1980

[16] Hindley J., Seldin J. *Introduction to Combinators and λ-Calculus* Cambridge University Press, 1986

[17] Kubiak R., Rudziński R., Sokołowski S., *An Introduction to Programming with Specifications: a Mathematical Approach* to appear in Academic Press, 1990

[18] Landin P. *The Next 700 Programming Languages* Comm. ACM 9, 157–164, 1966

[19] McCarthy J. et al. *LISP 1.5 Manual* The MIT Press, 1965

[20] Milner R. *A Theory of Type Polymorphism in Programming* J. Comp. Sys. Sci. 17, 348-375, 1978

[21] Mitchell J., Harper R. *The Essence of ML* University of Edinburgh, Laboratory for Foundations of Computer Science, Report ECS-LFCS-87-42, 1987

[22] Peyton Jones S. *The Implementation of Functional Programming Languages* Prentice Hall, 1987

[23] Reynolds J. *GEDANKEN: A Simple Typeless Programming Language Based on the Principle of Completeness and the Reference Concept* Comm. ACM 13, 5, 1970

[24] Sannella D., Tarlecki A. *Extended ML: An Institution Independent Framework for Formal Program Development* University of Edinburgh, Laboratory for Foundations of Computer Science, Report ECS-LFCS-86-16, 1986

[25] Turner D. *Functional Programs as Executable Specifications* in: *Mathematical Logic and Programming Languages* (ed. Hoare and Shepherdson), Prentice Hall, 29–54, 1985

[26] Wikström Å. *Functional Programming Using Standard ML* Prentice Hall, 1987

Appendix C

Index

This is not an exhaustive listing of all pages at which respective terms appear. Only the defining, the introducing, and the most important occurrences are mentioned.

det *54, 62*
determinant *54–55, 97*
diagonalisation of matrix *64*
DICT *123, 133*
dictionary *vii, 49–53, 62–63, 98, 123–124, 133–134*
differentiability *vi*
differentiation *44, 62*
directed graph *171*
discretisation *56*
disjoint union *67, 69, 94, 113*
disjunction *8*
div *9, 38*
divergence *16*
divides *11*
divisibility *3–4, 10*
drawcurve *56*
dynamic binding *233*

eager evaluation *15–17, 63*
Edinburgh University *vi, 56*
efficiency *v, 5, 11, 19, 23, 53, 64, 173–174*
entrance to graph *172*
entrance to subprogram *184*
enumerable sequence *62*
enumeration type *6, 67*
environment *113–115, 120, 159, 179–183, 185–186, 188*
equality *62, 90, 116, 118*
equation *149–150*
Eratosthenes' sieve *64, 202*
error handling *52, 72*
error in proof *44–45*
error message *v, 9, 72*
error of type *6, 81, 84, 87, 90, 145, 165*
Euclidean space *127*
eval *168–170, 177*
evaluation *v, 13–18, 63, 87, 113, 165–168, 170–171, 177*
evaluator *167–168, 170, 172, 177*
exception *17, 50, 72–74, 152–154*
exception handling *17, 50, 52, 72, 74, 153*
execution *19, 178, 180–182*
executor *177–178, 181, 230*
exn *50*
explicit polymorphism *vii, 86, 88, 94*
explode *53, 74*
expression *v, 6–7, 9, 13–14, 16–17, 30, 66, 70, 72–73, 81, 84–89, 92, 97, 113, 145–147, 154–156, 165, 167–170, 177–180, 185–187*
expression denoting type *67, 84–85, 88, 93–95, 147, 155*
expressive power *vi, 101*

fact *100*

factorial *55, 100*
Failure *17, 51–53*
false *8*
family tree *76*
field *126*
file *6*
finding a record *49, 124*
"first class citizen" *v, vii, 49, 62, 88, 94–95*
FIX *146, 167*
fixpoint *170–171, 187*
floor *9, 56*
fn ... => ... *50, 66, 147, 165*
forall *14*
forest *70*
for-statement *101*
Fortran *65*
free storage *173–174*
free variable *87–88, 95, 154, 169, 174, 178–179*
fun *4, 11*
function *v–vii, 4, 6–7, 10–11, 15, 17, 23–25, 29–31, 41, 49–51, 53–56, 60, 62, 64, 82–83, 146*
functional (applicative) *v–vii, 4, 18, 20–23, 53, 62, 101, 109, 145, 165, 233*
functional (high order function) *vi–vii, 49, 62, 99, 146, 153, 233*
functional abstraction *50, 66, 146–147, 154–155, 165, 186*
functional dependence *vii, 86, 96*
function as data *v, 49–50*
function definition *9–11, 17, 38, 53, 69, 100, 102, 105, 146*
function space *66–67, 91, 94, 99, 101, 106*
functor *vii, 129–132, 134–140, 152–153*

garbage collection *166, 172–174*
Gaussian elimination *55, 64, 203*
gcd *13, 83*
Gedanken *234*
generalisation *25–26*
generalised Cartesian product *93, 95*
generic *80, 139*
grammar *70, 72, 76, 156*
graph *165–166, 170–174*
group *125–126, 129–130*
GROUP *125*

handle ... => ... *17, 52, 73*
hash table *vii, 49*
Hd *72, 82*
hd *72, 82*
head 72, 82